CUMBRIA AIR
IN THE SECOND
WORLD WAR
including the Isle of Man

Martyn Chorlton

COUNTRYSIDE BOOKS
NEWBURY BERKSHIRE

COUNTRYSIDE BOOKS
3 Catherine Road
Newbury, Berkshire

To view our complete range of books,
please visit us at
www.countrysidebooks.co.uk

ISBN 1 85306 983 3
EAN 978 1 85306 983 3

The cover picture shows a Bristol Beaufort I of
1 (Coastal) Operational Training Unit on a
training sortie over northern Cumbria
and is from an original painting
by Colin Doggett

Produced through MRM Associates Ltd., Reading
Typeset by CJWT Solutions, Newton-le-Willows
Printed by Borcombe Printers plc, Romsey

CONTENTS

MAP OF THE SECOND WORLD WAR AIRFIELDS

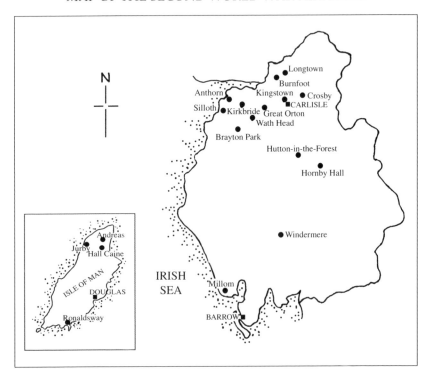

ACKNOWLEDGEMENTS

Thanks to Glynn Griffith and all at the RAF Millom Aviation Museum for the use of photographs. Thank you to Phil Paine and Ivor Ramsden for assisting Jarrod Cotter on the Isle of Man. Also to Jarrod Cotter and Key Publishing for the use of selected photography and to the staff of Hutton-in-the-Forest Hall for their hospitality and assistance.

Special thanks, once again, to my wife, Claire, who tirelessly edited my work making this book possible.

AUTHOR'S NOTE

At the beginning of the Second World War, the modern day Cumbria was made up of Cumberland, Westmorland and parts of Yorkshire and Lancashire. This remained the case until the nationwide boundary changes of 1974. For simplicity, I have referred to the area as Cumbria and apologise if this offends any resident of the original counties.

I

SETTING
THE SCENE

Pioneering Days

Several years before the reality of powered flight could be imagined, the only aeronautical events to be seen were performed by balloonists. In November 1902, the gunboat HMS *Renard* arrived at Douglas in the Isle of Man with a balloon on board. Also on board was the crew of the balloon, Mr Percival Spenser and the Revd J M Bacon. The balloonists were tasked with naval survey work of the coast of the island, and on 10th November, the weather conditions were good enough to fly. Over 15,000 people witnessed the ascent of the 60 ft high by 45 ft in diameter balloon, which sailed off across Douglas Bay and then disappeared into cloud. The balloon remained in contact with HMS *Renard* whilst crossing the Irish Sea before landing in a remote area of Dumfriesshire after a journey of 77 miles and four and a half hours.

It was not until the summer of 1911 that the islanders first saw a real flying machine. As part of the celebrations for the coronation of King George V, an aviation display was arranged in conjunction the steam packet *Ben-my-Chree*. The plan was for two famous aviators of the day, Claude Graham-White and George Barnes to bring their aircraft by ship to the island. Having recently competed in the *Daily Mail* Paris to London Air Race, the aircraft arrived on the morning of 4th July. Graham-White was to fly a Farman biplane and Barnes a Bleriot parasol monoplane. Unfortunately, the Bleriot had been damaged and it was up to Graham-White to entertain the crowds single-handed. The Farman took off from Nobles Park in Douglas, making this the first unofficial landing ground on the Isle of Man.

The 1910 *Daily Mail* air race, which offered £10,000 to the winner, involved flying a 1,010 mile circuit around Great Britain. Flown over five days, there were 13 compulsory stops including one at Carlisle. The exact location of the stop is unknown, it was simply called 'Carlisle Control' and at least 20 aircraft flew in and out during the race.

The majority of all aviation interests in Cumbria before the First World War centred on Lake Windermere, much to the annoyance of the 'Friends of the Lake District'. Oscar Gnosspelius of Hawkshead and Captain E H Wakefield were competing to be the first aviators to take off from the lake. Gnosspelius, who had been experimenting with models on the lake for several years, commissioned local boat builders Borwick & Sons to build him a full scale 'hydro monoplane', fitted with a 20 hp Alvaston engine. Gnosspelius was convinced that, as a result of his tests with models, the aircraft would make him the first man to achieve man-powered flight from the lake. On the day of the first flight test, the monoplane crashed on the first attempt, damaging the wing and destroying the propeller. Gnosspelius had the machine repaired at Borwick's and uprated the power of the monoplane with a 40 hp Clerget engine. In this new configuration, the monoplane went on to fly well, with Ronald Kemp at the controls. In the meantime, Capt. Wakefield, in an Avro biplane named *Waterhen*, piloted the first powered aircraft to take off from Windermere in November 1911. Wakefield went on to make many more flights in other aircraft with names such as *Lakes Waterhen* and *Lakes Seabird*. Gnosspelius developed his into the monoplanes No1 and No2 and made many flights from lakes until the outbreak of war.

Oscar Gnosspelius of Hawkshead. (via Stuart Leslie)

Not long after these pioneering activities, the Lakes Flying School was formed with Roland Ding as its Chief Flying Instructor. The school flourished under his guidance until he, like Gnosspelius and Kemp, were called for service with the forces.

The *Daily Mail* in 1912 was very keen to demonstrate the capabilities of flying machines. They enlisted the help of many of the leading aviators of the time to promote aviation, including the enthusiast Gustave Hamel. His aircraft and entourage arrived by steam packet

Gnosspelius on the edge of Lake Windermere with his No 1 Single-Float aeroplane in 1910. (via Stuart Leslie)

into Douglas on 3rd August 1912. His aircraft, a French-built Morane Saulnier parasol monoplane, was prepared for flight at Nobles Park. Hamel entertained a large local crowd as well as the thousands of holidaymakers on the island at the time. He demonstrated the aircraft all over the Isle of Man and, on a flight to Peel, was credited with making the island's first airmail flight.

The classic 1914 Schneider Trophy air race was won for the first time by an Englishman, Howard Pixton, from Jurby on the Isle of Man. His flying career began in 1910 at Brooklands, where he became a good friend of A V Roe. On 17th October 1910, Pixton attempted his very first take off, not fully understanding the effect of wind; thus a downwind take off resulted in a crash into the famous Brooklands sewage farm. Pixton was airborne again on 8th November, safely clearing the sewage farm, but subsequently side-slipping into the ground, whereupon the long-suffering Roe IV triplane caught fire. The aircraft was again repaired and, with Pixton at the controls, was in the air on 17th November and back in the sewage farm on 4th December! Despite early setbacks Pixton gained his airman's certificate on 24th January 1911 and Roe, demonstrating supreme confidence in his new self-taught test pilot, detailed him to make the first flight in March 1911 on his next design, the Avro Type D.

9

Born in Jurby on the Isle of Man, Howard Pixton (centre) started his flying career testing aircraft for A V Roe.

Pixton went on to become one of the best-known pre-war test pilots and a worthy early bearer of the Avro Chief Test Pilot title. He left Avro for Bristol's in 1911 and during that year earned more prize money for flying than anyone else in the country.

The First World War and the Interwar Years

The remoteness of both Cumbria and the Isle of Man resulted in very little aviation activity during the Great War. The old Lakes Flying School was renamed the Northern Aircraft Company and was used for a military purpose. It was one of many flying schools which taught the basics of flying to personnel from the Royal Navy who would go on to serve with the Royal Naval Air Service (RNAS).

A Home Defence Squadron landing ground was constructed near

Solway House in the north of Cumbria, located between Cardurnock and Anthorn. If used, it would have been an alternative landing place for a Scottish-based squadron tasked with defending the Glasgow area against Zeppelin attack.

The only tentative connection with aviation and the Isle of Man during the First World War was the steam packet. The Royal Navy requisitioned 14 and several, including the *Ben-my-Chree*, became seaplane tenders.

The draw of the Isle of Man Tourist Trophy Motorcycle Races brought a single de Havilland DH.9 to Douglas Head for the 1925 T.T. meeting. Flown by Mr C Barnard, the aircraft was chartered by *The Motor Cycle* to supply copies to the thousands of fans at the event. A second DH.9 repeated the event the following year and the flights continued, landing next to the main T.T. grandstand. In 1928, an Imperial Airways airliner delivered over a ton of motor cycle journals, landing on ground belonging to Ronaldsway Farm. The pilot of the airliner was Capt. G P Olley, who would become influential in developing Manx Air Services and Ronaldsway Airport.

Pleasure flying from Douglas beach, arranged by Surrey Flying Services Ltd, began in 1928. A hangar was constructed at Douglas Head making the site another unofficial aerodrome. An Avro 504 took passengers flying for five shillings a time.

An Avro 504K of Surrey Flying Services, similar to the aircraft that took passengers flying for the first time from Douglas Head.

11

A Saro Cutty Sark amphibian was operated from the Isle of Man by Flt Lt Monks' ground breaking British Amphibious Air Lines.

In 1932, Flt Lt R H C Monk was granted permission to use the foreshores at Blackpool and Douglas for the operation of a Saro A.17 Cutty Sark flying boat named 'Progress I'. Capable of carrying four passengers, the small amphibian cruised at 85 mph, taking on average 40 minutes to cross the Irish Sea. Monk set up British Amphibious Airlines Ltd, the first scheduled airline in Great Britain. The service continued until 1933 and Monk's efforts are commemorated on a plaque in the Ronaldsway Airport lounge.

As the nation's enthusiasm for civilian aviation gained momentum many major towns and cities wanted their own municipal airport. Carlisle was one of the earliest cities to establish an airport, albeit a small one at Kingstown on the northern side of the city. The small grass airfield opened in 1931 but it was not until 1933 that regular services began to Hall Caine and Ronaldsway on the Isle of Man. Ronaldsway was the first to open in 1933 followed by Hall Caine in 1935, both competing to be the island's main airport. At Kingstown, the Border Flying Club was formed, giving local people the opportunity to learn to fly. The first military flying unit to be formed in Cumbria, 38 ERFTS, began training pilots for the rapidly expanding RAF.

Meanwhile the competition between Hall Caine and Ronaldsway ended in the latter's favour in 1937. Ronaldsway continued to expand until the beginning of the Second World War but this did not stop at least one airline continuing to operate a scheduled service to the mainland.

Worthy of mention in this chapter are the Manx Air Races, five of which were organised. The course of the race followed the coastline of the island from Douglas Head via Maughold Head, Bride Church, Peel Castle, Tynwald Hill and then Ronaldsway. Aircraft were handicapped with starting times decided by the expected performance of each aircraft. The first race, on 18th June 1932, had nine entrants including Mrs Winifred Brown, the winner of the 1930 King's Cup air race. It was Mr A Cook in a de Havilland Cirrus Moth who won the event, averaging 102 mph around the course. The next race was in 1936 and was dominated by 19-year-old Alex Henshaw, who crossed the finish line three minutes quicker than his nearest rival. The 1937 race attracted two Messerschmitt Bf 108 Taifuns from the Aero Club von Deutschland. Races were held in 1938 and 1939, the latter event being won by Alex Henshaw's father, Albert, in a Percival Vega Gull.

The Second World War: Maintenance Command

Construction work began on Cumbria's two biggest Maintenance Units (MU) in 1938 as the storm clouds of war were gathering over Europe. Number 12 MU at Kirkbride and 22 MU Silloth would handle between them literally thousands of aircraft, during wartime and many years beyond. The two units opened on the same day, 5th June 1939, and both airfields, because of the nature of their work, were very well equipped with hangars, technical buildings and dispersal areas. Both units were civilian-manned, employing up to 750 skilled staff, many from the local area. Up to 300 aircraft were stored on the airfields, officially known as Aircraft Storage Units (ASU), during wartime. As wartime dispersal rules relaxed and aircraft could be parked closer together, over 1000 aircraft could be seen on either airfield. Preparation of aircraft for front-line squadrons was the main wartime role of the two MUs as well as modification and some repair work. The role played by this type of unit is never included in the big picture of the Second World War. After manufacture of the aircraft, the next step was the MU and it was units like 12 and 22 MU that kept the

There was no shortage of hangar space at Silloth or Kirkbride; virtually all are still in use today. (Author)

flow of operational aircraft going, which in turn contributed greatly to the eventual victory over the enemy.

Flying Training

Cumbria and the Isle of Man both possessed some very unforgiving terrain, which claimed the lives of many airmen. In contrast, the skies were and still are uncluttered and the weather, in particular in the north of Cumbria, was generally very good. Both regions' airfields contained a large number of flying training units. By the war's end, over 60 units had served at one or more of twelve different airfields within Cumbria and the Isle of Man.

Jurby on the Isle of Man was specifically built as 5 Armament Training Station in 1939, becoming 5 Air Observers School (AOS) and then 5 Bombing and Gunnery School before reverting to 5 AOS. The airfield hosted many visits by Flying Training Schools, Operational Training Units (OTU) and even the Armament Synthetic Development Unit, flying Vickers, Wellingtons and Warwicks. Gunnery schools

14

Gunnery training was carried out at Jurby, Millom and Ronaldsway. (RAF Millom Aircraft & Military Museum)

were well suited to the Isle of Man, with its abundance of both bombing and air-to-air firing ranges. A similar school, 2 AOS was established at Millom in the south of Cumbria. Initially the school struggled with the unreliable Blackburn Botha but the more purposeful Avro Anson eventually replaced these. Ronaldsway was the home of the Ground Defence Gunners School from 1940 to 1943 and Andreas was home to 11 Air Gunners School until September 1946. Millom, close to the coast in the south of Cumbria, was also perfect for housing a bombing and gunnery school.

It was unrealistic to expect a flying training school to operate safely in the south east of England, especially during 1940. In June 1940, 15 Elementary Flying Training School (EFTS) moved en masse with their large fleet of Magisters to the pre-war airport at Kingstown. The unit gained a Relief Landing Ground (RLG) at Burnfoot and the sight and sound of pilots learning their trade in the ubiquitous Tiger Moth around Carlisle continued until December 1947.

Fighter pilot training in Cumbria began when 59 OTU took over a new airfield at Crosby in 1941. Longtown was also used by the unit, which flew the Hawker Hurricane, until it moved across the border to

The Lockheed Hudson was one of the most common aircraft types to be seen in the area. However, it is particularly associated with Silloth, near the Solway Firth, which was renamed 'Hudson Bay' because of the number of crashes.

Milfield in Northumberland. 55 OTU at Annan in Dumfriesshire, also a Hurricane unit, took over Longtown as a satellite in April 1942 and then moved to Great Orton.

Coastal Command training was dominated by 1 (Coastal) OTU, based at Silloth. Its predominant aircraft type was the Lockheed Hudson, of which an alarming number were lost in training accidents. 1 OTU also used Kirkbride as an RLG and Longtown for night flying. Aircraft from Silloth would be seen operating in and out of virtually all the airfields in the area, including the Isle of Man. The Hudsons were operating from Silloth from 1940 to 1943, when they were moved to Thornaby in North Yorkshire. 9 (Coastal) OTU was the next big Coastal Command training unit to arrive in the area and it took over Crosby from 59 OTU to train crews on the Bristol Beaufighter. These big powerful fighters also operated from Longtown and, like the Hudson, suffered a high accident rate, which in 9 OTU's case, the Air Ministry frowned upon.

9 OTU dissolved seamlessly into 109 (Transport) OTU operating the Douglas Dakota. Remaining at Crosby, the unit was redesignated 1383 CU in August and was disbanded twelve months later.

Longtown briefly hosted 1674 Heavy Conversion Unit (HCU) in October 1943, operating the Handley Page Halifax, Consolidated Liberator and Boeing Fortress. However the stay was short-lived, leaving Longtown, the unit moved to Aldergrove to support a single Beam Approach Training Flight (BATF) and a few Dakotas from Crosby before closure.

Fighter Command

Jurby was one of the busiest training stations in late 1940, but this did not stop it from being the home of five different fighter squadrons. Fighter Command thought the Isle of Man should house fighter squadrons, not only for its own protection but to intercept any potential enemy over the Irish Sea. At the time, enemy activity was high in the region and the hope was that Jurby's squadrons would achieve many kills. 307 Squadron with the Boulton Paul Defiant was the first to arrive, followed by 258, 312 and 302 squadrons, all flying the Hurricane, and finally 457 Squadron, flying the Supermarine Spitfire. The main daily duties performed by these squadrons were shipping

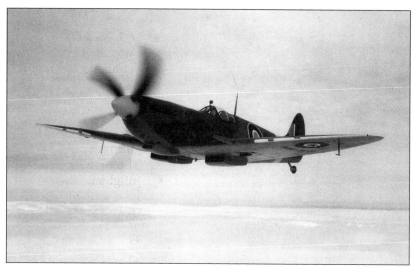

Several fighter squadrons were stationed on the Isle of Man from late 1940 to 1942.

17

patrols, convoy escorts, interception exercises and formation flying. Much to the pilot's frustration, no Jurby-based fighter encountered a single enemy aircraft.

Andreas became the island's main fighter defence station when it opened in September 1941. 457 Squadron moved its Spitfires to the new fighter station but the fresh surroundings did nothing to improve the squadron's luck against the enemy. 452 Squadron, also operating the Spitfire, took over in March 1942 and hopes were still high that an enemy aircraft would be shot down. Close contact with the enemy finally came on the 3rd May 1942 when the squadron was responsible for the entire Woodvale Sector. A Junkers Ju88 was engaged over the Irish Sea by two Spitfires, both claiming it damaged and silencing the rear gunner of the twin-engined bomber. Return fire from the Ju88 damaged one of the Spitfires, which had to ditch in the sea. 93 Squadron, also flying the Spitfire, replaced 457 Squadron in June 1942. No more enemy combats occurred, and with 93 Squadron's departure from Andreas in September 1942 all Fighter Command cover of the region ended.

Fleet Air Arm

Aircraft of the Royal Navy were not an uncommon sight from the beginning of the Second World War. Both Silloth and Kirkbride were handling Fleet Air Arm (FAA) types such as the Fairey Seafox, Blackburn Shark, Roc and Skua and the Fairey Swordfish throughout the war. Several FAA detachments were passing through Andreas and Millom and it was not until 1943 that the Royal Navy gained their own airfields.

The Admiralty first surveyed Ronaldsway in 1942 as a potential home for several Torpedo Training Squadrons. After a successful negotiation the RAF handed Ronaldsway over on 31st March 1943. Expansion of the airfield was not completed until mid 1944 and on 21st June, RAF Ronaldsway became HMS *Urley*, Royal Naval Air Station (RNAS) Ronaldsway. Between July 1944 and December 1945, nine FAA units operating a variety of types including the Fairey Barracuda and Swordfish would be stationed at Ronaldsway. The Admiralty relinquished Ronaldsway in 1946.

Like the MUs at Silloth and Kirkbride, the Admiralty needed an airfield in a remote yet accessible location that was capable of handling a large throughput of aircraft. A site was chosen on the northern shore of Moricambe Bay for a brand new purpose-built airfield to accommodate an Aircraft Receipt and Dispatch Unit (ARDU). Originally on the same short-list as Ronaldsway as a home for a Torpedo Training Unit, Anthorn was ready for occupation by the summer of 1944. RNAS Anthorn or HMS *Nuthatch* was commissioned on 7th September 1944. No1 ARDU worked in a similar way to 12 and 22 MUs and during the war years, the main aircraft types to pass through the unit were the Grumman Hellcat and Fairey Firefly. The ARDU continued its work until the last aircraft departed in 1957 and today is the only airfield in this book to still be retained by the Ministry of Defence.

Satellite Landing Grounds

The maintenance units at Silloth, Kirkbride and 18 MU at Dumfries would never have been able to handle as many aircraft without the support of the humble Satellite Landing Ground (SLG). By the war's end, northern Cumbria had four, all filled to the gunnels with aircraft without the knowledge of the Luftwaffe or even many local people. Not much more than fields, the SLG always made good use of natural camouflage. When this was not available every effort was made to conceal aircraft using hides or netting. All four SLGs opened between April and June 1941. 39 SLG at Brayton and 10 SLG at Wath Head were constructed for 12 MU while 8 SLG at Hutton-in-the-Forest and 9 SLG at Hornby Hall were allocated to 22 MU at Silloth. All four SLGs changed hands throughout the war; Hornby and Wath Head were also used by 18 MU when their airfield at Dumfries was overflowing with aircraft. Security was taken very seriously at all of the SLGs; in the early part of the war, army detachments carried out patrols until these were taken over by the RAF Regiment in 1942. SLGs also had their own Home Guard units drawn from the civilian workers.

An untold number of aircraft passed through the SLGs, from Spitfire fighters through to Halifax bombers, with remarkable efficiency and an incredibly low accident rate. When the war ended in Europe the dispersal of aircraft was no longer a necessity and the last SLG was closed by January 1946.

2
ANDREAS

During the early years of the Second World War, especially over the Isle of Man, the Luftwaffe appeared to rule the skies. Transiting the Irish Sea virtually unharrassed by our fighters, the German aircraft took full advantage, attacking targets in Northern Ireland and the north-western mainland of England. Jurby was already in place, but it was obvious that a second fighter station was needed, and quickly.

A site for a new airfield at the northern end of the island was located without great trouble, as the whole area was originally identified at the beginning of the war as a good landing area for enemy aircraft. The land on Ballaghue Farm, north-east of Andreas, was chosen for the new airfield and work began in late 1940 by local contractors Moss and Company. The design of the airfield was a typical triangular three runway layout, although all were slightly longer than normal, as plans were already in place for Andreas to become an emergency diversion airfield in the future. The runways were connected by a perimeter track, which in turn led to a selection of dispersals and blast pens of both fighter and bomber design.

The main technical and domestic site was on the western side of the airfield, almost within walking distance of the village of Andreas. However this could not have easily been penetrated, as the entire airfield was secured by several rows of barbed wire, with access via a single main entrance with a guardroom. A purposeful feel to the site was given with the construction of three Bellman hangars, which, at 175ft long and 95ft wide, were by far the largest buildings on the airfield. These were complemented later on in the war by eight Extra Over Blisters, which had a span of 69ft.

The airfield was completed by the end of September 1941 and was by now under the command of Wg Cdr Gomez, who took up residence in Glen Auldyn on the outskirts of Ramsey. Within days the first unit arrived and they did not have far to travel. The Australians of 457 Squadron, under the command of Sqn Ldr P M Brothers, who had been at neighbouring Jurby since August 1941, arrived at Andreas on 3rd October. Formed at Baginton, Warwickshire on 16th June, the squadron was made up of Australian pilots and RAF ground crew, initially flying the Supermarine Spitfire I. On their arrival at Andreas, the squadron had progressed onto the Spitfire IIA. Although their location had changed, the squadron's tasking had not and the bulk of their time was spent on shipping patrols, convoy escorts, interception exercises and formation flying. Whilst at Andreas the squadron was divided into two flights, 'A' and 'B' flights and subdivided again in four sections, namely Blue, Green, Red and Yellow sections. They were all on a state of high readiness at varying times of the day.

Airfields on the Isle of Man, and in particular Andreas, were used by squadrons either transiting through on cross-country exercise or flying on to stations in Northern Ireland. On 8th October, 133 'Eagle' Squadron was getting ready to move to a new home at Eglinton in Northern Ireland from Fowlmere in Cambridgeshire. 15 Hawker Hurricane IIbs, led by the Sqn Ldr G A Brown, left Fowlmere on the first leg to Sealand in Cheshire. After leaving Sealand, poor weather caused the group to split up and only six aircraft arrived at Andreas as planned. Two wisely turned back for Sealand and three others landed safely at Jurby. As night fell, four aircraft were still unaccounted for and a rescue launch from Douglas started searching off Maughold Head after reports were received of a pilot in the sea. At first light the following morning, more local rescue launches and two Spitfires from 457 Squadron continued the search for the missing pilots and their aircraft. Tragically, all four had crashed into the island; Z3253 came down on Snaefell, north-west of Laxey, Z3457 was abandoned and crashed at Ballafayle Farm near Ramsey, Z3677 was down at North Laxey and Z3781 ploughed into Ballaskeig Moor, also near Ramsey. Four pilots, Flt Lt Mamedoff, Plt Off. Stout, Plt Off. McCall and Plt Off. White lost their lives. To maintain morale, three Hurricanes from 133 Squadron joined 457 Squadron on a local flying exercise. However, when they left the island on 11th October it must have had quite an effect on the squadron to have lost almost a third of their strength without having encountered the enemy.

The daily routine for 457 Squadron was disrupted when they were called upon to join the search for three internees who had escaped from

Ramsey Internment Camp. The resourceful trio had 'acquired' a white cutter, in which they were making across the sea to the Cumberland coast. The squadron spent the whole morning of the 16th October looking for the escapees but, much to the annoyance of the Australians, the group was discovered by a lone Bristol Blenheim from Jurby.

The radar station at Bride caused some excitement on 25th October when it reported two unidentified aircraft 30,000ft over the island. Blue Section was scrambled but, just to add to the unit's frustrations, the enemy turned out to be 457 Squadron Spitfires!

Wg Cdr Gomez's time at Andreas came to a premature end on 27th November when he was posted to Valley, Anglesey as their new station commander. Wg Cdr E V Knowles DFC took over Andreas as Gomez left the airfield in dramatic style as a passenger in a Bristol Beaufighter.

A routine patrol turned to tragedy for the squadron on 29th November. Green Section was ordered to patrol base and then the Calf of Man at 10,000ft and, after being ordered to land, Sgt Brewin, in Spitfire IIa P7445, went missing. It is believed he lost control while descending through cloud and a rescue aircraft quickly reported wreckage and a body four miles west of Peel.

The Spitfires were joined by a long-term detachment of 275 Squadron on 30th November. This Air Sea Rescue unit had been formed at Valley only a few days before. Along with another detachment at Eglinton, the squadron was responsible for virtually the whole of the Irish Sea, approximately 60,000 square miles! The Westland Lysander III and Supermarine Walrus I and II were its main aircraft types, although Boulton Paul Defiants, Avro Ansons and the Spitfire Vb were also used by the squadron. The unit became operational at Andreas on 3rd December, with three Lysanders available.

457 Squadron and the station as a whole suffered a severe blow to morale when the B Flight commander, Flt Lt Edy was killed in Spitfire IIa P7502 on 5th December whilst performing aerobatics. The squadron sorely missed a popular character and his great experience.

A welcome distraction for the squadron came in December with the arrival of the more powerful Spitfire Vb. Fitted with a Rolls-Royce Merlin 45 engine producing 1,440 hp, this variant was over 400 hp more powerful than the Spitfire I.

The scrambles continued into the new year, all resulting in contact with friendly aircraft, although it was still counted as operational flying. At the end of January 1942 the final comment in the squadron's

The Spitfire VB was the most common variant of this classic fighter to be seen over the Isle of Man until the end of 1942.

official record stated 'No Hun was forthcoming!' The squadron did come as close as it ever would to actually seeing an enemy aircraft on 21st February. Red and Yellow sections were scrambled and were within minutes of making contact with a lone raider before he managed to escape by making use of cloud cover.

The station commander and the squadron commander led two sections of the squadron on a practice interception exercise on 24th February. The 'enemy' was six Handley Page Halifaxes, which were successfully intercepted over the Irish Sea. Annoyingly for the Australians, they were not destined to intercept the real enemy during their stay at Andreas. On a similar exercise on the 8th March, Sgt McDonnell was killed when his Spitfire Vb BL491 plunged into the sea off Ramsey.

Ten days later, the squadron received a movement order saying that the whole unit would be going to an airfield in the south-east of England. The same order announced that their replacement at Andreas would be another Australian fighter unit, namely 452 Squadron, based at Kenley in Surrey, also flying the Spitfire. This was deemed appropriate, as 457 Squadron was used by 452 Squadron as a clearing unit for feeding through their own operational pilots. The departure date was to be 20th March, however poor weather delayed this to 22nd March. 457 Squadron pilots flew out of Andreas for the last time, taking with them their new Spitfire Vbs, although several were left behind for the incoming unit. The ground crew and support staff followed in five Handley Page Harrow transports, arriving at their new home at Redhill a few hours later. They were destined to stay in the country only a few more months before being sent overseas, although for 457 Squadron it was back home as they left for Australia on 18th June 1942.

The following evening, the same five Harrows returned to Andreas filled with the ground crew of 452 Squadron and accompanied by the squadron's Spitfire Vbs. Formed on 8th April 1941 at Kirton-in-Lindsey in Lincolnshire, the squadron was operational on the Spitfire IIa by May and in action from Kenley in July 1941. Considerably more experienced than their predecessors from a combat point of view, with at least eleven enemy kills chalked up, the squadron was sent to Andreas for a rest.

Up until this time, aircraft had been operating from the main runway without incident, but a few minor accidents drew the Air Ministry's attention to the church. Andreas parish church had a tower which stood 120ft tall and was positioned only a few degrees from the centre line of the main runway. The ministry ordered that it either be removed or shortened and within a few weeks the tower was carefully dismantled, stone by stone. It was rebuilt to exactly half of its original height and the removed stones were stored and numbered in anticipation of its being rebuilt again. It is rumoured that after the closure of Andreas, the churchwardens elected for compensation rather than the rebuilding of the tower. The money was spent on a new electric-powered blower for the church organ!

Under the command of Sqn Ldr K W Truscott, 452 squadron quickly settled into the patrolling and exercise routine. This increased briefly on 31st March when 308 Squadron moved south from Woodvale in Lancashire. This left the Woodvale Sector completely devoid of fighter protection; so 452 Squadron brought an extra section in readiness to cope with the additional patrols.

The Fleet Air Arm made a brief appearance at Andreas on 1st April 1942. 825 Squadron brought its new Fairey Swordfish IIs from Lee-on-Solent in Hampshire for a brief stay. The squadron was virtually wiped out only a few weeks earlier after its brave but disastrous attack against

The Fairey Swordfish made several brief appearances at Andreas.

the German battlecruisers which were breaking out of Brest Harbour; an action which earned Lt Cdr Esmonde, the commanding officer, a posthumous Victoria Cross. The squadron returned to Lee-on-Solent on 8th April.

The first of several losses incurred by 452 squadron during their stay at Andreas happened on 10th April 1942. Sgt Waters in Spitfire Vb BL284, an ex 457 Squadron aircraft, was lost whilst returning from an exercise over the Cumberland coast. Waters, who was a non-operational pilot, was reported to have left the formation and crashed into the sea south approximately 8 miles south west of St Bee's Head. A ship nearby, the SS *Herbert Walker*, reported seeing an aircraft crash into the sea but saw no sign of the pilot. Before darkness fell, a Lysander of 275 Squadron, a Beaufighter from Valley and two seaplane tenders joined the search, but sadly all to no avail.

At 06:16hrs on 3rd May, Blue and Green sections were scrambled after reports that several enemy aircraft had been spotted crossing the Irish Sea. Blue Section, made up of Sgt Bassett and Plt Off. Lammerton in AD537, were off the Cumberland coast near Millom when they made contact with a Junkers Ju 88. Both pilots engaged the aircraft, claiming it damaged and silencing the rear gunner in the process. During the attack, Lammerton's engine was hit by machine gun fire from the Ju 88, causing a pipe to burst in the glycol system. Lammerton

25

nursed his engine for a further 10 minutes, but excessive fumes began to enter the cockpit and he had no choice but to bail out. A massive air and sea search was implemented immediately, involving other aircraft from 452 Squadron, Lysanders of 275 and aircraft from Jurby, Millom and Squires Gate. Luckily, Lammerton was spotted by an Anson from Jurby and was picked up by a naval launch some 5½ hours after he had bailed out.

The last fatal incident involving the squadron's aircraft occurred in public style directly over Andreas on 8th May. During a cine gun attack, Spitfire Vb AB171, piloted by Plt Off. Ford, collided with Spitfire Vb AB244, flown by Sgt Goodhew. Ford managed to bail out before his aircraft crashed on the edge of the airfield. Unfortunately, Goodhew made no attempt to escape his crippled Spitfire. He was killed outright when his aircraft came down one mile west of the Hall Caine airfield.

452 Squadron were officially stood down from all duties on 31st May, effectively leaving the entire sector and island without any fighter protection. The squadron left by sea and rail the following morning for a temporary stay at Atcham in Shropshire before departing for Australia on 18th June 1942. On this occasion, all aircraft and ground equipment were left behind at Andreas in preparation for the formation of a new unit at the airfield.

It was not until 5th June that Flt Lt Watson and Flt Lt Curtis, the flight commanders of the re-formed 93 Squadron, arrived by air. The next day the Commanding Officer, Sqn Ldr Nelson-Edwards also arrived, followed by the squadron's pilots on 9th June. 93 Squadron was originally formed on 7th December 1940 at Middle Wallop and equipped with the Handley Page Harrow. It was involved in the adventurous task of perfecting the art of laying aerial mines across the path of enemy aircraft. It actually achieved a success with this technique, destroying a single German bomber on 22nd December 1940. Douglas Havocs and Vickers Wellingtons followed before the squadron was disbanded into 1458 Flight on 24th November 1941.

In stark contrast to their previous aircraft, 93 Squadron were now equipped with the Spitfire VB, the majority of which had already seen service with 457 and 452 squadrons. Operational training began immediately for the new fighter pilots with exercises including air-to-ground firing, air-to-air firing, interceptions and formation flying. By 27th June 1942, twelve squadron pilots were categorised as operational.

The squadron suffered its first loss on the 29th June, during a practice interception. Yellow Section was acting as the target, when one of their group, Sgt Lowney in Spitfire VB AD570, went missing. A search discovered his body approximately eight miles south-west of the Calf of Man. It was assumed that he either bailed out too late or was thrown from his aircraft on impact. By the beginning of July, the squadron was fully operational, flying mainly convoy patrols with the occasional interception.

Andreas nearly provided a safe haven for an aircraft of the Aeroplane and Armament Experimental Establishment on 28th July 1942. Douglas Boston III W8291, with Plt Off. R H A Williams at the controls, was on a training flight from West Freugh in Dumfries and Galloway when on approach to Andreas the starboard engine failed. With flaps and undercarriage down, Williams was unable to maintain height on a single engine. The Boston came down in a field one mile north of Bride, injuring two passengers on board.

A similar emergency occurred on 4th August to Beaufighter IC T4715 from the station flight at Lyneham in Wiltshire. The aircraft was carrying out a fuel consumption test when the port engine cut. Whilst carrying out an emergency approach, the twin engined fighter crashed two miles north of Ramsey.

A routine flight around the island on 7th August resulted in the squadron's second and final loss while operating from Andreas. Red Section, composed of four Spitfires, was south of Maughold Head and on their return home when they ran into low cloud. Red 1, 2 and 3 climbed through the cloud without any problem but Red 4, Sgt Bickmore in Spitfire VB AB796, was nowhere to be seen. A large patch of oil and an unopened parachute was all that was found.

Radio transmissions (R/T) between the ground and aircraft had never been of a particularly high quality during the early years of the Second World War. This situation was radically improved for aircraft operating around the Isle of Man on 13th August. A new, permanent signals station was opened at Regaby just two miles from Andreas. This, combined with new equipment in the station operations room, made a huge improvement in the quality of R/T.

93 Squadron's future role was put to the test during an exercise on 19th August 1942. Six aircraft flew to Ballyhalbert in Northern Ireland, where they landed to refuel and rearm as though providing reinforcement for another squadron. Incredibly, all six aircraft were ready to take off again in 14 minutes, making the exercise a total success.

A routine flight to the mainland brought tragedy to the station on 23rd August. The station commander, Wg Cdr E V Knowles DFC, who was accompanied by his wife, Mjr Waite, Plt Off. Paton and four airmen took off in Armstrong Whitworth Whitley V BD417 of 296 Squadron. Two minutes after take off, the aircraft appeared to stall, and then it crashed in flames just outside the airfield's northern boundary. Only three airmen survived. Andreas was without a station commander until the arrival of Wg Cdr S G Beaumont on 1st September.

93 Squadron continued to cram in the training, which included a rendezvous with 41 Squadron from Llanbedr, Gwynedd on 28th August. The two squadrons then carried out a simulated enemy sweep over Preston. Two days later, the squadron was withdrawn from front line duties, and on the 4th September an advance party of 93 Squadron and No 3091 Servicing Echelon left for King's Cliffe in Northamptonshire. On 7th September, the main parties of both units as well as 16 Spitfires and one Magister of 93 Squadron left for King's Cliffe; the rear party left the following day. 93 Squadron were destined to leave for North Africa in October, going on to support the invasions of Sicily and Italy.

The airfield was put to the test for the first time as an emergency diversion airfield on 6th September 1942. A Boeing B-17E Flying Fortress from Westover Field in Massachusetts landed safely with ten crew on board; it left later that day. A few weeks after, a Douglas Dakota with 16 passengers on board used Andreas as a safe haven. En route from Ringway to Langford Lodge in Northern Ireland, the twin-engined American-built transport left the following day.

September was filled with visitors, including six Fleet Air Arm Spitfires, six Fairey Fulmars, and on 29th September, 13 Spitfires from 41 Squadron. The squadron was moving from Eglinton to Llanbedr and three Handley Page Harrows accompanied the unit. 41 Squadron would use Andreas for many exercises over the coming weeks.

With no resident fighter squadron, the airfield concentrated more on its own upkeep. From 22nd September, the first daily five-minute message was broadcast across the station tannoy system. The message covered a plethora of subjects including camp cleanliness, salvage, intelligence, security, 'war mindedness', fitness and sport, anti-gas, national savings, education and, last but not least, food production. Plenty for the permanent staff to think about! With regard to security, the following is worth quoting from official documents, '22:35 *hours "Bags of Panic". Light seen flashing on a hill in direction of Sulby – spies and fifth columnists? No – airmen rabbiting!!'* This could be interpreted either as vigilant security or a very bored sarcastic airman on duty that night!

Bad weather forced six Fulmar IIs from 808 Squadron to land here on 16th October 1942. The Fleet Air Arm (FAA) fighters were en route from Stretton in Cheshire to Peterhead in Aberdeenshire. The more cynical officers and airmen on station at the time suggested that the navy pilots had known about a big party that was to be held on Andreas that very night. The visitors must have had a good time because they did not leave until 19th October.

275 Squadron was very busy in October and the arrival of the first of two Supermarine Walruses came in very useful. On 21st October, ASR (Air Sea Rescue) searches were carried out for a Wellington and a Mustang I, sadly only an oil patch, which indicated the Wellington crash site, was found. The Mustang was AM241 of 169 Squadron, from Twinwood Farm in Bedfordshire. The American-built fighter hit the sea whilst flying low on a navigational exercise. On 27th October, 275 Squadron carried out a search for a missing Lockheed Hudson. Five airmen were picked up safe in Liverpool Bay, much to the frustration of 275 Squadron, whose search area ended 20 miles west.

41 Squadron's Spitfires used Andreas throughout December for interception exercises, practice 'Rhubarbs', and refuelling and re-arming exercises. They returned briefly in January 1943 for another exercise but by February the whole unit was moved to High Ercall in Shropshire.

A Fairey Swordfish arrived at Andreas on 1st February from the aircraft carrier HMS *Activity* that was steaming off the east coast of Ireland. The following day the 11,800 ton escort carrier had arrived in Ramsey Bay, arousing much interest among the locals and military alike. 275 Squadron quickly arranged a cooperation exercise with No 54 ASR Marine Craft Unit (MCU) based at Ramsey so as to get a good look at the carrier. On 3rd February, the Swordfish at Andreas, which was now accompanied by a Fulmer, returned to the carrier and HMS *Activity* went on to survive the war.

On the morning of 9th February 1943, Andreas hosted a very unusual aircraft, which had arrived from Defford in Worcestershire. The aircraft was Boeing 247D DZ203 (former NC13344), a twin-engined American airliner, which was impressed into RAF service in July 1941. DZ203 belonged to the Telecommunications Flying Unit (TFU) and it was generally used for blind approach landing experiments. On this occasion, the Boeing was carrying out tests with HMS *Saltburn*, a minesweeper which was launched back in 1918. DZ203 returned to Defford on 22nd February.

Throughout early 1943, Andreas played the role of an enemy airfield in numerous exercises flown by Spitfire and Curtis Tomahawks from

Ballyhalbert and Typhoons from Woodvale. On several occasions these fighters would land and be quickly turned around by their ground crews, who had been transported from their home airfields.

Worthy of mention was the momentous occasion when communications from Andreas were improved on 3rd March 1943. Flt Lt Laven had the honour of releasing the first carrier pigeon from the airfield. The bird's destination was No 58 Carrier Pigeon Loft on the mainland, it was not recorded whether its flight was a success or not.

275 Squadron, although generally very busy, had much of its spare time taken up by training and exercises, usually involving its aircraft. On 30th March 1943, an exercise with a difference was held, involving personnel from the squadron. A large number of officers and airmen were dropped at various points around the island. Dressed in uniform, but without their 1250 identity cards, the object of the exercise was for them to find their way back to the operations building at Andreas without being caught by the local police or Home Guard. Only two airmen successfully arrived at the operations guard room.

Air gunners were still in high demand in mid 1943, with Bomber Command still not quite gaining the upper hand over the enemy and losses remaining high. The amount of space at Andreas and the unrestricted air space with access to several ranges, both air-to-ground and air-to-air, meant that it was the prime candidate for a new air gunners school.

No 5 Air Gunners School (AGS) was originally meant to form at Castle Kennedy in Wigtownshire on 24th July 1941. This was cancelled and a second attempt at forming 5 AGS at Andreas on 1st May 1943 was short-lived. 5 AGS was never to be and the following day the unit was officially renamed 11 AGS, within 29 Group. The AGS equipment was simply an aircraft with the ability to tow a drogue target and another to carry pupil air gunners, with a fully mobile gun turret. The Miles Martinet provided the target towing and the Avro Anson I proved to be a reliable gunnery trainer and could carry at least four pupil gunners plus an instructor. Within a few weeks, the school had 25 Martinets, 23 Ansons and a single Miles Master on strength.

The accident-free record of 275 Squadron was blighted for the first and only time on 21st July 1943. Anson I EG548 suffered an engine failure and made a successful ditching four miles south of Scarlett Point, near Castletown. No one was injured and all four on board were quickly rescued by an RAF launch.

The new year started badly for 11 AGS when a completely avoidable accident occurred between two aircraft on 6th January 1944. Martinets

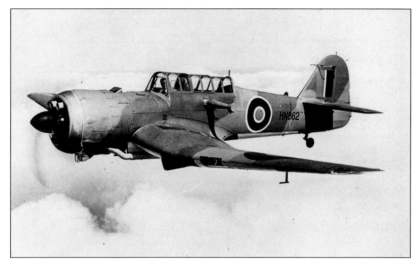

11 AGS spent three years at Andreas and the unit's Miles Martinets target tugs flew, weather permitting, every day.

JN448 and JN492 were in tight formation returning to the airfield when, in a moment of madness, one decided to make a mock attack on an unsuspecting Anson. The two target tugs collided, both spiralling down in flames into the sea off the Point of Ayre.

As anticipated back in 1940, Andreas was officially made an emergency landing ground and diversion airfield. Andreas was in a particularly useful position for aircraft travelling 'over the pond' on the Atlantic Ferry Route. B-17 Flying Fortresses and B-24 Liberator bombers were predicted to be the main aircraft to be diverted, but only a few ever arrived.

Several interesting aircraft, mainly American types, found sanctuary in Andreas throughout 1944 including, on 24th January, a USAAF Lockheed P-38 Lightning with engine trouble . A Grumman Martlet, basically a Royal Navy version of the Wildcat, also paid a visit on 17th March. RAF visitors were just as prolific; on 13th June 1944, two Beaufighters from 9 OTU at Crosby made precautionary landings at Andreas. Beaufighter XI JM117 landed with engine trouble and Beaufighter X JM327, piloted by Plt Off Menaul and navigator Flg Off. Webster, had an overheating cockpit. Both returned to Crosby the same day, ground crew of 11 AGS having rectified both aircraft.

Mosquito XII HK119 of 307 Squadron was destined not to return

B Flight of 772 Squadron brought their Supermarine Sea Otters to Andreas.

home on 27th June 1944. 307 Squadron's home base was at Church Fenton in Yorkshire but at that time this aircraft was on detachment at Coltishall in Norfolk. On approach to the airfield, the port engine cut at a critical moment and the twin-engined night fighter undershot the runway and plunged into the ground.

The Avro Anson, which had performed sterling work for 11 AGS and many other gunnery schools and units, was steadily phased out from September 1944 onwards. Its replacement was the Vickers Wellington III, X and XIV, the school having 19 on strength by the end of November while still retaining at least 25 Martinets as target tugs. The school also operated a single Handley Page Halifax, bringing added diversity to the air gunners' training.

By January 1945, twelve Supermarine Spitfire VIIs could be seen at Andreas, there being fighter affiliation against pupil air gunners in the Wellingtons as well as extra target tugs for the steadily dwindling population of Martinets.

On 17th April 1945, B Flight of 772 Squadron moved to Andreas from Ronaldsway. They were equipped with the Vought Corsair, Douglas Boston and the Supermarine Sea Otter, the last providing air sea rescue cover until they returned to Ronaldsway on 6th September.

11 AGS lost its only Spitfire VII on 11th October 1945. MD169 had just taken off when the Merlin engine cut, forcing the pilot to make an

32

Spotting a Seafire on land was a rare sight in 1946, but several could be seen on Andreas during 772 Squadron's stay.

emergency belly-landing on the beach south of Shellag Point. The following day, Wellington X JA346 overshot a single-engined landing, causing the undercarriage to collapse. The bomber skidded down the runway on its belly, luckily without harming the crew and pupil air gunners on board. The final aircraft loss of 11 AGS occurred on 31st May 1946 when Wellington X NC767 overshot its landing and raised its undercarriage to stop itself from careering off the end of the runway. Once again, all on board were unhurt, but the aircraft was a write-off.

A detachment of 772 Squadron arrived at Andreas on 7th March 1946. The squadron brought the Seafire L.III, Mosquito PR.XVI, B.25 and PR.34 as well as a return of the Avro Anson. A section of the detachment left for Anthorn on 3rd May while the remainder stayed at Andreas until 15th August 1946, when they made the short flight to Jurby.

The gates of the airfield opened for the first time to the general public on 14th September 1946. It was the annual Battle of Britain Day flying and static display, which in the post-war years was organised on almost every active RAF airfield. This was to be the only event of its kind held at Andreas because, on 19th September 1946, 11 AGS was moved to Jurby, bringing an end to military aviation on the airfield.

Although in a very poor state of repair, the type 518/40 fighter station control tower at Andreas still stands. (Jarrod Cotter, www.flypast.co.uk)

Placed under care and maintenance, the airfield was closed in February 1947, there being no justification for having two military airfields so close together in the north of the Isle of Man.

The Isle of Man Government bought the 400 acre airfield back from the Air Ministry for a mere £23,700, the price that was actually paid for it back in 1940. All technical and domestic buildings were included as a goodwill gesture for the island's cooperation during the war. The Air Ministry did place a clause on the actual airfield, saying that no development work should take place within the perimeter track and that all three runways should be kept in a useable condition. Eventually this area was put up for auction by the Isle of Man Government Property Trustees; it was sold for £33,000 to the Morrey family, who still own it today.

Today, two of the three original runways remain in reasonable condition; one is still used by the Andreas Gliding Club and a few microlights. The perimeter track and several dispersal areas still remain and so do many buildings, including the control tower, firing butts and innumerable small huts.

3
ANTHORN

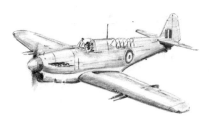

Anthorn's role during the Second World War was rather short, the bulk of activity occurring during the post-war years. Anthorn was the last airfield to be built in Cumbria and the only one used solely by the Royal Navy. However, it is the only airfield in this book that is still retained by the Ministry of Defence but not, unfortunately, in the role of a flying station.

Located on the northern shore of Moricambe Bay, which flows into the Solway Firth, Anthorn can trace its aviation past back to the First World War. A landing ground was located between the hamlets of Cardurnock and Anthorn, near to a property called Solway House, which was demolished to make way for the new airfield. Not much is known about the landing ground, but it is highly likely that it would have been used by a Scottish-based Home Defence Squadron tasked with defending the nation against Zeppelin attack.

While still only a collection of fields, it allegedly served as an emergency landing ground for aircraft from Silloth. No records acknowledge its existence or use at the time but it is quite possible. Several aircraft did force-land near to the site but this was probably without realising a landing ground existed. One of these was Armstrong Whitworth Whitley V Z6748, which force-landed near to Solway House at 06:00 hours on 15th July 1941. The crew was uninjured and despite the aircraft being severely damaged it was repaired and remained in RAF service until 1945.

The Admiralty first surveyed a site at Anthorn, along with locations at Scotsdyke and Kirkandrews, for a new airfield on 18th September 1942. The inspecting group included the Admiralty's Director of Air Material and the Civil Engineer in Chief.

Initially the Royal Navy was looking for a new station to train their aircrews in the art of dropping torpedoes. The remoteness, relatively clear skies and great areas of water made Anthorn perfect for the task and work began on the airfield in December 1942. Construction progressed at a painfully slow rate, with the contractor's and the Admiralty's ever-changing priorities distracting both the civilian workforce and the military planners.

1943 passed and it was beginning to look like the work at Anthorn was going to be abandoned. The Admiralty had, by now, found an alternative for its torpedo-training unit at Ronaldsway and Anthorn was without a future unit. It was not until the spring of 1944 that civilian contractors, John Laing & Son, started work on three concrete runways and the usual network of perimeter track. The main runway was only 1,400 yards in length, supported by two 1,200 yard runways in a traditional triangular pattern. Dispersal areas were limited, with a few extensions of the perimeter track for the parking of aircraft.

In the summer of 1944, the Admiralty announced that Anthorn would become the home of an Aircraft Receipt and Despatch Unit (ARDU). This changed the specification for the local contractors, especially with regard to hangarage. An ARDU would need as much cover as possible, as aircraft modifications and upgrades would be the main work carried out. 21 Fromson type hangars were constructed, all 60ft wide and 84 ft long, as well as a collection of technical buildings, very few of which were of brick construction. Accommodation was also classed as temporary, which normally meant Nissen huts. Enough were constructed to accommodate 87 Royal Navy Officers and 906 other ranks. Accommodation for 13 WRNS Officers and 226 other ranks was also provided.

Keeping with the naval tradition of naming their airfields after birds, Anthorn was commissioned as Royal Naval Air Station (RNAS) or HMS *Nuthatch* (known as a 'Stone Frigate') on 7th September 1944. No 1 ARDU was the first unit to occupy Anthorn with the main task of bringing new Fleet Air Arm (FAA) aircraft up to an operational standard.

The first aircraft, ten Grumman Hellcats, were supposed to arrive at Anthorn. Unfortunately they had to divert to nearby Kirkbride because the runway that was into the wind that day was still unfinished. This situation continued for a few more weeks, with all crosswind landings being carried out at Kirkbride.

The Hellcat was the main type passing through the ARDU in late

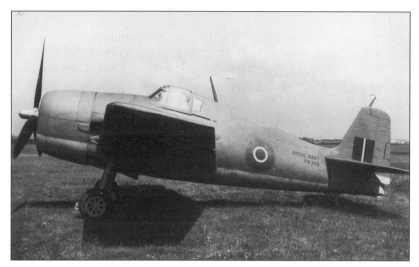

Several Grumman Hellcats were the first aircraft to arrive at Anthorn; many passed through the ARDU before the war's end.

1944. The Royal Navy was a heavy user of this successful American-built fighter. 252 F6F-3s entered service from the beginning of March 1943. The FAA designated it the Hellcat I but had originally wanted to name it the Gannet I. By this stage of the Second World War, the Admiralty was beginning to realize that changing the names of American aircraft was causing more confusion than it was worth. A further 930 F6F-5s, known as Hellcat II, were also used by the FAA with great success, especially against the Japanese. Both marks went through Anthorn, many of them arriving too late from the USA to see active service. One particular aircraft, Hellcat II KE209 arrived at Anthorn on 1st September 1945 for storage. It was sent to Stretton in Cheshire a few months later and then Lossiemouth for long-term storage in June 1946. Incredibly, it remained at Lossiemouth until April 1970, when it was passed to the FAA Museum at Yeovilton, where it survives to this day.

The all-British-built Fairey Firefly was also common at Anthorn during the last few months of the Second World War and beyond. Developed as a replacement for the Fairey Fulmar, the Firefly first took to the skies on 22nd December 1941. This two-seat tactical reconnaissance aircraft, powered by a Rolls Royce Griffon engine, was far superior to its predecessor in virtually all respects. It entered service

The Fairey Firefly was a common sight at Anthorn during the last few months of the Second World War and for many years after.

with the FAA in October 1943; however its first real combat was not until July 1944 when Fireflies from HMS *Indefatigable* attacked the *Tirpitz* in a Norwegian fjord. It continued to serve with distinction against the Japanese in the Pacific, remaining in service with the FAA until 1950. One famous aircraft which passed through Anthorn was Firefly AS5 WB271 belonging to the FAA Historic Flight, which sadly crashed with the loss of both crew at Duxford in Cambridgeshire in July 2003.

The very nature of an ARDU was to receive aircraft, often direct from the manufacturer, and prepare them for operational service. The aircraft usually carried their own equipment, which was supplied as a modification kit. Batches of aircraft that needed the same weapon fit would pass through the unit, this would include machine guns and/or cannon, bomb racks and/or rocket rails. Gun sights were also fitted, plus the testing and harmonising of the weapons on the ground in one of the many Fromson gun-butts. Radios and radar were fitted, and a specific area of the airfield was allocated for their testing, although the danger to human health caused by standing in front of radar was not understood as it is today.

RNAS airfields were always located in the most extreme points of the United Kingdom and Anthorn's position made it a useful stopping off point for many FAA aircraft. A comprehensive Station Flight was formed at Anthorn, mainly for the large number of liaison duties which the ARDU demanded. The station's aircraft would fly as far south as Culdrose in Cornwall and as far north as Hatston in the Orkneys. The flight operated several Avro Ansons, Airspeed Oxfords, Tiger Moths and a selection of American-built aircraft which included a Stinson Reliant, Grumman Avenger I and a Beech Traveller. Designated UC-43 by the United States Navy, the Traveller was transferred to the Royal Navy with the registration FT498. This popular aircraft managed to escape the scrap men at the end of the war and was returned to the USA via Abbotsinch in Renfrewshire in late 1945. Another important task performed by the Station Flight was the collection of goods which were rationed in England. When visiting Northern Ireland, aircraft were loaded with eggs, and trips to the Isle of Man were always encouraged, as they would return with kippers.

With the Second World War at an end, the only dispatching the ARDU was performing involved the scrapping of endless lines of aircraft. Many Grumman Hellcats returned to the unit only to be flown to Sydenham in Northern Ireland, placed on an aircraft carrier and dumped at sea. This was in line with the Lend-Lease agreement, which called for all aircraft supplied by the USA to be either returned or destroyed at the end of hostilities. Other naval air stations were rapidly closing down around the country and many of their aircraft were flown to Anthorn for long-term storage. The airfield was quickly covered with aircraft but there was still plenty of room for the first of several operational squadrons to arrive. 772 Squadron brought a collection of aircraft including the Mosquito PR34, PRXVI and B25 plus an Anson and Spitfire LIII on 3rd May 1946. The squadron spent most of its time on detachment at Andreas and Jurby before departing for Arbroath in Angus on 26th June 1947. 813 Squadron, with the powerful Blackburn Firebrand TF5, and 801 Squadron, with the Sea Hornet F20, both followed from Arbroath on 21st May 1948, with a detachment to Bramcote in Warwickshire before departing for Culdrose. The Sea Fury FB2s of 802 Squadron arrived next, from HMS *Vengeance* on 6th October 1949. These superb naval fighter aircraft returned to HMS *Vengeance* on 24th January 1950. Fairey Firefly AS6s of 812 Squadron from HMS *Theseus* made Anthorn their temporary home from 4th June to 3rd July 1952, followed by Sea Fury FB2s from Stretton in Lancashire. 807 Squadron arrived on 14th January 1954, leaving for Brawdy in Pembrokeshire on 5th May 1954. The final operational FAA squadron to arrive at Anthorn was 824 Squadron from Eglinton in Northern Ireland, on 17th July 1954. The squadron operated the

It was a Fairey Gannet AS1 that became the very last aircraft to depart from Anthorn in December 1957.

American specification Grumman Avenger TBM-3E, returning to Eglinton on 28th July 1954.

Two Dutch naval squadrons were stationed at Anthorn in late 1957. 860 and 861 Squadrons were converting to the Armstrong Whitworth Sea Mk.50 and both air and ground crew training was being given on the station.

The ARDU continued its work for many years after the war's end, handling a diverse range of aircraft. Aircraft types included the Avenger, Gannet, Firefly, Sea Balliol, Firebrand, Seafire, Sturgeon, Seamew, Harvard, Martinet, Sea Hawk, Sea Fury, Barracuda, Sea Hornet, Dominie, Tiger Moth, Anson, Oxford and SG.38 Glider.

The last aircraft to leave the unit was Fairey Gannet AS1 WN448. The Gannet arrived at Anthorn on 8th January 1957 and flew out on 2nd December 1957 for the AHU (Aircraft Holding Unit) at Culdrose.

The airfield was quickly run down and was closed to flying by March 1958. Retained by the Ministry of Defence, the airfield is now covered in myriad aerials for producing Very Low Frequency (VLF) radio transmissions. The system is specifically used for transmitting orders and messages to Royal Navy submarines as well as for relaying reports from Fylingdales in North Yorkshire to the USA Defense HQ in

One of four surviving Fromson hangars, three of which are outside the radio station's boundary. The Fromson provided substantial protection for a single aircraft and also doubled as a firing butt for testing aircraft guns. (Author)

Colorado. The radio station is strictly out of bounds to the general public and is currently controlled by the Defence Communications Service Agency (DCSA).

Many of the original runways, perimeter tracks and dispersals remain in reasonable condition but very few wartime buildings of significance still exist. Several of the Fromson hangars remain and a few static water tanks. Admiralty houses, which were constructed in 1952, make up the bulk of the accommodation which today is Anthorn village. The aerials still give the airfield a Cold War feel and access is usually discouraged.

One rather intimidating proposed use for Anthorn, was the consideration of the airfield for Project Isolus. ISOLUS stood for Interim Storage of Laid-up Submarines, which was to provide temporary storage of radioactive waste from decommissioned Royal

Only the sheep are allowed onto the airfield; visitors are not encouraged. (Author)

Navy nuclear-powered submarines. The plan was then for the final processing or disposal of the waste to be sent to a national facility when it became available. This post-Cold War use did not materialise, however, and, without it, it would seem that Anthorn will be remaining in military hands for many years to come.

4
Brayton Park

On 30th April 1941, Wg Cdr J M Mitchell, the Commanding Officer of 12 Maintenance Unit, inspected a new Satellite Landing Ground at Brayton Park. Mitchell was expecting the SLG to be up and running no later than June of that year, however local politics and difficulties with contractors severely delayed its use.

Located one mile east of Aspatria, sandwiched between the B5299 to the south and the A596 to the north, the airfield was known as Brayton Hall during its construction. Its official title was 39 SLG and, along with 10 SLG at Wath Head, its role was the dispersal of aircraft from the parent unit at Kirkbride.

Throughout May and June of 1941, several senior officers, all of whom were in deep discussion with various contractors, made visits. Despite the SLG being in a state of flux, the Marshal of the RAF, Sir Edward L Ellington GCB, CMG, CBE, accompanied by the CO of 12 MU, requested to visit the site on 6th June. The airfield was not a pretty site and the situation did not improve a few days later when, on 18th June, the CO visited the SLG with Superintendent Graham of Wigton Police. For the landing ground to function a minor road needed to be closed, a decision that Graham wholeheartedly objected to. The superintendent's objections delayed the opening until he was eventually overruled by the 'unseen powers from above'.

Work continued through 1941, although at a very steady pace, as many people thought that the whole idea of an SLG at Brayton would be abandoned because of the road issue, which had still not been resolved. As late as February 1942, hard standings and dispersal areas were still being constructed and marked out, eventually being completed at the end of March. With an indication that the SLG may be nearing completion, Flg Off. G E Mason was named as the officer in charge, with Plt Off. S P Pallot acting as administration officer. Finally, on 23rd April, the SLG's status rose to the ability to be 'opened within 14 days for partial dispersement if necessary'.

A trial landing by an Avro Anson from 12 MU took place on 14th May, followed by No 39 SLG's official 'long awaited' opening on 29th May 1942. The first aircraft to arrive for dispersal was a Wellington at 14:30hrs, followed by a second a few minutes later. A pair of Avro Ansons dropped in moments later, both filled to the brim with Air Transport Auxiliary (ATA) pilots from 16 Ferry Pilots Pool (FPP) at Kirkbride. Such was the need to relieve the pressure on Kirkbride, the ATA planned to deliver aircraft direct to 39 SLG.

Inspection followed inspection throughout June 1942, the main thrust being camouflage and more permanent hard standings for dispersed aircraft. On 22nd June Lt Col W G Clark from the RAF Regiment HQ of 41 Group visited to discuss the defence of the SLG and potentially accommodating an RAF Regiment Squadron at Brayton. Local Home Guard training was also discussed and recruitment of the civilian workforce immediately began.

By the beginning of July a second runway was completed at a length of 1,100 yards, complementing the original, which was slightly longer, at 1,300 yards. Wellingtons were arriving virtually on a daily basis since the SLG's opening; however on 17th August 1942 the first of many Spitfires landed at Brayton. It was envisaged from a very early stage that Brayton would accommodate four-engined aircraft. With this in mind, a safety 'run-off' area of 350 yards was added to the end of the main runway and on 2nd September an RAF Flying Fortress I landed with room to spare.

While Spitfires were no stangers to Brayton, the one and only occasion an operational aircraft arrived was on 7th September 1942. A Spitfire Vb of 154 Squadron at Wellingore in Lincolnshire ran into a storm and Brayton provided a safe haven while the weather cleared. The crew of a Beaufighter were not so fortunate on 23rd September. They crashed in flames on the edge of the landing ground with no chance of survival.

Drainage was becoming a recurring problem, with large waterlogged areas beginning to appear on the runways. Contractors were commissioned to lay more drainage pipes but it appears that the satellite's civilian staff carried out the bulk of the work. On 29th September it was recorded that 24 of Brayton's employees were furiously working on the drainage to solve the problem. The amount of water on the surface of the runways continued to disrupt operations

The first Handley Page Halifax flew into Brayton in late 1942 and several were dispersed in the surrounding woodland.

from the SLG until well into November. Surface conditions began to improve after a Pierced Steel Planking (PSP) perimeter track was laid and this put the SLG in a better position to receive larger aircraft.

The first Handley Page Halifax arrived from 12 MU on 30th November, experiencing no difficulty on landing and little damage was caused to the surface of the landing ground by the big bomber.

A new type of aircraft arrived for the first time on 26th June 1943. The American-built North American B-25 Mitchell, with its tricycle undercarriage, was quite a head-turner for the staff of Brayton. The model being dispersed at Brayton was the B-25C, simply known in RAF service as the Mitchell II. This was the most frequent mark in the RAF, 542 serving from late 1941 through to late 1945.

18 MU based at Dumfries was approaching its maximum capacity in June 1944. On 23rd June, arrangements were put in place to disperse over 40 aircraft and Brayton was the best candidate to receive them. By the end of July, 18 MU had created sufficient space at Dumfries, and Brayton could now boast nearly 200 aircraft of various types dispersed around its perimeter.

One of the last aircraft to leave the SLG was the Vultee Vengeance, which, by the end of war, was relegated to target towing duties.

The old SLG has not changed over the years; the landing ground remains as does the Robin hangar. (Author)

46

With the war now at an end, so was Brayton's usefulness as an SLG. It was now a case of flying the dispersed aircraft – the bulk of which were Vickers Wellingtons belonging to 12 MU – back to their parent units. It was recorded on 22nd October 1945 that 63 Wellingtons had returned to Kirkbride. On 16th November, a further 69 Wellingtons made the short and final flight to 12 MU. On 19th December 1945 the last aircraft left Brayton, a single Wellington and a pair of Vultee Vengeance target tugs.

Today, a single Robin hangar still remains in reasonable condition, with a few ancillary buildings. A fitting memorial to the site is the naming of Wellington Farm located near to the A596, which, hopefully, will survive as a small clue for future generations as to Brayton Park's wartime role.

5
BURNFOOT

On 15 Elementary Flying Training School's (EFTS) arrival at Kingstown on 3rd June 1940, a priority was to find at least one Relief Landing Ground (RLG). The main reason being poor drainage but also the Air Ministry's unwillingness to provide a perimeter track at Kingstown. These should have been obvious problems to rectify, you would have thought, however, the short term solution was solved with the acqusition of a pair of RLGs. One at Kirkpatrick, north of Gretna Green, and a second located south-west of Longtown, where the River Esk and River Lyne meet between Burnfoot and Hopesike Woods.

Burnfoot RLG was first occupied on 5th July 1940. With only a flat area of rolled grass and a few huts, facilities consisted of billets for airmen, a small mess hall and at least one lecture room. The local farmhouse was used as the watch office and at least five Robin type hangars were scattered around the perimeter. However limited these facilities may sound, the fact that any aircraft that could operate from here was relieving the pressure from Kingstown.

The first aircraft to move in was a flight of Miles Magisters and the first of the usual batch of accidents associated with a training airfield began on 24th July 1940. Whilst under instruction, LAC Andrews was attempting a sideslip in Magister I R1905. He mishandled the controls and ended up cartwheeling across the airfield, thankfully without injury to himself or the instructor.

Practice forced-landings were an important part of basic flying training and Burnfoot was a good location to learn the fundamentals of this skill. A few airmen came to grief at Burnfoot demonstrating how not to land a Magister. L8335 stalled and sideslipped into the ground on 2nd September, followed on 11th September by LAC C. Szymen in Magister I L8335. The last incident involving a Magister occurred on 25th February 1942 to N3961. Having survived the Battle of Britain

The Magister was the first monoplane trainer to be used by the RAF.

whilst on Biggin Hill's strength, the small trainer's flying career ended in Hopesike Wood after a failed overshoot. From June 1942 onwards, the Magister was superseded by the Tiger Moth which was virtually the only aircraft type to be seen at the airfield until the war's end.

Wg Cdr Bolan from HQ 51 Group inspected the RLG on 4th September 1942 and was sufficiently impressed to suggest that the airfield was suitable to house permanent staff. A conference at Kingstown, hosted by Wg Cdr D C M Homersham, Officer Commanding 15 EFTS, was held on 11th September to discuss how Burnfoot's facilities could be improved. Raising the status of the RLG would involve better medical facilities and the Senior Medical Officer (SMO) from Kingstown was a key player in improving Burnfoot. The farmhouse on the airfield, whose first floor was being used for the watch office, gained a medical room and officer billet on the ground floor. NCOs were accommodated in new hutments and in the old officers' accommodation, which was originally in the mess block. The RLG was inspected on the same day by OC 15 EFTS and the SMO, who found all current living, messing and sanitary facilities to be excellent. A target date of 1st October 1942 was set for full permanent occupation.

Crosby-in-Eden was located 8 miles to the south-east of Burnfoot and the residents in October 1942 were the Beaufighters and Beauforts

The Magisters of 15 EFTS were the main aircraft at Burnfoot until mid-1942. (Author)

of 9 (Coastal) Operational Training Unit. Burnfoot's Chief Flying Instructor, Sqn Ldr Morris AFC, visited the Station Commander of Crosby on 2nd October to discuss the demarcation of flying areas in order to avoid the possibility of air-to-air collisions in both of the airfields' circuits. Strict flying zones were agreed and, thankfully, no aerial accidents occurred. The rules and regulations agreed would have applied to Longtown as well, which was a satellite of Crosby. Considering that Longtown's main runway was only two miles away and almost in line with Burnfoot, they would have been very strictly adhered to.

Burnfoot officially opened as a Satellite Landing Ground on 25th October 1942, slightly after the original ambitious target date. The camp now had 20 flying instructors and 90 pupils living at the RLG, complete with two flights of Tiger Moths, which had become the unit's sole type of aircraft in June 1942.

The daily routine of pilot pupils cutting their teeth on the rudiments of flying a Tiger Moth was disrupted in dramatic style on 13th January 1943. Tiger Moth BB755 was landing when another Tiger Moth, T6499, taxied into its path. The resulting collision looked horrific and none of those who witnessed the accident expected any of the four airmen to survive. Remarkably, only the two flying instructors, Flt Sgt Gourley

The Magister was superseded by the ubiquitous Tiger Moth, which was virtually the only aircraft type that could be seen at Burnfoot until the airfield's closure in mid-1945.

and Sgt Bryson, were injured, both pupils walking away from the wreckage without a scratch.

Only three more Tiger Moths were involved in accidents at the airfield, none of them serious, which, considering the amount of take-offs and landings, was quite an achievement.

Burnfoot's small but important contribution to flying training during the Second World War came to end on 9th July 1945, when it closed to flying. The final task was the removal of medical supplies from Kingstown's other RLG at Kirkpatrick and from Burnfoot on 18th July 1945.

No buildings remain today and the land has returned to farming. It is not difficult, however, to imagine the sound of a Gipsy Major engine passing overhead.

6
CROSBY-ON-EDEN

Affectionately known as the 'Lake District Airport', Crosby-on-Eden is now officially labelled Carlisle Airport. Averaging 30,000 aircraft movements per year, the airport is the only major airfield now open to flying in Cumbria and as such is thriving. It offers general aviation pilots easy access to the north-west of England and promotes itself as a gateway to southern Scotland.

Located between Carlisle and Brampton off the A689, it has Hadrian's Wall on the northern edge of the site and the path of a Roman road passes directly through the middle. Work began on the new RAF airfield at Crosby-on-Eden in the summer of 1940. The country was fighting for survival in the Battle of Britain and many pilots and aircraft that served in the conflict would end up flying from Crosby.

Occupying 512 acres, the airfield was constructed by John Laing and Son Ltd, a rapidly growing company that would make millions out of the construction of airfields during the Second World War. Crosby alone cost £879,000 and was built with three runways made of asphalt and laid on a hardcore base. The main runway was 1,600 yards long with two shorter runways at 1,100 yards each, all bounded by the usual perimeter track and a few dispersals.

A 'Q' decoy airfield was also constructed at Scaleby, two miles north-west of Crosby. The decoy could be lit up at night, the theory being that an enemy would bomb Scaleby and not the main airfield at Crosby. It was manned by two airmen until at least the middle of 1942 and was never attacked by the Luftwaffe.

The airfield was hastily opened on 20th February 1941 and Crosby prepared to receive its first unit. Formed on 16th December 1940, 59 Operational Training Unit (OTU) was assembled at Turnhouse, Midlothian within 13 Group Fighter Command. Before arriving at Crosby, the OTU was transferred to 81 (Training) Group and was without aircraft on arrival at the airfield. Wg Cdr J I T Jones DSO, MC, DFC, was 59 OTU's first commanding officer but he was replaced almost immediately by Wg Cdr A F Scroggs, who took over as temporary station commander as well. Within days, Wg Cdr Scroggs was replaced as station commander by Wg Cdr F G A Robinson DFC, who was promoted to the more appropriate rank of group captain on 1st March.

The advance party of 59 OTU, comprising 40 officers and men, arrived on 21st February. A lack of completed accommodation on Crosby meant that the party was moved to Carlisle and billeted with the army at Hadrian's Camp. It would be another three weeks before they could finally settle in at Crosby.

After heavy snow had delayed work on the airfield, local contractors announced that Crosby's runways were serviceable on 10th March 1941. Station headquarters (SHQ) was the only permanent building actually completed and, as this provided a comfortable place for the senior staff to operate, Crosby was announced operational. Forty non-commissioned officers (NCO) and airmen arrived the same day and were moved into quarters on camp. They were faced with very grim conditions; no light, no permanent water supply, no finished roads, drainage still to be connected and laid in some areas, and no telephones!

The first aircraft to land at Crosby arrived on 11th March, a Hurricane I, flown by Flt Lt Orton DFC, made the short flight from Silloth. Orton was the first of many highly experienced pilots who all OTUs needed to pass on their skills to future fighter pilots. Orton returned to operations with 73 Squadron after his tour as an instructor and by the war's end achieved 17 victories flying the Hurricane.

Over the next two days, 64 Hurricanes descended upon Crosby, followed by a few Miles Masters and a pair of Fairey Battle Target Tugs. On the second day of this mass movement of aircraft, Sgt Elkins became lost and was killed when his Hurricane crashed into a barrage balloon over Newcastle upon Tyne.

Despite the airfield still resembling a building site, the OTU was ready to receive its first training course. Course No 1, the first of 21 which would pass through Crosby, arrived on 24th March and was made up of 37 pupils, 13 of them Canadian. The following day, more instructors moved into quarters on camp, but light and water was still lacking, although a single temporary telephone was now available.

Flying training started on 26th March but to enable this to happen the 12 airmen's barrack huts had to be reallocated. One became the

The Hurricanes of 59 OTU were the first aircraft to make use of Crosby. Typical of all OTUs, the training was tough and the loss rate was high.

officers' mess, another the sergeants' mess and two more were designated as the airmen's mess. Two more were converted into a temporary NAAFI with a games room, and six were used for ground training. Cooking for everyone on the station was carried out in a field kitchen and over 200 airmen had to be accommodated in Kirklinton Hall near Smithfield. It was not an ideal situation but everyone worked hard to overcome and adapt, and morale was high, with all focussed on getting as many pilots as possible safely through their training.

The first course was successfully completed on 5th May, with 34 of the pupils passing, and the course establishing a group record for the lowest accident rate per hours flying time. This was quite remarkable considering four Hurricanes were lost, including one involved in a fatal accident with Plt Off. B W Vickers in Hurricane I V7237 on 16th April.

Throughout May 1941, conditions began to steadily improve, including the completion of a permanent NAAFI, which was celebrated at an airmen's dance. In June, the officers' mess was ready for occupation, with the luxury of hot water in the bathhouse but, unbelievably, not in the mess itself.

By the end of June, the airfield was covered with aircraft, including

66 Hurricanes, 17 Masters, 1 Battle, 1 de Havilland Dominie and a solitary de Havilland Tiger Moth. Personnel strength had also expanded, with 71 officers and 1529 other ranks, the majority of whom by now were living on Crosby. Space at Crosby was created with the allocation of D Flight on 14th July at nearby Longtown as a satellite airfield for 59 OTU.

Royalty arrived for the first and only time during the war years on 2nd July 1941. Gp Capt. HRH The Duke of Kent arrived in a Lockheed Hudson, accompanied by Wg Cdr Fielden, who was the Captain of the King's Flight. Gp Capt. Robinson met his highness, who then inspected a guard of honour. After various officials had been presented to him by the High Sheriff, P A Carr, the royal visitors left by road for Hadrian's Camp.

The unit was beginning to expand its training programme by July, with the first daily practice of low dive-bombing over gunposts beginning on 24th July. Sqn Ldr D P A Boitel-Gill DFC, who demonstrated these exercises with great enthusiasm, taught this particular technique. Exercises were becoming more tactical with more and more cooperation with army units on the ground. Battle Station exercises also began in the same month but the big one for instructors and pupils alike occurred on 23rd and 24th August. Exercise Hadrian was part of an even bigger exercise which had actually begun on 21st August with 'enemy' landings on the east and south-east coast of England. The scenario continued when the 'enemy' successfully landed on the Yorkshire coast, penetrating 20 to 30 miles inland on 22nd and 23rd August. This was when the Hurricanes and ground defences of both Crosby and Longtown came into play. The intention was to deny the enemy use of both airfields and to enable our own aircraft to use these airfields for as long as possible. 59 OTU would also support the Home Guard in their defence of the river crossing over the Irthing at Ruleholme Bridge. Defenders at Crosby included No 711 Defence Squadron, RAF, one troop from B Sqn 11th Btn Royal Armoured Corps, a mobile company from the 234th Light Anti-Aircraft Regiment Royal Artillery plus four Bofors Anti-Aircraft guns from the same regiment. The exercise was a total success for all concerned and ended for 59 OTU on 24th August when six Hurricanes, led by the chief flying instructor, Sqn Ldr W D David, DFC, carried out a dive-bombing and low-level attack on Carlisle.

Many of the training courses which passed through Crosby had an international feel to them and No 8 Course was typical of the time. Among the 44 pupils on the course were 20 Canadians, 19 New

Zealanders, 3 Australians, 1 Belgian and 1 American. Other nationalities included French, Polish, Czech and South African.

Morale for the permanent staff was struck a blow on 18th September 1941. Recently promoted Wg Cdr Boitel-Gill, who was now Officer Commanding Flying Wing, was killed carrying out a mock attack on a fuel dump near the airfield. Having joined the RAF in 1929, Boitel-Gill then became a pilot for Imperial Airways before the war. Recalled to the RAF in 1939, he joined 152 Squadron at Acklington as a flight commander, becoming its commander in November 1940. Boitel-Gill was credited with eight enemy kills during the Battle of Britain.

General de Gaulle, accompanied by Marshal General Vallin and the AOC, 81 Group, paid an official visit to the airfield on 16th October. His main interest was in the training of Free French pilots, who provided a flypast of Hurricanes. The general went on to inspect a guard of honour and to have a tour of the ground school. He made a short speech in French to the Free French pupils in the officers' mess and was entertained with sherry.

Gp Capt. Robinson relinquished command of 59 OTU on 17th November 1941. His replacement was Gp Capt. C R Keary, who, like Robinson, joined the RAF in the 1930s as a fighter pilot and rose quickly through the ranks.

The unit performed a flypast over Carlisle on 14th February in support of the of the 'Warship Week' celebrations. That same evening, the airfield and 59 OTU took part in a large 81 Group exercise which was designed to test the defences of the airfield. At 18:10hrs, as part of the exercise, a message was received from the duty pilot that 'enemy' aircraft had been spotted 30 miles away, heading in a south-westerly direction. Eight minutes later, the air raid siren sounded and within two minutes three 'enemy' Hudsons swooped low over the airfield attacking the hangars and various other technical buildings. A single Boulton Paul Defiant of 410 Squadron from Ouston in Northumberland, which was on patrol in the area, simulated a lone attack on the bombers. The Hudson attack lasted until 18:40hrs and the main criticism of the personnel on the ground at Crosby was the fact that they were too slow in taking cover. It was later reported that if live ordnance had been falling then the airmen concerned may have moved a little quicker!

The exercise continued into the next day, 'enemy' aircraft being reported at 08:24hrs at ten miles approaching from the west. More 'enemy' Hudsons approached the airfield at very low level, attacking the hangars and runways. Before they were clear of the perimeter of the airfield, they were attacked by three 59 OTU Hurricanes which had been on patrol since 08:00hrs. Each Hurricane selected one of the Hudsons, while a fourth fighter, which was taking off during the attack, joined in the fray. A running fight developed with the bombers making various attacks on the aerodrome whilst being vigorously pursued by the Hurricanes. The exercise was a success and the final conclusions stated that the Hudsons would have caused considerable damage to the airfield, although they would probably have all been shot down by the combined efforts of the airfield defences and the attacks by the Hurricanes.

The international flavour of the courses that passed through Crosby continued with the arrival of No 15 Course on 10th March. The 31 pupils had the usual Commonwealth participants including a Rhodesian, but also this time a student from the USA and more unusually a French-Argentine. Sadly, Sgt W O Kreugar, the American on the course, was killed in a flying accident a week later. The majority of successful pilots were posted to home fighter squadrons but an increasing number were being retained as staff pilots, going on to attend instructor courses. This was not ideal, as senior staff preferred pupils to be instructed by individuals who had at least experienced flying with an operational squadron. However, an increasing shortage of instructors forced the issue.

59 OTU was at the peak of its strength by the end of March 1942, with 80 Hurricanes, 21 Masters, five Battles, one Dominie, one Tiger Moth and a single Lysander at their disposal. Personnel totalled 2,250 officers and other ranks and the newly formed RAF Regiment 2711 Squadron, which took over airfield defence, added a further two officers and 211 other ranks.

Gp Capt. Keary was well aware of the fact that 59 OTU would be moving in the near future. Back in March, he had already visited the partially completed airfield at Milfield in Northumberland, which was to become the unit's new home. 59 OTU had plenty of time to prepare for the move and the first indication was the formation of an advance party, formed under Cpl Wright, on 8th June. The party was formed specifically for taking over Brunton, also in Northumberland, which was being constructed as a satellite airfield for Milfield. On 28th June, 2711 Squadron RAF Regiment left the airfield to take up duties at Croydon in Surrey, leaving Crosby lacking any significant airfield defence.

The expected signal from HQ Fighter Command for the unit to move was received on 21st July. It ordered 59 OTU to move to Milfield between 5th and 10th August 1942. Already prepared, the first of several daily Motor Tranport (MT) convoys began on 25th July, moving equipment to Milfield even before the usual advanced party was dispatched. The first aircraft to move, eleven Hurricanes, six Masters and five Battles, flew out of Crosby for Milfield on 2nd August, followed by a similar number the following day. Flying training was suspended at Crosby on 5th August and the advance party left the airfield by special train the following day. The main party departed on 8th August and all the remaining aircraft left Crosby for Milfield on 9th August. 59 OTU's efficient departure was completed on schedule on 10th August and Crosby stood silent.

Crosby was now handed over to 17 (Training) Group of Coastal Command, whose HQ was at the Mackenzie Hotel in Edinburgh. The airfield was now being hurriedly prepared for a Coastal OTU, with longer runways, a more complicated perimeter track system, additional dispersals and three extra Type T2 hangars. The additional building work continued unabated when the advance party of 9 (Coastal) OTU under the command of Sgt Hart, arrived on 5th September 1942. The unit was formed at Aldergrove in Northern

Beaufighter trainers did not exist; so 9 OTU used several dual-control Beauforts. The Beaufort was less powerful but was a good representation of the flying characteristics of the Beaufighter.

Ireland on 7th June 1942 to train long-range fighter crews for Coastal Command. The Bristol Beaufighter was the unit's main aircraft type. It was also one of the most powerful and versatile combat aircraft produced during the Second World War. When it was first developed back in 1938, the aim was to build a twin-engined fighter that was heavily armed, fast and had a good range. With the tail-plane, wings and rear fuselage of the Bristol Beaufort, a redesigned forward fuselage and new, more powerful Bristol Hercules engines, it was first flown on 17th July 1939. The Air Ministry had already placed an order for 300 aircraft before the prototype took to the air. The Beaufighter went on to become effective as a night fighter, fighter-bomber, torpedo bomber, ground attack aircraft and anti-shipping aircraft. Final production totalled over 5,500 and the Beaufighter was not withdrawn from RAF service until 12th May 1960.

Aircraft from 9 OTU had actually been arriving since August. The first Beaufort I, L4477, arrived from Aldergrove on 5th August, L9883 arriving the following day. Despite the construction chaos, the first Beaufighters, dual control Beauforts, Airspeed Oxfords and a pair of Lysander Target Tugs arrived over the next few days. The Beauforts, which were usually laid out in a single control configuration, were converted as trainers, making an ideal stepping stone before progressing to the more powerful Beaufighter. The Beaufighter had a single seat for the pilot; so an instructor would demonstrate the aircraft

A Coastal Command takeover saw the arrival of 9 OTU from Aldergrove, with the Beaufighter as its main type; pictured is a Mk VI.

9 OTU flew several different versions of the powerful Beaufighter, including this Mk XI.

to a trainee while he stood behind the pilot's seat and held on as best he could.

The main party of 9 OTU, made up of 200 officers and other ranks, arrived at Crosby on 6th September. The party was under the command of Wg Cdr P H Woodruff, the Chief Flying Instructor (CFI). Gp Capt. F Woolley OBE, DFC took over command of Crosby and 9 OTU from Wg Cdr Woodruff on 19th September. By 22nd September only one pilot had arrived at Crosby, making it impossible for the first course of seven Beaufighter crews to start their operational training. Limited ground training began, but there was still a shortage of equipment and the airfield was effectively unserviceable because of the construction work. The satellite airfield at Longtown had received the first Beaufighters a few days earlier and, despite the runways still being worked on, they moved to Crosby in an effort to start the training programme. It was not long before the unit suffered its first casualty, when a Beaufighter crashed during circuit training. Plt Off. Lyon in Beaufighter VI T5286 stalled during a turn at low altitude and spun into the ground at Longpark, near Haughton, four miles west of Crosby, on 4th October. The pilot had no chance of escape at such a height and was killed instantly.

The situation began to improve enough for a specialist night flying unit, named 'N' Squadron, to be formed at Crosby on 22nd October.

Under the command of Plt Off. Nelson, the unit began experimental night flying the following evening, although many difficulties were experienced. Even the simple task of positioning the Chance light, which was usually used to guide pilots to a runway when in distress, was complicated by newly ploughed soft ground. A shortage of personnel to man the flare path and fire tender, plus a general shortage of equipment, initially restriced the night flying to one aircraft in the circuit at a time. 'N' Squadron later found more success operating from Longtown.

After several accidents caused by Beaufort engine failures, including one involving L4455, which occurred on approach to Crosby on 23rd October, instructions were received from 17 Group that the flying of Beauforts with the Bristol Taurus II and IV engines should be stopped immediately. This grounded all of the 9 OTU's Beauforts, and dual training would have to rely on the unit's Airspeed Oxfords, the handling of which was considerably different from that of a Beaufighter. It would be several months before all of the unit's Beauforts were either modified or had their engines changed to the more powerful 1,130hp Taurus XII or the Pratt and Witney Twin Wasp.

The construction work was beginning to make life very difficult for 9 OTU. Several cases of aircraft being damaged as a direct result of faulty work by contractors came to a head on 28th October. Two aircraft were damaged: one taxied into an unfilled, unmarked trench, while another became stuck in a manhole which had been covered by a thin concrete slab. The decision was made for the current Beaufighter course to continue at another airfield whilst the construction work was completed. On 10th November, Wg Cdr Woodruff, accompanied by Sqn Ldr Godbury, went by air to Thornaby in North Yorkshire to arrange for an attachment to proceed there. An air party departed the following day and Thornaby became a temporary satellite to Crosby while the first course was completed.

For 9 OTU to operate effectively they needed the ability to have access to at least two air firing ranges, preferably not to far away. On 23rd November, Flt Lt Miller from Coastal Command and Mr Andrews, an Air Ministry specialist on air firing ranges visited a new site at Rockliffe Marshes. The site was also approved by Gp Capt. Woolley and was officially named Burgh-by-Sands. A second range at Caerlaverock on the edge of the Solway Firth, between the villages of Blackshaw and Bowhouse in Dumfriesshire, also became available early the following year.

By the end of November, construction work was nearing completion. Crosby now had 'Drem' night lighting installed, laid out in a curved approach, and the runways were serviceable. The main runway had been extended from 1,600 to 2,000 yards and the two shorter runways were lengthend from 1,100 to 1,400 yards, bringing Crosby up to a heavy-bomber-sized airfield. A re-organisation of the Flying Training Wing could now take place. On 27th November 1942, the following squadrons were brought into use: a Beaufort Conversion Squadron, a Beaufighter Conversion Squadron, an Air Fighter Squadron, a Night Flying and an Instrument Flying Squadron. When the first Beaufighter course was completed on 3rd December a semblance of order took over Crosby and all future training courses continued without disruption.

On the evening of 9th January 1943, a distress signal was received by Crosby that a Lancaster from Skellingthorpe in Lincolnshire was lost on a night cross-country exercise. A 'darky' bearing was transmitted, which enabled the Lancaster to home in on Crosby's flarepath and the main runway. All seemed well as the pilot, Sgt L A Smith in Lancaster I ED394 of 50 Squadron, made a normal approach, touching down on the runway. The bomber was then seen to bounce, followed by the sound of all four Merlin engines opening up for a go around. The bomber never gained enough height and crashed into a house on the outskirts of Brampton, a few miles east of the airfield. Four crew were killed instantly. Sgt Smith survived the intial crash but died of his injuries four days later. Incredibly, two aircrew, Sgt T A Williams and Sgt G A Hobson, survived.

Flying tests on the two new air firing ranges were carried out by Wg Cdr Woodruff and Sqn Ldr Holland on 3rd February 1943. They performed low flying within the air firing areas and simulated dive bombing attacks. Both Burgh-by-Sands and Caerlaverock were found suitable and pronounced ready for use the same day. It was while returning from an air firing exercise on 4th March, that Sgt Ellsworth and Sgt Glayton received the endorsement of 'Very Creditable Performance' in their logbooks. The starboard machine gun panel of Beaufighter VI EL305 became partially detached in flight and the pilot, Sgt Ellsworth, had great difficulty controlling the aircraft. The crew tried everything to remove the panel, the observer, Sgt Glayton, sending signals back to base right up to the point that the crew decided that bailing out was the only option. Both survived without injury and the crippled Beaufighter dived into the ground near Canonbie in Dumfriesshire.

The aircraft establishment of 9 OTU in March 1943 consisted of 42 Beaufighter VIs and VICs, 15 dual control Beauforts, a handful of Oxfords and Ansons and a pair of tired Lysander target tugs, which were being steadily replaced by the purpose-built Miles Martinet.

It was always good for morale when news got back about the exploits of former pupils. On 30th March news was received that Sgt Jordan and Sgt Oakley of No2 Course had been credited with helping to shoot down a Junkers Ju 88. The pair had been posted to 235 Squadron at Leuchars in Fife operating the Beaufighter VIC.

While brand new Beaufighters continued to arrive at Crosby, the CFI became increasingly concerned about the shortage of serviceable Beauforts. From April onwards the Beaufort was the only aircraft operating from Longtown, specifically with 'A' and 'N' Squadrons. Night flying from the satellite was also improved when sodium lights were fitted, allowing for a more concentrated effort on this aspect of the training. From 6th April 1943 all Beaufighter flying was carried out from Crosby, as the airfield was now in a more suitable condition to cope.

The accident rate at Crosby rose to at least one Beaufighter crash per week, many of them fatal. One particular incident on 15th May 1943 was the very first solo for student pilot Sgt Chalmers. Having succesfully taken off in Beaufighter I T3292, Chalmers was told to carry out two circuits and then land. After his first landing, the Beaufighter bounced badly and, slamming the throttles too hard, Chalmers choked both engines, stalled and dived into the ground. The big fighter caught fire immediately with Chalmers trapped inside. He was rescued by AC2 H Kay, whose brave and quick actions saved the pilot's life. Kay was suitably awarded the British Empire Medal (BEM) on the 31st July 1943 for Meritorious Service. It was a sad end for T3292; the Beaufighter had seen operational service with 272, 143 and 235 squadrons before being withdrawn to training duties with 2 (C)OTU at Catfoss in North Yorkshire.

More replacement Beaufighters arrived in June 1943, several of them ex-operational aircraft from Predannack in Cornwall. It was becoming a struggle to keep up with the loss rate, which, by the late summer of 1943, was outstripping the supply of replacements. A particularly tragic accident involving another Beaufighter occured on 11th July. Beaufighter VIF X8036 'X', piloted by Sgt M M Vinton, lost power and hit high tension cables in the ensuing forced-landing at Harby Brow near Wigton. The navigator, Sgt H J Shallow, was killed instantly in the crash while Sgt Vinton survived the impact. A civilian who witnessed the accident rushed to the scene only to be electrocuted by a hanging cable, while Sgt Vinton died from burns in hospital twelve hours later.

As the various training squadrons and courses got into full swing, the unit's hourly flying increased to reflect this. On 22nd July 1943 a station record was set at 149 hours 5 minutes of day-time flying. Over 30 hours were achieved that night and this particular record was surpassed again on 6th August by a time of 36 hours 35 minutes. During this busy period only two Beaufighters were lost in accidents, with only one fatality among the four aircrew involved.

Fighter affiliation exercises were introduced into the curriculum from August. The very latest fighter tactics and evasive actions were demonstrated by instructors to each course which passed through Crosby. Torpedo training exercises and RP (Rocket Projectile) training was introduced the following month. The Beaufighter could carry up to eight 60lb RPs, four under each wing, for use against enemy surface ships, of which thousands of tons were sunk by the end of the war.

Air Vice Marshal A O A Maynard from HQ Coastal Command visited Crosby on 15th October to discuss the handing over of the Longtown satellite to Silloth. Longtown was to receive a Heavy Conversion Unit (HCU); so Crosby would have to become even busier as the Beaufort squadrons returned to the airfield. By 27th October, Longtown was no longer under 9 OTU's control and all training was now crammed into Crosby.

By November 1943, 9 OTU was supplying crews to five United-Kingdom-based fighter and RP squadrons plus a further two units in North Africa. Despite this, senior staff were unimpressed by Crosby's production rate of fully trained crews and considered closing the unit down. Proposals were seriously put forward to split 9 OTU's workload between 2 OTU at Catfoss and 60 OTU at East Fortune in Lothian. However, this did not happen and 9 OTU continued its work unabated at Crosby.

A Halifax from Rufforth in North Yorkshire arrived at Crosby on 22nd November with only the pilot onboard and the port outer engine on fire. The pilot of the Halifax had cautiously ordered his crew of six to bail out, all of whom landed safely. Longtown was returned as Crosby's satellite on 5th January 1944, the Beauforts vacating the airfield for a second time the next day.

Because of the Beaufighter's excellent range, which was nearly 1,500 miles, navigational exercises and Operational Flight Exercises (OFE) were flown the length and breadth of the country, both day and night. Two aircraft were on an OFE on 5th February when, on the return leg to Crosby, Beaufighter XI JM126 suffered engine problems. The pilot, Flg Off. Stevens and navigator Flg Off. Parker successfully ditched off the coast of Northern Ireland and took to their dinghy. The entire event was witnessed by Flt Sgt Kimberley and Sgt KcKnee in Beaufighter X JM220, who immediately carried out an Air Sea Rescue (ASR) procedure. Stevens and Parker were just about to drift ashore at Rathlin Island when they were picked up by a rescue boat.

Longtown not only served as a satellite but also made a good diversionary airfield if a problem occured at Crosby. On 9th April 1944, emergency services were dealing with Beaufighter VI T5349, piloted by Flg Off. Cosman, which had crash-landed after overshooting the main runway. A few moments later, Beaufighter VI T5014, flown by Flg Off. Grant, entered Crosby's circuit with its undercarriage unlocked. T5014 made a near perfect belly-landing on the main runway but unfortunately completely blocked its use for three other Beaufighters trying to land. Low on fuel, they quickly diverted the short distance to Longtown, where they landed safely.

The unit received a visit from Air Chief Marshal Sir W Sholto Douglas, KCB, MC, DFC, Air Officer Commanding in Chief of Coastal Command, on 19th April 1944. He was accompanied by the AOC of 17 Group plus several other senior staff, who inspected the station. William Sholto Douglas served in the Royal Field Artillery at the beginning of the First World War, transferring to the Royal Flying Corps in 1915. He joined the RAF in 1920, later becoming an instructor at the Imperial Defence College. During the Second World War he was promoted to Air Vice Marshal and was one of several senior staff who were highly critical of the strategy implemented by Sir Hugh Dowding and Air Vice Marshal Keith Park during the Battle of Britain. Douglas was made the head of Fighter Command in place of Dowding in 1941 and then Commander in Chief of the RAF in the Middle East in 1943. He retired from the RAF in 1948, going on to serve as the chairman of British European Airways from 1949 to 1964.

Unit aircraft establishment peaked in April 1944 with 55 Beaufighter ICs, VICs, Xs and XIs, 17 Beauforts, three Oxfords and nine Martinets. The few Martinets that 9 OTU possessed were airborne virtually every day flying target-towing sorties over the ranges. The safety record of the Martinet was almost impeccable with only one minor incident recorded at Crosby on 29th May 1944. Flg Off. Barrett in Martinet TTI HP129 burst a tyre on landing and swung off the runway slightly damaging the aircraft.

At 01:18hrs on the morning of 8th June 1944, the entire airfield was

Oxfords were used by 9 OTU in a supporting role at Crosby.

thrust into total darkness. Several Beaufighters that were returning from night operational flight exercises had to divert to Longtown because of the power failure on the airfield. The loss of power had been caused by a Stirling from 1654 HCU at Wigsley in Nottinghamshire severing power lines on the edge of the airfield. Plt Off. D C Gundry RAAF was at the controls of Stirling III LK515 with seven crew aboard when, at 15,000ft, the inner port engine failed. Gundry headed for Crosby, where, on approach, the inner starboard engine also cut. The bomber undershot the runway and crashed into an irrigation ditch; the sudden drop was sufficient for the aircraft's undercarriage to collapse causing minor injuries to one of the air gunners and to the wireless operator.

Another bomber made an unexpected arrival at Crosby on 17th June: Halifax I W7881 from 1652 Conversion Unit at Marston Moor in North Yorkshire. Plt Off. O C Cronshaw, the pilot, was forced to land at Crosby owing to an internal glycol leak in the port engine, which caused a fire. W7881 was a veteran of three operational squadrons and two conversion units; repaired at Crosby, the bomber went on to serve the RAF until removed from service in February 1945.

The strength of the unit began to decline through the summer of 1944 as aircraft that had been written off or damaged were not being replaced. Plans were already in place to change the role of 9 OTU and its aircraft and on 10th August 1944 staff officers from 17 Group and 44 Group visited the station. The next day Crosby and Longtown were transferred from 17 Group Coastal Command to 44 Group Transport Command, whose HQ was at Barnwood in Gloucester. The same day, 9 OTU was disbanded, the majority of its personnel passing to 109 (Transport) OTU, which was formed at Crosby that day as a transport training unit.

9 OTU had a busy time at Crosby, mainly owing to the fact that the unit had lost an incredible 61 Beaufighters and eleven Beauforts in a variety of flying accidents. On the day of their disbandment, only 30 serviceable Beaufighters and 15 Beauforts remained at Crosby. These were quickly removed to other training units.

109 OTU was equipped with the Douglas Dakota III and IV, effectively a C-47A and a C-47B respectively. 1,895 Dakotas served the RAF in 25 squadrons, the first joining 31 Squadron on the Burma front in June 1942. It continued in RAF service until 1950, when the Vickers Valetta replaced it. A single airworthy example is still on RAF charge today, with the Battle of Britain Memorial Flight at Coningsby in Lincolnshire.

As the allies made good progress through Europe, demand was high for trained Dakota crews, especially with the number of airborne

Douglas Dakotas of 109 (Transport) OTU supported Operation Market *in September 1944, their crews gaining valuable operational experience.*

operations and the general logistical needs of an army on the move. 109 OTU was formed on a half stength basis but this still meant that 20 Dakotas descended upon Crosby, with a few Oxfords and a single Miles Magister in support.

An influx of personnel who were more familiar with the workings of the Dakota began to arrive on 16th August. The majority were posted from 105 (Transport) OTU at Bramcote in Warwickshire. They had been trained on the Dakota but their old unit had not yet received the aircraft.

A distinct shortage of RAF transport aircraft meant that even training units like 109 OTU became involved in operational duties. During September 1944, 46 Group Transport Command was at full stretch because of its involvement with Operation 'Market Garden', the largest airborne assault the world had ever seen. Seven 109 OTU crews were assembled for a detachment from 22nd to 28th September to carry out operations detailed by 46 Group. After a briefing at 09:30hrs on 22nd September, the first four crews flew to Down Ampney in Wiltshire, followed by three more to Blakehill Farm in the same county. Later the same day all of the 109 OTU crews flew an average of 4,500lbs of freight to airfield B.56 at Evere on the outskirts of Brussels. From this airfield, the Dakotas flew a variety of sorties, including ferrying more freight, removing casualties, moving prisoners, soldiers and even VIPs. When the detachment ended, the Crosby Dakotas had moved 260 casualties, 113,000lbs of freight and 78 passengers, flying a total of 130 hours 25 minutes.

By the beginning of October, sufficient aircraft, which totalled 15 Dakotas (five more were unserviceable), an Airspeed Oxford II W6638 and a lone Miles Magister I N3957, and personnel were available for training to begin. No 1 Course 109 OTU officially began on 3rd October and, to augment training, three Airspeed Horsa gliders arrived for basic training for airborne forces work. The unit was organised into two flights, 'A' Flight for type conversion and 'B' Flight for operational training.

Poor weather over east and central England resulted in a large amount of aircraft being diverted to airfields in the north of the country on 18th November. Nine Halifaxes from 415, 424 and 433 (RCAF) squadrons, based at Linton-on-Ouse and Leeming in North Yorkshire, were diverted to Crosby. Five Wellingtons from 105 OTU at Bramcote in Warwickshire also found a safe landing place at Crosby.

During December, the unit lost two Dakotas in serious flying accidents. The first was Dakota III KG639, which flew into high ground near the airfield on 6th December 1944. One of the crew was killed. The second incident occurred on 13th December, when Dakota III KG661 stalled after take off, injuring two, and then was destroyed by fire. KG661 was the serial issued to the current BBMF Dakota back in the 1970s when it served with the RAE (Royal Aircraft Establishment). Later research uncovered the fact that KG661 was actually destroyed at Crosby; so a new serial, ZA947, was issued and remains on the aircraft today.

January 1945 saw the formation of a daily shuttle service. A route was flown to Nutts Corner in Northern Ireland and Pershore, Worcestershire, to give new crews experience in Transport Command operations. The flights always carried passengers and rarely operated without carrying actual freight. A new passenger and freight section was also formed at the same time. The section was up and running very quickly and by the end of the month was operating successfully. Three Dakotas were permanently fitted with dummy loads and these were flown for additional training on every possible occasion. Pupil crews were briefed and instructed by personnel from the freight section in all aspects of loading the Dakota, including Jeep loading exercises, which were introduced in May.

Poor weather conditions over East Anglia forced six Lancasters to divert to Crosby after a raid on Gelsenkirchen on 23rd February 1945. The bombers were from 186 Squadron at Stradishall in Suffolk and 195 Squadron from Wratting Common, also in Suffolk. These were the last operational aircraft to arrive at Crosby before the end of the Second World War.

May 1945 was the busiest month so far for 109 OTU with regard to the daily service to Nutts Corner and Pershore. The route was flown for 18 days of the month, with 335 passengers and 7,768lbs of freight carried. The unit also assisted others to move, including 1332 Heavy Conversion Unit (HCU) between 19th and 21st May. The HCU was moving from Nutts Corner to Riccall in North Yorkshire. The Dakotas of 109 OTU made a total of 19 lifts over the three days, comprising 79 passengers and an impressive 98,000lbs of freight in all.

A post-war reshuffle of commands resulted in Crosby and Longtown being transferred from 44 Group to 4 (Transport) Group on 1st June 1945. Less than a week later, the AOC of 4 Group, Air Vice Marshal H S P Walmsley CB, CBE, MC, DFC, plus several staff officers visited the unit. One of the visitors was the group captain in charge of training for 4 Group and he spent a further two days later in the month at Crosby, inspecting all sections. During this time, 109 OTU gained a new navigation section, which was first used by No 14 Course. The section had three good-sized classrooms, which were fully equipped.

Another major change to the unit occurred on 10th August 1945. 109 OTU was redesignated No 1383 (Transport) Conversion Unit (CU) with the same task of training Dakota crews for Transport Command. The unit was reorganised so that 'A' Flight was still used for conversion training while 'B' and a new 'C' Flight taught route training. Additional aircraft from another Dakota unit arrived on 8th August from Bramcote. 105 (Transport) OTU was a large unit and a single flight from it was transferred to Crosby, raising the number of Dakotas on 1383 CU to over 30 aircraft.

From 14th August, the first of many flights to and from Prague in Czechoslovakia began. Stirling IV and V transport aircraft from 38 Group arrived on a daily basis, filled with Czech and Polish refugees, the majority of whom were children. At least 150 were moved to Britain on flights that took nearly seven hours. Many of the children had recently been inside concentration camps and on arrival at Crosby they were transferred to a hostel in Ambleside. The following month, 1383 CU produced a record 1,748 flying hours and there seemed to be no let up in the demand for transport crews.

On 15th September 1945, virtually every RAF station throughout Britain celebrated the ending of hostilities with a Battle of Britain air display. Crosby opened up to the public for the first time and over 2,200 people visited the show, contributing £36 to various service charities. Visiting aircraft at the airshow included a Lancaster, a Halifax, a York, a Spitfire and a Mosquito. A single 1383 CU Dakota was open to the public, while the rest of the unit was airborne in the circuit for most of the day.

In early 1946, Crosby and 1383 CU suffered the single worst aircraft accident in their combined histories. Dakota III KG502 was returning to Crosby after a night cross-country flight when, while descending through cloud, the aircraft crashed into the 2,400ft summit of Cold Fell, east of Castle Carrock, on 3rd February. All six onboard stood no chance of surviving the impact, which scattered the Dakota over a wide area; several small parts of the aircraft remain on the mountain today. A second, less serious, accident followed on 28th March when Dakota III KG660 force-landed after take off near Brampton. This was to be the last military accident from Crosby and as the year progressed the throughput of crews rapidly declined. The need for RAF transport crews lessened and the large number of instructors being demobbed made further training increasingly difficult.

No 26 Course proved to be the last at Crosby and, at the end of May 1946, it was transferred to 1382 CU at Wymeswold in Leicestershire for completion. The Dakotas of 1383 CU were flown to 22 MU at Silloth for storage and eventually disposal, the last leaving the unit at the end of June 1946. Crosby was swiftly placed under care and maintenance, although 1383 CU was not officially disbanded until 6th August 1946. That same day the RAF left the airfield for good, leaving Crosby to its fate.

The newly nationalised British European Airways (BEA), who, under a different guise before the war, operated several aircraft from Kingstown to Ronaldsway in the Isle of Man, looked at using Crosby. BEA considered resuming this route from Kingstown but the airfield was found to be too small with no real room for expansion. From October 1946, BEA, equipped with the de Havilland Dragon Rapide, began using Crosby for its operations, with an additional route to Nutts Corner in Northern Ireland via Woolsington (later Newcastle Airport) in Northumberland. Sadly, BEA withdrew a large number of its United Kingdom domestic services and, on 6th October 1947, the airline stopped using Crosby.

The airfield returned to its original agricultural use and the farmers who had their land requisitioned were brought back as tenants. The airfield's buildings were deteriorating fast by the mid 1950s but the Town Clerk of Carlisle still saw potential in Crosby as an airport. In November 1954, Mr H D A Robertson approached the Ministry of Transport and Civil Aviation to enquire about the possibility of Crosby or Great Orton becoming a municipal airport. The following year, a

An original Type T2 hangar, still being put to good use after 60 years. (Author)

71

The original wartime tower still serves the modern airport. (Author)

conference was held, with all interested local authorities attending. At this stage, Great Orton looked like the favourite with Silloth as second choice. A second conference in April 1955 pushed Crosby forward as the preferred site, mainly on the grounds that the strength and condition of Crosby's runways were superior to the other options, thus reducing the cost of bringing the airfield into service again.

On the 7th December 1960, the airfield was purchased by the Carlisle Corporation and a wave of small aviation-related businesses moved into Crosby. The airfield was renovated sufficiently for it to receive a Category 2 operating licence on 3rd January 1961. A new passenger reception, office facilities and new VHF/DF radio aids were added within the control tower. The first scheduled service began a few days later from Crosby to Ronaldsway Dakota 3 'City of Lancaster' G-AMWV from Silver City Airways flying the route. An official opening ceremony was carried out by the Mayor of Carlisle, A T L Macdonald, from the cockpit of a Rapide on approach into the airport on 15th June 1961.

Various scheduled services followed, bringing a steady increase in passengers through the airport. Increasingly, larger airliners such as

The future for Carlisle airport is bright, with potential investment and expansion looking very likely in the near future. (Author)

the Vickers Viscount became a common sight throughout the 1960s but less so during the 1970s. Military visitors, including a Blackburn Beverley, Ansons and the odd Jet Provost, also made use of the airport. On 8th January 1979, the first jet airliner, a VFW 614 of Cimber Air visited, but this was still a rare event. The management of the airport was taken over by CSE Aviation in 1980 and a resurgence of services followed during that decade.

The airport is also the home of The Edward Haughey Solway Aviation Museum. This excellent museum has nine complete aircraft on display, including the largest ever aircraft to land at the airport, the Avro Vulcan. A veteran of the Falklands War, Vulcan B2 XJ823 made its spectacular arrival on 24th January 1983.

Border Air Training was established at Carlisle in 1991 and offers potential pilots flying courses, air experience flights and much more.

Carlisle Airport has had its ups and downs over the years but still survives with much of the original wartime layout of the airfield still intact. Expansion of the airport complex has done nothing to detract from the strong historic aviation atmosphere that is still very much present.

7
GREAT ORTON

RAF Great Orton did not have a particularly glittering career and it is a shame that the airfield is now more associated with a national event that occurred in 2001. In an attempt to stop the spread of foot-and-mouth disease, a nationwide cull was implemented and several airfield sites were chosen to bury the carcasses. Nearly half a million animals are buried in the middle of the old airfield, which has now also become home to a collection of wind turbines.

The search for a site for a new airfield in the already crowded area of northern Cumbria began in early 1942. A location on the Solway Plain, 3 miles west of Carlisle, between the villages of Great Orton and Wiggonby was chosen. The bulk of the land belonged to Mr Timperon of Watchtree Farm. Locally, the airfield was always known as Wiggonby and a signpost still exists today directing you to 'RAF Wiggonby'. Work began in August 1942 for an airfield that was intended to be a new satellite for Silloth. Another new airfield was to be constructed on the coast at Mawbray, also intended as a satellite for Silloth. Once completed, Great Orton would be transferred to Crosby-on-Eden's control. However, Mawbray never left the drawing board and Great Orton was destined to remain under Silloth's control for its entire existence.

Great Orton, although only intended as a satellite, was built larger than its parent unit but had considerably fewer facilities at its disposal than Silloth. A three-runway layout was constructed with runways of four-engined bomber standard, the main one being almost 2,000 yards long with the two subsidiary runways at 1,400 yards each. Only a single frying pan and 20 loop dispersals were built and hangarage was provided by just three blister hangars.

Before the airfield was actually opened, Sgt Hughes, in Hawker Hurricane I W9348 of 55 Operational Training Unit (OTU), became the first person to land at Great Orton after the fighter's engine failed on

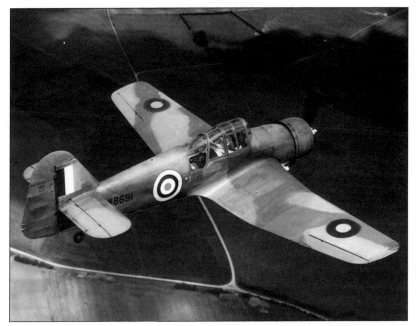

Miles Masters were used as transitional trainers, supporting 55 OTUs Hawker Hurricanes.

29th May 1943. The official opening ceremony in early June 1943 was purely a paper exercise, as the airfield was far from ready and certainly in no fit state to receive aircraft.

It was not until 20th October 1943 that the first aircraft officially arrived. 'E' and 'F' Flights of 55 OTU, whose parent unit was Annan in Dumfries, arrived from Longtown with eight Hurricanes and a single Miles Master. It was an inauspicious arrival, as one of the group, Hurricane IIA Z2822, piloted by Flt Lt F S Perkin, swung off the runway after catching a strong cross wind. A similar incident occurred two days later, setting the tone that was typical of the high accident rate associated with a fighter OTU.

A second unit arrived at Great Orton on 17th November in the form of No 1 (Coastal) Engine Control Demonstration Unit flying a handful of Vickers Wellingtons. Formed within 1674 Heavy Conversion Unit at Longtown, the unit had left for Aldergrove in Northern Ireland by 19th December.

Four more Hurricanes were lost from Great Orton in a variety of incidents before the year was out, including a mid-air collision on 27th December 1943. Hurricane I V7010, piloted by Flt Sgt O E D Louden RNZAF, and a Hurricane X, flown by Plt Off. S F Cleworth, came together during dog fighting practice over Dalston, south of Carlisle. Both pilots were killed instantly.

By the beginning of 1944, 55 OTU was downgraded to a Day Pilot Holding Unit, but, between Great Orton and Annan, the unit had 60 Hurricanes, 18 Masters, 5 Martinets, 1 Dominie, 1 Lysander and a single Typhoon still on charge. On 26th January, the unit was redesignated 4 Tactical Exercise Unit (TEU) and 'E' and 'F' Flights became 'B' Squadron, 4 TEU, still flying the Hurricane.

Life continued at Great Orton much as it had before the unit's name change, though the accident rate seemed to significantly decrease. Only three Hurricanes were involved in accidents throughout February, none of them causing injury to their pilots, and all of the aircraft were repairable.

The unit was renamed again on 28th March 1944, this time only numerically as 4 TEU became 3 TEU. The sole aim of the unit was to train fighter-bomber pilots for ground-attack squadrons, which were increasingly operating the Hawker Typhoon in this role. These ground

The Hawker Typhoon was not a common sight in Cumbria but several made a brief appearance at Great Orton with 3 TEU.

attack units would play a crucial role during the Normandy invasion in June and continued to harass German armoured units until the war's end. By the end of March, 25 Typhoons were on strength, which justified the formation of 3 TEU Typhoon Conversion at Great Orton on 7th April 1944. Not much is known about Typhoon operations from the airfield other than that 3 TEU had vacated Great Orton by the middle of May 1944.

The first of several detachments by Air Sea Rescue (ASR) squadrons came on 18th April 1944 with the arrival of 281 Squadron from Davidstow Moor in Cornwall. Their main equipment was the Vickers Warwick I, which was a development of the Wellington. Like many other ASR squadrons, they were affiliated to a parent station but spent most of the war flying from station to station providing ASR cover where it was needed most. 281 Squadron, whose home airfield was Tiree in Argyllshire, spent most of its time operating over the Irish Sea before departing for Wick in Caithness on 17th September 1944.

282 Squadron from St Eval in Cornwall followed, also equipped with the Warwick I. 281 Squadron in turn replaced them in November 1944, once again providing ASR cover from the airfield until they left for Mullaghmore in Northern Ireland on 2nd January 1945.

Three detachments of Vickers Warwicks passed through Great Orton during the latter years of the Second World War.

The Wellingtons of 6 OTU at Silloth used Great Orton as a satellite airfield from June 1944 until at least April 1945. Navigators' 'W' Holding Course took up residence at Great Orton on 1st October 1944. Having arrived from Haverfordwest in Pembrokeshire, this small unit departed for Killadeas in Northern Ireland.

Once 6 OTU ceased to use the airfield, it was briefly placed under care and maintenance on 16th April 1945. Within weeks, the airfield was taken over by Maintenance Command and Great Orton became a Satellite Storage Site for 219 Maintenance Unit (MU) from 4th May. The parent unit was based at the Falcon Hotel in Settle, Yorkshire, and its main role was as an Explosives Storage Unit. 219 MU was joined by 249 MU, which was formed at Great Orton on 27th May, initially as an Air Ammunition Park but was later renamed an Ammunition Depot. Under the command of Flt Lt Fantini, 249 MU was responsible for the storage and eventual disposal of thousands of tons of bombs not dropped on the enemy by Bomber Command. In June 1945 alone, the unit handled 8,884 tons of bombs. By the end of 1945 the unit was also receiving depth charges, depth charge primers, photographic flash bombs, various projectiles, signal cartridges, incendiaries, smoke floats and marine markers to name a few. Most of the ordnance received by

Specifically designed for fighter satellite airfields, the Type 3156/41 control tower still stands today. (Author)

The only propeller blades turning at Great Orton today belong to a cluster of six wind turbines. (Author)

the MU was destined to be dumped in the sea off Northern Ireland. To make this task easier, a permanent detachment was organised at Shane's Castle on Lord O'Neill's estate near Coleraine.

The first of several visits by Wg Cdr Potter, the airport manager of Kingstown, was made on 31st July 1945. He wanted to discuss the future use of Great Orton for civil aviation purposes and, rather than tackling the subject of actually purchasing the airfield, he seemed more interested in what furniture the RAF personnel were going to leave behind. He also suggested that certain MT vehicles should be left behind as well for when the airfield was taken over. He returned on three more occasions, each with more senior local officials, culminating in a visit on 11th October 1945 with the Carlisle Borough Surveyor, the Treasurer and 20 other personages in tow. All were from the Carlisle Borough Council and Cumberland County Council and, as history has shown, neither Kingstown nor Great Orton was chosen as a civilian airport.

Auster I LB286 had to land at Great Orton owing to lack of fuel on 11th August 1945, becoming the last recorded military aircraft to do so. Once refuelled, permission had to be sought from HQ 42 Group for the light aircraft to take off again. This it did safely the following day and headed for Silloth.

The final unit to arrive at Great Orton was a detachment from 60 MU. The repair and salvage unit consisted of one officer, two SNCOs and 12 airmen arriving on 31st July 1946. 219 MU had cleared up their operation on 20th May 1947 when the unit was disbanded. 60 MU had gone by 1950, leaving 219 MU to close the airfield down on 15th August 1952.

Today, only remnants of the runways remain, and the bulk of the perimeter track, part of which is used by a minor road. The control tower still stands but few other buildings of significance remain. In an attempt to disguise events of recent years, DEFRA are attempting to promote the site as a tourist attraction, called Watchtree Nature Reserve, after Watchtree Farm. The entrance to the reserve has a memorial and a visitors' centre. A long bank runs alongside the entrance road and this gives an excellent view of the old airfield. The six turbines of the Great Orton 'Windcluster' only help to draw the eye to another piece of Cumbria's aviation history.

8
HALL CAINE
(Cold Lake)

Named after the novelist Sir Hall Caine, who died in 1931, but known locally as Cold Lake, this small grass airfield in the north of the Isle of Man is still marked as 'disused' on modern aviation maps. This is more than can be said of the hundreds of other such sites which have disappeared into obscurity. It did not have a major role to play in the Second World War; however, it was in the running to become the island's second civilian airport.

A group known as The Hall Caine Manx Airport Ltd was first formed on 27th March 1935 with £2,000 to its name. The two sons of the late author, G R Hall Caine MP and Sir D Hall Caine bought £650 worth of shares each. 45 acres of land was acquired north of Cold Lake Farm on the A13 between St Judes and Ramsey. The field was levelled and a limited amount of drainage was put in place. A small hangar and a wooden hut were also constructed on the site, which received a restricted licence from the Air Ministry at the end of April 1935.

All operations from the airfield, officially opened on 3rd May 1935, were controlled by Capt. J W Spinner, and the same day the first aircraft landed, with Capt. O Garden at the controls.

Construction work on the airfield continued to raise the standard sufficiently to apply for a full aerodrome licence, which it received on 13th July 1935. From April, several regular services were being flown from Hall Caine but the airfield's new status made it an attractive proposition to bigger airlines. Companies using the airfield included United Airlines Ltd (former Spartan and Hillman's Airlines), the Whitehall Securities Group and Northern and Scottish. United's services included flights to Belfast and Blackpool, flying a variety of aircraft including de Havilland Dragons and Rapides, a Spartan

81

Quite possibly the biggest, and certainly one of the earliest, aircraft to fly into Hall Caine was the Armstrong Whitworth Argosy.

Cruiser and an ex Imperial Airways Armstrong Whitworth Argosy. The last was by far the largest aircraft to operate from Hall Caine, flying mainly to and from Blackpool and on local pleasure flights.

In January 1936, construction of a larger hangar began, but poor weather disrupted its completion until May. In fact the weather was so bad that the River Sulby burst its banks after several days of heavy rain. Despite this, services from the airfield were still maintained.

British Airways increased its flights through Hall Caine from May 1936. Extra services added included Carlisle (Kingstown), Liverpool and Blackpool, reaching a peak of activity in August. The following month, Northern and Scottish, which was a subsidiary of British Airways, took over most of the routes. These were maintained into early 1937 but a wave of corporate restructuring by the Whitehall group resulted in a steady downturn in operations from the airfield.

Northern and Scottish was dissolved into Northern Airways Ltd and Scottish Airways Ltd on 12th August 1937. The main shareholders of these two airlines had interests in Ronaldsway airport, Hall Caine's main competition on the island. The last scheduled flight from the airfield was on 2nd August 1937, with more and more focus on Ronaldsway as the island's main airport. The airfield remained open mainly for the use of private aircraft, one of which was a Luton Minor owned by J E Carine from Douglas.

Like all other civilian airfields in Great Britain, Hall Caine was closed when war broke out on 3rd September 1939. The airfield only remained dormant for a few weeks, its fortunes set to change with the opening of the Armament Training Station at Jurby and the formation No 5 Air Observers School (AOS) on 18th September. Hall Caine was quickly occupied by the RAF. They immediately recognized its usefulness as a Relief Landing Ground and a safe location for the dropping of target-drogues from the nearby air-to-air gunnery range north of Ramsey Bay.

No 5 AOS became No 5 Bombing and Gunnery School (B&GS) on 1st December and it was the unit's Westland Wallace, Fairey Battle and Hawker Henley target tugs that would be most often seen flying low over Hall Caine.

Hall Caine featured prominently in the local flying regulations at the time. The airfield was used as a starting point for target towing aircraft when approaching the Ramsey Bay range. The routine was for the aircraft to stream its target drogue at 2,000ft over the airfield (not below 1,000 ft) and then fly in a northerly direction across the range. When the air-to-air firing exercise was completed, the towing aircraft

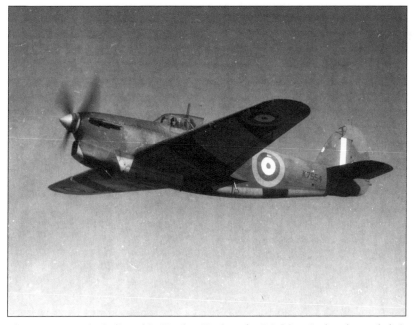

The target tugs, including this Hawker Henley of 5 B&GS at Jurby, dropped their target drogues onto Hall Caine airfield.

would return to Hall Caine, dropping the drogue at not less than 500 ft. A control officer was employed at Hall Caine with responsibility for the control of signalling between the RAF ground party and the target towing aircraft. The target drogue was quickly recovered and the pupil gunner's score could be promptly reported to Jurby almost before they had landed.

Accidents during drogue recovery were rare considering the number of air-to-air firing sorties flown, and only two occurred at Hall Caine. The first was on 27th September 1940 when Battle I L5671 of 5 B&GS was dropping its drogue. The Battle approached the airfield too slowly; it then stalled and dived into the ground half a mile west of the airfield, killing both the pilot and drogue operator instantly. A similar accident happened a few days later to another Fairey Battle from Jurby. The pilot, Sgt S Osmala (Polish) and the drogue operator AC2 A Sharp were the crew of Battle I L5672 on 1st October. On the

The original booking office at Hall Caine was a wooden hut. It was replaced by a more inviting brick building, which still survives today. (Jarrod Cotter – www.flypast.co.uk)

return to Hall Caine from the range, they crashed near the airfield with fatal results.

The airfield lost its RLG status when Andreas opened in September 1941 but continued to operate in support of the target-towing aircraft for a short time. Once the RAF left Hall Caine, the landing area was obstructed with a variety of obstacles in order to prevent it from being used by the enemy.

With the war at an end, the Air Ministry returned the airfield to its original owners, who continued to register Hall Caine as an airport until the company was closed down in February 1971.

Aviation has since returned to the airfield; in recent years it was home to the Islanders Gliding Club and local microlights occasionally visit the old site, which is still intact. The original brick-built booking office remains, the concrete base to a hangar and a flagpole, all dating back to the pre-war days of the airfield. The hangar, although modified, still survives at Ronaldsway airport.

9

HORNBY HALL

Originally intended for the sole use of dispersing aircraft from 22 Maintenance Unit (MU) at Silloth, Hornby Hall was also used by 18 MU at Dumfries and 12 MU at Kirkbride.

Officially designated No 9 Satellite Landing Ground (SLG), Hornby was located off the A66, approximately 3 miles east of Penrith. Virtually surrounded by woodland, with the added distraction of the River Eamont, Hornby was able to capitalise on this natural camouflage, especially from the air.

The first two aircraft arrived on 17th March 1941. They were Wellingtons from 22 MU, the lead aircraft being flown by one of the unit's test pilots, Flt Lt H H Grieg, the second with Plt Off. J Hughes-Evans, also a test pilot, at the controls. No problems were encountered and Flt Lt Grieg cleared the SLG for full operations on 25th March.

Camouflage was a crucial defence to any airfield and full advantage was made of Hornby's surroundings for the dispersal of aircraft. Dispersals were carved out of the woods and potential sites for hides were also looked at by a number of senior RAF Officers during April.

It was not long before the Commanding Officer of 12 MU, Wg Cdr Mitchell, visited the SLG, as their own airfield was rapidly filling with aircraft. He was accompanied by Wg Cdr D W Dean, the CO of 22 MU, on 27th April and special emphasis was placed on visiting the dispersal areas and potential new areas around the SLG.

By the end of May 1941, aircraft dispersed at Hornby included ten Fairey Battles, three Bristol Blenheims, one Lockheed Hudson, one Hawker Hurricane and three Wellingtons, with space for many more, as additional dispersal areas were being completed.

Airfield defence was taken very seriously in the early days of the Second World War and, on 9th July 1941, Hornby gained its very own platoon of the Home Guard, made up of 28 civilians from the

SLG's workforce. These volunteers were in addition to the small detachment of the Border Regiment, who were already carrying out guard duties. The CO of the 8th Battalion, The Border Regiment, Lt Col Browning, arrived on 17th July to inspect the army guard detachment at Hornby.

By the beginning of August 1941, 32 aircraft were dispersed at Hornby and it was becoming obvious that more dispersal space was needed. Wg Cdr Dean and Flt Lt Blomfield from the Ministry of Aviation Production (MAP) visited the SLG on 6th August. Extending the dispersal areas was the main topic of conversation and, within two days, Mr Dockson from MAP began to arrange for the requisitioning of additional land around the SLG.

An Anson from 2 Air Observers School (AOS) at Millom with the unit's CO and Sqn Ldr Gardener landed at Hornby on 14th August. Another of the unit's Ansons had force-landed at Kirkby Thore on 8th August and, after an inspection was made, the aircraft was transported by road for repairs at Hornby. A similar visit occurred again on 22nd August when Sqn Ldr Gardener, accompanied by Sqn Ldr Christmas, the Senior Engineering Officer (SEO), landed in a 2 AOS Anson. This time it was a Blackburn Botha L6416 from the same unit at Millom which had crashed on Castle Moss; the Botha was beyond repair and was only good for salvage. L6416 was carrying out a navigation exercise when the pilot, Sgt W Wasilewski, lost control in cloud. Wasilewski and three other crew members were killed. A third incident involving 2 AOS took place on 28th November. Sgt Coleman in Battle I R7401 force-landed in a field near the SLG. The following day, the Battle was moved a short distance to a dispersal area for repair to the port wing, aileron and flaps. Battle R7401 was an unlucky aircraft because, when it was air tested on 3rd December, after the repairs, it crashed again on landing at Hornby.

Hornby Hall was never criticised for its camouflage, especially from the air. A good example of its success occurred on 3rd September 1941 when 1st Officer James ATA from 5 FPP at Kirkbride in a Piper Cub landed at Hornby. James could not distinguish the positions of the runways and made a safe landing in No 3 Dispersal Field instead. James landed at Hornby to collect 1st Off. Chater ATA, who had force-landed a Spitfire near Appleby.

An indication that the SLG could possibly be changing hands in the near future came on 8th December 1941. Wg Cdr Starling, Sqn Ldr Wyatt and the CO of 18 MU at Dumfries, with an assortment of officers, visited Hornby and inspected the runways and dispersal

Although the good-looking Westland Whirlwind looked every inch a fighter, it was not particularly successful in RAF service. A few Whirlwinds were dispersed by 18 MU at Hornby.

areas. Two days later, four test pilots from 18 MU visited in an Anson, also to inspect the runways and dispersals.

The dispersed aircraft belonging to 22 MU began to be flown back to Silloth from the middle of December. The last 22 MU aircraft left Hornby Hall on 9th January 1942. From the beginning of February 1942, aircraft from 18 MU began to arrive for dispersal. They included Battles, Wellingtons, Hurricanes and the occasional Westland Whirlwind twin engined fighter. Wg Cdr Poole, the CO of 18 MU, inspected the dispersed aircraft on the SLG on 19th February. He was accompanied by Mr Hone, the 9 SLG site engineer who carried out a survey of sites for several proposed blast-proof hides. The threat of air attack was still high and a well placed enemy bomb could damage several aircraft.

Kirkbride was becoming inundated with Halifaxes and Wellingtons by April 1942 and the CO of 12 MU was getting desperate for dispersal space. To solve this, Hornby was temporarily handed over to 12 MU on 2nd May. Two days later, a couple of Wellingtons arrived from 12 MU but the unit's test pilot found that Hornby was unsuitable for the larger Halifax.

From 5th May, 18 MU aircraft began returning to Dumfries. Two Battles departed first and a Wellington from 12 MU immediately filled the space they had created. This coming and going of aircraft continued until the Wellingtons of 12 MU became the most prolific type on the SLG. An unusual visitor from 12 MU arrived on 9th May.

Miles Mentor L4415, piloted by Flt Lt Farquarson, was delivering stores from Kirkbride. Only 45 of these three-seat single-engined monoplanes were built, with only a handful entering RAF service at the start of the Second World War.

The risk of fire was taken very seriously at Hornby. The Right Honourable Lord Geddes, the National Fire Service (NFS) Regional Controller, carried out regular inspections and checks. The surrounding woodland, especially during the summer months, was a potential tinderbox. A major fire practice was held at the SLG by the combined fire brigades of Appleby and Penrith on 24th May 1942. Water was drawn from the River Eamont, with hoses running to Hornby Hall Farm through farm buildings via a disused road to the SLG's HQ. Water was made available from the river within 25 minutes of the arrival of booster pumps and hose tenders. Only a few days later, the CO of 22 MU sent a message to Hornby to say that a large number of fires had been reported in the district. The SLG responded by doubling the amount of patrols around the airfield.

On 26th June, a Hurricane became the last 18 MU aircraft to leave Hornby, leaving a total of 11 Wellingtons and three Bothas occupying the SLG.

To aid camouflage from the air, the dispersal areas were fenced off and sheep and cattle were allowed to graze these areas. Up until the arrival of the Wellingtons, resident aircraft had been quite easy to camouflage. However, these large bombers were particularly visible from the air, especially when aerial photographs were taken on 10th July.

12 MU relinquished its use of Hornby on 11th July 1942, control of the SLG being returned to 22 MU at Silloth. The Wellingtons and Bothas which had been flown in from Kirkbride were taken over by 22 MU.

41 Group sent its own test pilot to Hornby on 25th July to once again assess its suitability to receive large four-engined aircraft. Flt Lt Ashton, the officer in charge of flying at 22 MU, brought Flt Lt G F R Duffy in an Airspeed Oxford. Duffy carried out several test flights in the Oxford and concluded that a landing by a Halifax should be carried out in the near future. This was contrary to the advice suggested by the 12 MU test pilot back in May, but in the end a more than suitable alternative SLG at Wath Head became available for the big bombers.

The resident army unit guarding the SLG at the end of August 1942 was No24 Platoon G Company, 30th Battalion of the Manchester Regiment. On 31st August, the unit became No17 Platoon E Company

Several RAF Mustangs were dispersed at Hornby in 1942, probably the SLG's busiest period.

with the company HQ at Hornby, under the command of Capt. Maylor. This unit took part in a major battle exercise on 5th September 1942, named 'Apple'. Exercise 'Apple' was under the direction of the sub-area commander and lasted from 19:30hrs through to 08:30hrs the following morning. The exercise consisted of an attack from Penrith, from the east and north-east, 17 Platoon at Hornby effectively lying in the path of this 'enemy' attack. A small attack was made on the SLG at midnight and was successfully repelled by the platoon and the resident Home Guard.

The first of several North American Mustangs arrived for dispersal from 22 MU on 24th September 1942. They joined an increasing number of Hurricanes, Wellingtons, Hudsons and Bothas.

Facilities at Hornby continued to improve; the fire section in particular was given a boost by the arrival of a Weeton Fire Tender, which was collected from 25 MU at Hartlebury in Worcestershire on 7th November. Security was to be improved with the siting of dog kennels and accommodation for their handlers on the SLG. The dogs were specifically employed for anti-sabotage duties and all were in place by 1st December.

By 1944, 22 MU at Silloth began to concentrate on specific types, including the Sea Hurricane. When naval fighters began to arrive at Hornby, additional staff were employed.

The army left Hornby on 13th November 1942, handing over responsibility for security of the SLG to the RAF Regiment. The army had occupied two Nissen huts and the local parish hall; these were taken over by the RAF Regiment on 17th November.

The number of aircraft held at Hornby reached its peak on 20th November 1942, with 47 aircraft stored on the SLG. 18 Hurricanes, 13 Mustangs, seven Wellingtons, seven Bothas and two Hudsons were carefully concealed, many local people not even knowing of their existence, let alone the enemy.

A pilot from 78 Squadron, based at Breighton in North Yorkshire, proved that a Halifax could land at Hornby. The reason for the landing was a drop in oil pressure on both inner engines. This was rectified by the pilot's own ground crew with the help of SLG personnel and equipment. The pilot stated on landing that, if it had not been for the fact that he saw a smoke generator burning and a Hudson and an Oxford from 22 MU land, he would not have recognised the place as an airfield. He considered the camouflage excellent.

The average personnel strength, not including the defence force at

Hornby, remained consistently at one RAF officer, nine other ranks and an average of 37 civilians. When 22 MU became a specialist Hurricane and Sea Hurricane unit in late 1944, the SLG began to employ more technical civilian trades. In December, Hornby gained an additional shop foreman, three electrical fitters, two airframe fitters and three extra labourers. This was to be one of the busiest periods in the SLG's history and the workload continued unabated until the end of the war in Europe in May 1945.

By June 1945, only 19 civilians remained at Hornby and many of the aircraft had returned to Silloth for long-term storage or scrapping. Hornby Hall was officially closed on 2nd July 1945 and placed under care and maintenance under the Ministry of Works, despite the fact that several aircraft were still on the landing ground.

The now-vacated accommodation huts served as a temporary German prisoner of war camp from 25th July, and the last aircraft, an Anson, left the SLG on 31st July. Three civilians were still looking after the site in August 1945 but from then on the site was completely vacated as an airfield.

Today, a single Robin remains in good condition and is put to good use by the local farmer. The layout of the original runways and surrounding dispersal areas is virtually unchanged, having long since returned to agriculture.

10
HUTTON-IN-
THE-FOREST

The second of 22 Maintenance Unit's Satellite Landing Grounds was surveyed in late 1940. The landing ground was located on land near Hutton Hall, which was owned by William Vane, who later became Lord Inglewood. The hall itself was viewed for occupation as well and, on 1st June 1941, 8 Satellite Landing Ground (SLG), and then the hall were taken over by 50 Wing Headquarters.

Hutton Hall was the temporary home of 50 (Maintenance) Wing in 1941 and several army units throughout the Second World War. (Author)

Before the official opening, an Anson piloted by Flg Off. R H Ashton, the Officer in Charge of Flying at 22 MU, became the first aircraft to land on the SLG. Flt Lt E I Treasure accompanied him while Gp Capt. Hanson-Abbot of HQ 50 Wing watched the testing from the ground. Given the all-clear for use, within a few days several Blenheims, Hudsons, Bothas and a single Hurricane were dispersed around the landing ground. The natural cover of the surrounding woodland provided good protection from enemy eyes above and regular aerial reconnaissance by friendly aircraft ensured the site was well camouflaged.

The original site was furrowed land, which gently undulated. At least 100 men were employed to level the site with thousands of tons of rubble from Flusco and Blencowe limestone quarries near Greystoke. Once levelled, the site was covered in thousands of sections of Weldmesh and grassed over. The landing strip was approximately 1,000 yards long, so care had to be taken, especially on landing. A single Robin hangar was built along with a few hutments.

Within a matter of days, several senior officers visited the fledgling airfield, including Wg Cdr D W Dean OC 22 MU, who inspected the rapid progress of work on the dispersal areas and provisional 'hides' which were being experimented on in the woods. The following day, Col Thompson, Mjr Lancaster and Capt. Bunbury of the Penrith Home Guard visited Hutton to ascertain particulars as to the defence of the SLG.

On 6th June, the Marshal of the RAF, Sir Edward Ellington GCB, CMG, CBE visited Hutton, accompanied by Wg Cdr Dean. The same day Lt Col Brown arrived from the Border Regiment to discuss more aspects of the SLG's defence and Flg Off. Freer from the Ministry of Aircraft Production (MAP) arrived to discuss the dispersal and camouflage of the site.

Despite Hutton's being a few days old, it welcomed a visit by Newcastle Royal Grammar School Squadron ATC, under the command of E R Thomas. The following day, Flt Lt Longstaff and cadets of No 1028 (Eden Valley) Squadron ATC also visited. For such a small airfield it was certainly attracting a lot of interest.

Only one accident occurred during the SLG's short history; three weeks after opening Flg Off. Antolak crashed on landing in Hurricane I Z3404. Antolak was uninjured; Z3404 was seriously damaged but later repaired and despatched to Russia on the 28th November 1941.

Since opening, the SLG was protected by its own Home Guard unit, which was initially made up of 30 civilians from a total workforce of 43 who were billeted near the landing ground. Military staff was on average made up of two RAF officers and ten other ranks. The Home Guard unit's duties were relieved slightly on 10th November 1941 when a platoon of 'L' Company, Border Regiment, under the command of Lt King, took up residence in Hutton Hall. By 24th November, the army unit had taken over protection of the site at night and would eventually become solely responsible for 8 SLG's security. Hutton's Home Guard was now reduced to almost half of its original strength and remained so until disbandment in December 1944.

The usefulness of such a well-camouflaged landing ground did not escape the attention of other maintenance units in the area. On 8th December, Wg Cdr Poole and Sqn Ldr Beattie, from 18 MU at Dumfries, visited the SLG and inspected the runway. This was followed on 26th February 1942 by W E Sisson from the Ministry of Aircraft Production (MAP) and Flt Lt F Morgan from nearby 50 Wing at Hutton Hall. They had just visited Hornby Hall with a view to taking over both landing grounds for the use of 12 and 18 MUs, establishing a permanent maintenance party at both SLGs. Flt Lt R A F Farquharson and Flt Sgt J K Arber from 12 MU at Kirkbride carried out a similar visit on 14th March. Both unit test pilots, they also inspected the runway with a view to dispersing the swelling number of Wellingtons at Kirkbride.

The aircraft held in dispersal at 8 SLG in early 1942 averaged ten Blenheims, ten Bothas and three Hudsons, and regular inspections by Gp Capt. Hanson-Abbot of HQ 50 Wg ensured both camouflage and the efficient running of the SLG were maintained.

A spate of thieving did not go unnoticed in March 1942. On 31st March, a Geoffrey Allison, who was employed at the SLG as a fitter 'E', was charged at Penrith Petty Sessions with stealing Air Ministry property. It is not known what he stole but he was sentenced to three months in prison. A few days later, on 4th April, a J P Bell, who was also a fitter 'E' was charged with being in possession of aircraft spirit. He appeared in Penrith Petty Sessions on 14th April; his sentence is not known. However, he was informed the following day that, in view of his unsatisfactory conduct, he would not be retained in employment and that his name had been removed from the books of the establishment, which would have been the parent unit of 22 MU at Silloth.

As a direct result of these cases, Officer Commanding 22 MU, Wg Cdr E J H Starling, investigated procedures and key personnel at

The Lockheed Hudson was another regular visitor; many were hidden in the woods around the SLG.

8 SLG. The matter was discussed between Starling and Gp Capt Hanson-Abbot at HQ 50 Wing on 7th April. A decision then followed to replace the current officer in charge of 8 SLG with Flg Off. E F Drew and to replace the foreman of trades. Both postings were implemented swiftly and no further thefts were ever reported at the SLG.

Airfield defence was taken seriously during this period of the war and, on 10th April 1942, several Beaverette Reconnaissance Cars arrived from 22 MU at Silloth. Named after Lord Beaverbrook, the Minister of Aircraft Production, the Beaverette was a small armoured car used for the defence of airfields and factories. For an SLG like Hutton to receive such vehicles was quite unusual, although they were supplied completely unarmed, as a visual rather than an aggressive deterrent.

Hutton's location in woodland made it rather vulnerable to fire and regular testing and inspecting of fire services at all SLGs was always taken seriously. On 12th May at Hutton, Wg Cdr Starling met The Right Honourable Lord Geddes, the National Fire Service (NFS) Controller for the north-west. Lord Geddes found all the fire equipment to be satisfactory but recommended that the surrounding woods be cleared of bracken and brushwood to reduce the fire risk. His comments were implemented the next day when Section Leader F Jopson of the NFS and a party of 17 firemen reported to the unit to start work clearing the woods.

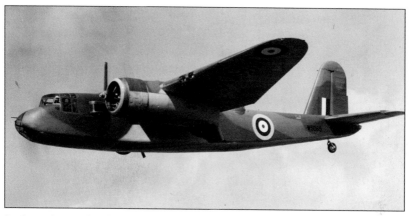

In the early months of Hutton's existence, a number of Bothas were transferred from Silloth. Along with the Blenheim and Hudson, the Botha was the most common aircraft to be seen at Hutton.

'L' Company, which had been looking after the security of the SLG since November 1941, was relieved by 'G' Company of the same regiment on 4th June 1942. The same day, contractors began measuring up for accommodation for a squadron of the RAF Regiment. The first of many visits and discussions by Sqn Ldr Blomfield occurred back in March with regard to accommodating a squadron of the RAF Regiment at Hutton. Their role would be to relieve the resident army unit of its anti-sabotage and guard duties. However, they would have to be accommodated on the landing ground and new buildings constructed to house them, all of this taking an agonisingly long time.

A new type of aircraft arrived for the first time at Hutton on 8th July 1942. Lockheed Ventura I AE669 was the first of many of these American aircraft to be dispersed and modified at 8 SLG. The Ventura was the result of a September 1939 proposal by the Lockheed Aircraft Company to the Air Ministry for a military version of the Model 18 Lodestar; this in turn was viewed as a successor to the Hudson, of which the first had been delivered to the RAF in February 1939.

Larger, heavier and more powerful than the Hudson, the Ventura had the same general layout as its older brother. It first entered service with 21 Squadron at Bodney in Norfolk. Despite being 50 mph faster and carrying a larger bomb load than the Hudson, Venturas were not popular with RAF crews and high losses reflected its unsuitability as a bomber.

Very similar in appearance to the Hudson, the Lockheed Ventura was a development of its older brother. The first arrived at Hutton in July 1942.

The difference between the Hudson and the Ventura was demonstrated when Flt Lt Ashton flew AE669 into Hutton. Landing in a north-westerly direction with a south-westerly crosswind, Ashton skilfully brought the aircraft to a halt with only 70 to 80 yards to spare. All future Ventura arrivals would be carried out only with a headwind directly down the main runway. After travelling by ship across the Atlantic Ocean from the USA, AE669 never served with an RAF unit. The Ventura was ferried by air to Canada, where it served with 34 OTU at Yarmouth in Nova Scotia.

Despite the fact that the Ventura tested the very edge of the limitations of the SLG, Flt Lt G F Duffy, a 41 Group test pilot, visited on 25th July 1942 to assess the airfield for larger aircraft. Duffy was brought into Hutton by Flt Lt Ashton in an Airspeed Oxford to test the feasibility of the satellite receiving four-engined types. 8 SLG must have been found unsuitable for such aircraft, as none was ever recorded to have used it.

The largest regular user was the Vickers Wellington III, the first of which arrived in the capable hands of Flt Lt Ashton on 5th August 1942. Ashton made several test flights in and out of the airfield, finding both the landing and take-off run satisfactory. The resident population of dispersed aircraft now began to rise rapidly with an average holding of 11 Hurricanes, 2 Wellingtons, 2 Hudson, 14 Ventura and 5 Bothas throughout August.

Another American-built aircraft arrived for the first time on 19th September 1942. A North American Mustang, flown by Plt Off. E Cleife was the first of many of this successful single-engined fighter to pass through Hutton. Within a few days, nine more followed, bringing added diversity to the work already being carried out on the SLG.

With their accommodation finally completed at the end of October 1942, a contingent of one sergeant, one corporal and ten airmen of the RAF Regiment arrived at the unit on 11th November. They took over anti-sabotage and guard duties from a company of the 39th Manchester Regiment on 15th November and remained in this role until the SLG's closure. Security was given another boost the following month with the arrival of a pair of dog handler teams, who were also accommodated on the SLG.

Turnover of aircraft steadily increased towards the end of 1942, with a peak output of 32 aircraft dispatched in a single month. No great figure compared to the output of the parent unit, but still a valuable contribution, of which Hutton's small civilian workforce was proud.

Work continued steadily throughout 1943, the only event worthy of note being the arrival of Air Officer Commanding 41 Group Air Vice Marshal G Laing, who inspected 8 SLG on 28th October.

Hutton featured in a large exercise organised between the local army units and the Home Guard on 26th March 1944. The SLG was one of the enemies' objectives during the exercise and the signal 'action stations' was received several times at Hutton; the SLG's own Home Guard unit manned defensive posts.

Hutton began to wind down from May 1945 onwards. With hostilities at an end in Europe, the need to disperse aircraft far and wide had ended. Over the next few months all of 8 SLG's aircraft were flown to the parent unit at Silloth and military and civilian staff alike were moved out. The SLG closed in August 1945, but the land was retained for the Admiralty, who stored munitions on the site until at least 1947.

Today very little remains, primarily because very little existed in the first place. The most prominent building is a well-built set of gun butts used for aircraft firing, which today serves a more quiet role as a store for farm machinery. The runway is still in place and the land is now back in the hands of the current Lord Inglewood.

11
JURBY

Work began on a new airfield in the north of the Isle of Man in late 1938. Located near to the coast, north-west of Sandygate, Jurby was planned as one of nine new Armament Training Stations. All of these training airfields were well equipped with several hangars, brick-built technical buildings and good quality domestic accommodation. All were positioned close to a bombing range, which, in Jurby's case, was only a walk away, as it was located at Jurby Head. There was a second at Ramsey Bay.

Jurby was ready for occupation as the Second World War began on 3rd September 1939. It was not until 16th September that No 5 Armament Training Station (ATS) arrived from Penrhos in Caernarvonshire, only to be redesignated two days later. The opening-up party, under the command of Sqn Ldr B B Dowling of No 5 Air Observers' School (AOS), was beginning its journey from Sealand in Flintshire by road with two 3-ton lorries and a van containing seven officers, one warrant officer and 34 other ranks, to arrive at Jurby the following day.

The station itself was officially opened the same day, with acting Gp Capt. T S Ivens, the Chief Instructor (Armament) of 5 AOS, and 25 officer and 16 sergeant pilots on strength. By 2nd October, Gp Capt A P V Daley AFC took over command from Ivens, who reverted to his original rank of Wing Commander to continue his Chief Instructor duties.

The first aircraft arrived on 10th October when Blenheim Is K7129 and L1287 and Magister I P2442 were delivered. A steady flow of aircraft continued to arrive until the end of November, the bulk of which were Blenheims, but also several Fairey Battles, Hawker Henleys and a few obsolete Westland Wallaces.

The airfield was busy with aircraft movements in no time and on 9th November the first serious accident occurred. Henley I L3391 struck Battle I K7620, piloted by Sgt Watson, whilst landing; the latter

The Blenheim was the mainstay of 5 AOS at Jurby until it was superseded by the Anson.

had arrived on station only three days earlier. Both aircraft were seriously damaged but luckily the crews escaped unharmed.

On 1st December 1939, 5 AOS was redesignated No 5 Bombing and Gunnery School (B&GS), operating the same aircraft for armament training. Within three days of forming, an aircraft of 5 B&GS went into action against the enemy for the first time. A signal was received at 09:00hrs from 15 Group HQ at Aldergrove that an enemy submarine had been sighted off the east coast of the island. This was confirmed 45 minutes later when the Chief Constable of Douglas phoned the station adjutant with the news that a 'reliable' civilian had reported seeing an enemy submarine in Dhoon Bay, midway between Laxey and Ramsey. The station adjutant reported this straight to 15 Group and Gp Capt Daley ordered a 5 B&GS Blenheim into the air to keep an eye on the submarine. Frustratingly, no more was seen of it but this incident highlighted that the war was close and even training units must be prepared for action.

Because of its great gunnery facilities, Jurby hosted several detachments from Flying Training Schools (FTS) for armament training. The first arrived on 2nd January 1940 in the shape of the Advanced Training Squadron of 5 FTS stationed at Sealand. 14 aircraft arrived first, with nine more on 4th January, supported by nine officers, 21 SNCOs and 19 airmen. The 5 FTS detachment included the school's Oxford flight plus several Hawker Audax biplanes, which soldiered on into the Second World War as gunnery trainers. On 8th January, Sgt Ken in Audax K5151 took off from Jurby at 15:15hrs and was never seen again. The 5 FTS detachment came to an end on 11th January, but sadly not before the unit lost another aircraft. Oxford I N6263 was carrying out a night flying exercise when it crashed at Ballamodha.

The next detachment to arrive was that of 12 FTS, from Grantham in Lincolnshire, bringing 12 Ansons and five Audaxes on 18th January. Staging through Sealand for the aircraft, and road and rail for the ground party, meant that the contingent was not complete until 23rd January. By the 27th, the airfield was snowbound and completely cut off, bringing all flying training to an abrupt halt. By 5th February, it was obvious that the detachment would not achieve anything by remaining at Jurby and the officers began to return to Grantham without their aircraft. It took until 25th February before 17 pilots were brought over from Grantham to collect the unit's aircraft.

The ground party, consisting of three officers and 32 airmen of the No 4 Group Pool Squadron, arrived from Abingdon in Oxfordshire on 16th February. This party was followed on 23rd February by six Armstrong Whitworth Whitley III twin engined bombers on 23rd February with a further five officers and 27 other ranks.

More bombers arrived on 16th March 1940 when 11 Operational Training Unit (OTU) from Bassingbourn in Cambridgeshire brought five Vickers Wellingtons with 19 officers and 42 other ranks.

166 Squadron from Abingdon brought more Whitleys into Jurby on 1st April and, along with 4 Group Pool, was disbanded into 10 OTU, which was officially formed at Abingdon on 8th April 1940. The two units, while at Jurby, were merged into 'C' Flight detachment and remained at the airfield until September 1940.

In these early days of the war, the threat of invasion was ever present and reports of a possible enemy attack occurring were frequent. On 16th May, a report was received from the Government Secretary that he had information from Whitehall which indicated an enemy landing at Ronaldsway between dusk and dawn. The incredibly specific time and location came to nothing but it made senior military and civilian staff on the Isle of Man think about how to defend the island. In response, a cooperation-in-defence exercise was organised on 10th June. Jurby's role was to detail six Fairey Battles with six crews for defensive action only at the discretion of the General Officer Commanding (GOC) Land Force, Isle of Man. The Chief Instructor of 5 B&GS was made responsible for the armed readiness of these aircraft, which should be available within 30 minutes of the sounding of the alarm, although, in hindsight, this would have been a token gesture if a real invasion of the island had occurred. The military felt they were slightly better prepared than having no aircraft at readiness at all.

A detachment from the Central Flying School (CFS) at Upavon in Wiltshire arrived on 4th June. Known as the CFS Attached Instructional Flight, they were at Jurby to instruct and give refresher flying to 5 B&GS's instructors, using three Fairey Battle dual control trainers. Night flying instruction began on the 5th June when six pilots were given both dual by day and then by night until the required standard was achieved. The CFS left on 13th June, having given the unit's pilots 33.35 hours of dual instruction by day and 25.05 hours by night.

On the afternoon of 13th June the 11 OTU detachment lost its first Wellington whilst at Jurby. Wellington Ia N3102 was returning to Jurby after a range-firing exercise when the starboard engine failed. The pilot successfully ditched the crippled bomber in shallow water 60 yards off shore near Orrisdale Head, north of Kirk Michael, with all on board taking to the aircraft's dinghy and safety. When the salvage crews and vessels arrived, which included the *Victoria Regina* from Ramsey, they found the Wellington was lying in only 11 ft of water at the high water mark but was still virtually submerged. Wire ropes were attached to the boss of each propeller with marker buoys. Instruments and guns were removed when the tide receded and a shore salvage party started work during the night on separating the starboard engine and port mainplane, complete with engine, from the bomber. The following morning, the engines and port wing were raised onto the *Victoria Regina,* which returned to the Queen's Pier at Ramsey. Both engines were transferred to a seaplane tender, ferried to a three-ton crane on the pier and then lifted onto the pier tramway. The port wing, which was found to be buoyant, was towed into the harbour by a seaplane tender and then hauled up the slipway of the Marine Craft Section.

The *Victoria Regina* returned to the Wellington wreckage that evening and made an attempt to lift the fuselage. A combination of a falling tide and an obstruction on the seabed, meant that the attempt was postponed until 17th June. However, Mother Nature took over on 15th and the wreckage was driven high up on the beach by a strong westerly wind, making it possible for the shore party to recover the rest of the aircraft. Where possible, every attempt was made to recover crashed aircraft and the recovery of N3012 is quite typical of the effort salvage teams put in.

Security around the island was improved slightly from 20th June, when a Ramsey-based seaplane tender began patrols around the coast. The 37½ ft long vessel had a pair of Vickers machine guns added and patrolled from Ramsey to Jurby Head twice daily at dawn and dusk.

Royalty paid a visit for the first time to Jurby on 11th July 1940. Gp Capt. HRH The Duke of Kent KG, KT, GCMG, GCVO, who was being employed by RAF Training Command, arrived by air to inspect the station. Tragically, the duke was killed when the 228 Squadron Short Sunderland flying boat he was travelling to Iceland in, crashed at Eagles Rock near Dunbeath, Caithness on 25th August 1942.

The number of aircraft now parked on the airfield surpassed three figures in the summer of 1940 and a decision was made to expand the airfield. In July, fourteen fields which adjoined the airfield boundary, were selected for dispersing aircraft. An order was signed by the Governor of the Isle of Man and the requisitioning was quickly carried out. Within days, all of the necessary work to cut gaps through hedges and walls was completed, allowing aircraft to be dispersed over a wider area rather than being concentrated around the large concrete apron in front of the hangars.

It was a wise decision to disperse the aircraft because the presence of Luftwaffe bombers had been steadily increasing. It was seen as only a matter of time before the island became a target, and the first of many air raid warnings was sounded in the early hours of 22nd July. In response to this, a test of the station defence scheme was organized a few days later. Army units based in the north of the island carried out exercises and a simulated air raid warning 'yellow' was received by the station. To add realism to the exercise, trainees from HMS *St George*, which was Cunningham's holiday camp before the war, acted as the 'attackers' attempting to penetrate the army defences and access the airfield. Approximately 50 prisoners were taken, all of whom were held at Jurby until the exercise ended. Valuable experience was gained by all who took part but, as usual, the question is how would they have fared if the naval trainees had been heavily armed German paratroops?

Thirteen Ansons from the School of Navigation at St Athan descended upon Jurby on 29th July 1940. The intention was for the group to return to St Athan in the early hours of the following morning. Heavy rain delayed their departure until 04:45hrs and all thirteen Ansons took off at one-minute intervals with only marginal visibility. Plt Off. Wigley-Jones in Anson I L7963 was one of the departing group who set course down the west of the island before rounding the Calf of Man and flying an easterly course towards the mainland. Unfortunately, the pilot mistook Dalby Point as the south of island and set his easterly course too early. The Anson, after entering low cloud, crashed into the side of Dalby Mountain, totally wrecking the aircraft. Miraculously, all on board escaped with just cuts and bruises.

From May 1940, there had been a series of incidents involving general thieving of aircraft parts and at least one incident of attempted destruction by fire of an aircraft. The situation arose when aircraft began being more dispersed, many of them left unattended for long periods. On one occasion, 23 spark plugs from a Blenheim were stolen and in July a Wellington in a dispersal field was nearly set on fire with some oily rags, which luckily only managed to destroy a hedge. In August, clocks and instruments were stolen from Blenheim Is L1304, L1198 and K7129, rendering the aircraft unserviceable and costing valuable man-hours to repair them while diverting airmen from other important tasks.

The first of many Handley Page Herefords arrived at Jurby on 14th September 1940. The Hereford was virtually identical to the Hampden, the main difference being the engines, which were a pair of Rolls Royce Daggers. These in-line air-cooled engines were incredibly unreliable and prone to catching fire, making the Hereford very unpopular with its crews. Herefords never saw front line squadron service; all of the 150 produced saw service only with training units, many ending their days with student pilots at the controls.

Wellingtons of 215 Squadron, based at Bassingbourn, were the next aircraft to use Jurby's facilities. Their detachment lasted four weeks, from mid October to mid November 1940.

Back in August, Sqn Ldr Oliver from HQ Fighter Command arrived to carry out a preliminary investigation into the question of siting fighter squadrons at Jurby. This came to fruition when, on 7th November, the main party of 307 Squadron arrived with eight

The Handley Page Hereford was very unreliable and prone to engine fires; several were lost in flying accidents from Jurby.

officers and 59 airmen in the ground party, followed by the air party with 11 officers and 31 airmen and finally by the air transport party with one officer and 35 airmen. The unit brought nine Boulton Paul Defiants, making it the first Polish night fighter squadron. Initially under the command of Sqn Ldr G C Tomlinson, the squadron was formed at Kirton-in-Lindsey in Lincolnshire on 5th September. The squadron was moved to Jurby to continue their training on the Defiant. There they found that conditions were far worse than at their previous home. Jurby did not suffer from daily air raid warnings but the personnel of the squadron complained about the weather. It rained almost constantly and the whole airfield was muddy. Accidents were frequent and the overall value of the squadron was becoming questionable. Rotations among the flying personnel were constant as the Polish aircrew desperately tried, often successfully, to be posted on to an operational front line squadron. Sqn Ldr Grodzicki shared the command of the squadron from 15th November and at the same time several keen young pilots came to the unit, making an immediate impact on both the morale and capability of the squadron. On 4th December, 307 Squadron was declared operational and, on 8th December, the unit made its first sortie. Three Defiants were

307 Squadron was the first fighter unit to be based at Jurby with the Boulton Paul Defiant.

scrambled to intercept a single enemy aircraft but, due to poor radio contact with ground control, the aircraft escaped detection. In an effort to gain combat experience, a section of Defiants was sent for a brief detachment to Cranage in Cheshire, where enemy activity was more frequent. Frustratingly, despite several patrols, the aircraft returned to Jurby without gaining an enemy kill.

Excitement was caused on the airfield when an air raid warning 'Red' was received on 20th December 1940. Several enemy aircraft dropped parachute flares all over the island but luckily no bombs. 307 Squadron was scrambled but once again they were either too late or in the wrong place to achieve an interception.

At the beginning of January 1941, five aircraft were detached to Squires Gate in Lancashire and on the 23rd the rest of the squadron left Jurby to join them. Positioned to defend the cities of Liverpool and Manchester, the squadron achieved several successful interceptions in this area.

258 Squadron was the next fighter squadron to arrive at Jurby. Re-formed at Leconfield in North Yorkshire on 20th November, the squadron was equipped with the Hurricane I and its pilots were mainly New Zealanders. 12 Hurricanes arrived at Jurby on 1st February from Acklington in Northumberland, with the task of carrying out defensive patrols over the island.

A major search was launched off the coast of the island when Sgt D Sutherland, flying a Blenheim of 5 B&GS from Squires Gate, went missing on 13th March 1941. Sutherland was presumed lost but

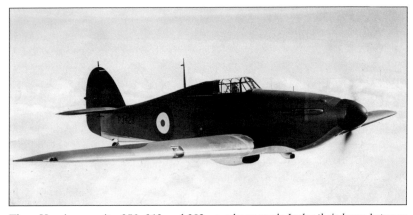

Three Hurricane units, 258, 312 and 302 squadrons made Jurby their home between February and August 1941.

the next day an Irish Republic wireless broadcast reported that an unidentified aircraft had forced-landed in County Louth and the sole occupant was taken to hospital. Jurby asked the Air Ministry if they would enquire if the aircraft was the Blenheim piloted by Sgt Sutherland. It was another four days before it was confirmed that the pilot was Sutherland. He had suffered a leg injury in the crash, was taken to a local hospital and was later interned by the Irish authorities.

Rationing on the Isle of Man was slightly less restrictive than in the rest of the United Kingdom, but this did not stop a station farm being set up on the airfield to complement the diet of the personnel at Jurby. Two large pigsties, a shed for storing food and a shed for boiling swill were constructed. Ten Large White pigs, about twelve weeks old, were also purchased and arrangements were made with a contractor who purchased station swill to relinquish a certain quantity for the feeding of these pigs. Crop production included a two-acre field which was cleared and ploughed so that it could be sown with barley. A 1½ acre field, which was ploughed the previous year for vegetables, was re-ploughed so that one acre could be sown with potatoes and the rest used for various other vegetables. All gardens at the station's married quarters were dug over and were developed as individual allotments for the cultivation of vegetables.

On the night of 15th April 1941, a large number of enemy aircraft passed over the Isle of Man during the hours of darkness. A single high explosive (HE) was dropped near Ramsey and several incendiary hombs (IB) fell around Scarlett, one mile south-west of Castletown. The Belfast blitz was at its height at this time and it is highly probably that the bombs that fell that night were simply being discarded by the Germans on their way home.

258 Squadron's uneventful tour of duty at Jurby ended on 17th April when the land party departed for Valley, Anglesey. The Hurricanes flew out on 19th April, their replacement, 312 (Czech) Squadron, arrived the same day, also equipped with the Hurricane I. 312 Squadron was formed at Duxford on 29th August 1940 with Czechoslovakian personnel as a fighter unit. It was first sent to Speke to defend Merseyside, then it operated from Valley before arriving at Jurby for defensive patrols.

5 B&GS, like so many other units, was having major problems operating the Hereford. Sgt J Astbury was at the controls of Hereford I L6075 when the port engine burst into flames whilst returning to the airfield on 26th April. To enable the crew to leave the crippled aircraft, Sgt Astbury successfully kept control of the Hereford, despite the

cockpit rapidly filling with smoke and flame. Astbury bailed out at a height of not more than 600 ft and survived; the rest of the crew all landed safely.

A demonstration of various synthetic training devices produced by Jurby was given to about 30 officers representing the majority of commands in the RAF on 6th and 7th May 1941. The proceedings commenced with a short introductory talk by the commanding officer and the visitors were then separated into small parties and taken around the various displays. In the Bellman hangar they found the panoramic trainer, tracer trainers (for both fixed and free guns) and a device for range estimation and aircraft identification. They were also taken to the 200yd moving target range and the 400yd fixed target range at Jurby Head and completed their tour by visiting the cine spotlight trainer.

312 Squadron left for Kenley, Greater London, on 29th May for a slightly more eventful tour of duty. 302 (City of Poznan) Squadron brought their Hurricanes to Jurby the same day from Kenley. This famous Polish fighter squadron was formed in time to see action in the later stages of the Battle of Britain, in which it performed exceptionally well. The Polish pilots quickly became frustrated at Jurby, performing the daily ritual of defensive and convoy patrols. Initially equipped with the Hurricane I, the squadron began to receive the Hurricane IIB whilst at Jurby. The main advantages of the IIB were an improved Merlin XX engine, which was fitted with a two-speed supercharger that improved the aircraft's performance at all altitudes. Its armament was also increased from the original eight 0.303 Browning machine guns to an impressive twelve.

Flying hours by 5 B&GS were recorded at a respectable 2,153 hours 40 minutes during May 1941, a record for the unit. This was not without cost, as it also suffered its highest accident rate, with one Henley and four Blenheims lost in flying accidents. 5 B&GS changed its name back to 5 AOS on 19th July 1941 and the training programme was simplified to a single course covering navigation and weaponry. During the month, the aircraft establishment of the school stood at 73 Blenheims, 26 Hampdens and Herefords, six Ansons and 12 Henley target tugs. Such was the high standard of training being delivered at Jurby, that a Mjr Kenney from the USAAC reported for attachment to study the training of air gunners on 8th August 1941. A second USAAC officer, Mjr Jenkins, also arrived on attachment on 22nd August 1941.

As 302 Squadron's association with Jurby was drawing to a close, the unit lost one of its Hurricanes. On 21st July, whilst returning from a convoy patrol, a 302 Squadron Hurricane suffered an engine failure and appeared to make a good ditching in the sea. The pilot was rescued but died from his injuries later that day. On 7th August, 302 Squadron left Jurby for Church Stanton in Somerset, to be replaced by 457 Squadron the same day. The squadron arrived from Baginton in Warwickshire with the Spitfire I, although it would re-equip with the more powerful Spitfire IIA before leaving Jurby. The squadron left Jurby on 3rd October 1941, making a short flight to Andreas. 457 Squadron was to be the last fighter squadron stationed at Jurby.

Personnel from the airfield were increasingly involved in the rescue of airmen who either crashed on the island or ditched at sea. An unofficial mountain rescue team was formed, which became officially recognised only after the war, when their work decreased dramatically. With no local maintenance unit, Jurby also became responsible for the salvage of wrecked aircraft. The first instance of this work occurred on 8th October 1941 when four Hurricanes from 133 'Eagle' Squadron and a Wellington crashed on the island. Salvage assistance was rendered by personnel from Jurby all through the night and continued the following day.

On the night of 15th/16th October, three inmates managed to escape from the Ramsey Internment Camp. Despite efforts by Spitfires from 457 Squadron at Andreas to find the group, who had stolen a boat from Ramsey, they remained undetected. On the morning of 17th October, a Blenheim, piloted by Flt Lt Godwin from 5 AOS, was on an early navigation flight when he reported seeing a small yacht off the Cumberland coast. Godwin had found the three internees, much to the chagrin of the Australian fighter pilots, and they were later captured by an army unit when they came ashore.

The mountain rescue team was put to the test on 17th January 1942. Anson I N5030 from 27 OTU at Lichfield in Staffordshire crashed into Snaefell at approximately 20:00hrs. Three of the crew of seven were killed but, despite heavy snow, the Jurby team rescued the survivors. During the ensuing salvage operation the weather deteriorated and the party ended up having to rescue one of their own. On 19th January, one of the salvage party, Cpl A Eedle, was in charge of the Anson's IFF equipment, which he was carrying from the scene of the crash to an MT vehicle which was parked two miles away. During a strong blizzard, Eedle became lost and the other members of the group lost contact with him. Another search party was sent out from Jurby but failed to locate Cpl Eedle. A second party including Flt Lt J N Paton,

Cpl MacPherson and nine other ranks set out from Jurby at 00:10hrs on 20th January under the command of Sqn Ldr Revd G L Horricks, the station SMO. In very risky conditions the party found Snaefell on snowbound roads, the last two miles of the journey were covered on foot in a raging blizzard. Cpl Eedle was found in a mountain bungalow semi-conscious and suffering from exposure and frostbite, but still in possession of the salvaged IFF equipment, which he insisted on bringing with him back to camp. Eedle was carried by the search party to a waiting lorry two miles away and eventually returned to Jurby at 06:30hrs. The station commander stated that the devotion to duty of Cpl Eedle and of all ranks concerned in his rescue was worthy of commendation.

Despite a tough winter, 5 AOS managed to achieve a record-breaking 3,000 flying hours in the month of February 1942. This figure was not achieved without cost: the unit lost three Ansons and two Blenheims. Only one was fatal when Anson I N5346 crashed into North Barrule while night flying, killing the pilot, Sgt Henderson, wireless operator Sgt Anderson and air observer LAC Carter instantly. The unit lost a further ten Blenheims and a single Hampden before 5 AOS was given the opportunity to take part in a historic Bomber Command operation.

Operation 'Millennium' was the brainchild of Bomber Command's new Commander in Chief, Air Marshal Sir Arthur Harris. The operation involved massed formation of bombers concentrating all their fire power on a city and several of the raids involved over 1,000 aircraft. To achieve such large formations of aircraft, Harris called up resources from conversions units, operational training units and even schools like 5 AOS at Jurby.

The first raid of the campaign was to involve over 1,000 aircraft, with Cologne as the target, on the night of 30th/31st May 1942. Three Hampdens were prepared to take part in the massive raid and on 25th May the aircraft left Jurby for Syerston in Nottinghamshire, home of 61 and 106 Squadrons operating the Avro Lancaster. The trip did not go well because Hampden I L6011, piloted by Sgt Hodgkinson, crashed near Syerston after hitting power lines. LAC Griffiths was killed in the accident while the rest of the crew escaped uninjured. On 26th May two more Hampdens followed to Syerston for operational experience. The same day a Hampden pilot was attached to Sutton Bridge in Lincolnshire and a Whitley pilot was sent to Llandwrog in Gwynedd.

The day of the biggest bombing raid in world history was an anticlimax for many of the aircrew of 5 AOS. Two of the Hampdens attached to Syerston had to return to Jurby for technical reasons, making it impossible for them to take part in the raid. A single Observer, Flg Off. D H Brewer, did take part in the raid as one of the crew of a 106 Squadron Lancaster.

The second 'thousand-bomber' raid was to Essen on the night of the 1st/2nd June 1942, although Harris could only muster 956 aircraft on this occasion. Two senior officers and crews took part in this raid. A single all-Jurby crew with Wg Cdr H R A Edwards as the pilot joined 70 other Hampdens taking part in the raid. Over the target, one engine failed and, after coming down to 600 ft over the English Channel, Edwards managed to reach the English coast. The bomber struggled on at tree-top height until the second engine failed and Edwards carried out a successful forced-landing in Norfolk. Wg Cdr G E MacDonald flew the same raid as bomb-aimer in a Lancaster and returned safely to Syerston. Further operational experience was gained by Plt Off. T D Robertson over Bremen on 4th June. Robertson flew as a second pilot in a Lancaster on the comparatively smaller raid, which still involved 170 aircraft.

Jurby became the home of a very unusual unit in the summer of 1942. The Armament Synthetic Development Unit was first formed at Dumfries in 1941, operating the Vickers Wellington. Little is known about this unit but its name implies it was involved in development of new teaching aids for air gunners, possibly working closely with 5 AOS. By June 1943, the unit had moved to Manby in Lincolnshire.

5 AOS received a visit from one of the RAF's great fighter pilots on 25th June 1942. Wg Cdr A G Malan DSO, DFC was an outstanding fighter pilot who achieved great success during the Battle of Britain. By the end of June 1941, he was the RAF's highest scorer, with 29 enemy aircraft destroyed, a record he held for three years. The South African was nicknamed 'Sailor' Malan and his famous 'Ten Rules for Air Fighting' were replicated in squadron crew rooms throughout the country. Wg Cdr Malan was at Jurby to inspect the unit's synthetic training equipment and view various training methods in place at 5 AOS. The day was marred when Blenheim Is Z6191 and K7084 collided during a cine-gun practice. Tragically, the pilots, Flt Sgt Kilian and Sgt Pawlowski, and four pupils were killed.

The Jurby mountain rescue team's work rate continued to increase throughout 1942. The team was spending as much time searching for aircraft from other units as it had been for 5 AOS. The loss rate was getting so high at 5 AOS that air gunners who had been flying front-line operations described the training as being the most dangerous part of their flying career!

On 3rd February 1943, aircraft belonging to 5 AOS totalled over 60 Ansons, 21 Blenheims and at least ten Lysander III target tugs. Within a few months, the Ansons would be the sole type as the ageing Blenheims were steadily retired from RAF service.

With so many aircraft ditching in the Irish Sea, making sure aircrew could survive a successful ditching was vital. On 27th February 1943, Flg Off. Siedlecki found himself volunteering for an unusual test. Siedlecki tested a new buoyancy suit in the cold sea-water in Ramsey Harbour. The test went better than imagined because Siedlecki spent ten hours in the water without any ill effects. The following day, Anson I EG300 from the unit ditched in the sea off the Isle of Man coast. The Anson was a good aircraft to ditch and quite often remained afloat for a significant period of time, enabling the crew to escape. The Anson came down around 21:30hrs and with efficient cooperation between flying control, 5 AOS aircraft and Air Sea Rescue, the crew were rescued unharmed and were on dry land by 23:00hrs.

As the Anson became the dominant aircraft, its reliability began to be reflected in the number of flying hours achieved by 5 AOS. Total flying time for February 1943 was a respectable 4,000 hours. The unit was congratulated by HQ 29 Group on reaching this figure, particularly because it was achieved with only one flying accident.

A Short Stirling, one of the biggest aircraft to land at Jurby, made an emergency landing with three engines on 19th April 1943. A second Stirling followed, also with one of its Bristol Hercules engines unserviceable. Mechanics from 5 AOS managed to repair one of the aircraft, which left later in the day. However, the other Stirling would require a complete engine change, which would be delivered the next day by very novel means. The remarkable sight of an Armstrong Whitworth Albemarle GTV, from 42 OTU at Ashbourne in Derbyshire, towing an Airspeed Horsa II glider came into view over the airfield. The Horsa, with a spare Hercules engine on board, was unhitched and glided down onto the airfield, followed by its tug a few moments later. The Albemarle and Horsa returned later that day, and the Stirling received a new engine and left Jurby on 26th April.

A spate of belly-landings, taxiing accidents and undercarriage-related incidents occurred throughout the beginning of 1943. They were occurring to such a degree that it became necessary to ground all of the RAF's Ansons for checking. All of 5 AOS's aircraft were cleared for service but two more crashed in May because of an undercarriage collapse and a burst tyre.

The airfield provided an impressive detachment of 400 RAF and 100 WAAF for the Douglas 'Wings for Victory Parade' and 15 Ansons for a flypast on 5th June. Another large parade was supported by the unit on 26th September 1943. 100 RAF and 40 WAAF, under the command of Sqn Ldr W H Emmett, paraded in Douglas for Battle of Britain Sunday. The Lt Governor of the Isle of Man took the salute at the parade.

A 17-year-old Princess Elizabeth flew into Jurby from Yeadon in Yorkshire for a four day visit to the Isle of Man on 11th October 1943. HRH The Princess Royal was met by His Excellency The Lt Governor, and a guard of honour of 100 airmen, under Sqn Ldr E E M Angell, was provided by the station. On 13th October, Jurby sent a detachment of 50 WAAF personnel, under Sqn Ldr B Vaughan, to take part in a review by the Princess Royal in Douglas. The princess left Jurby on 14th October and the unit provided another guard of honour of 100 airmen.

By the end of 1943, the remaining Blenheims had gone and the Lysander target tugs had been replaced with a few Miles Martinets. The pace of training was slowing down by the beginning of 1944 and the unit was set for yet another change of title. On 1st February 1944, 5 AOS was disbanded and redesignated the Air Navigation and Bombing School (AN&BS). All basic navigation training was now being provided at overseas units under the Empire Air Training Scheme (EATS). The new school at Jurby was the only one of its kind in the United Kingdom and its main task was to develop new training methods and measure the standard of navigators from the EATS units.

During March 1944, the flying commitment of the school had fallen to 2,500 flying hours and the aircraft establishment of the unit was to be reduced. At the end of the month, 67 Ansons, three Martinets and a single Avro Tutor made up the school's aircraft. On 1st April this was reduced to 46 Ansons and a single Miles Magister.

Operation 'Sonnie' began on 20th April 1944 with the arrival of four Lockheed Lodestars from Norway. The operation involved 90 flights, via Leuchars in Fife, into one of the many internment camps on the Isle of Man. The Lodestar was a development of the Lockheed 18 airliner and 25 served with three squadrons of the RAF, all in the Middle East. The RAF's Lodestars remained in the Middle East throughout the war; so the aircraft that flew into Jurby were most likely being operated by BOAC. It seems no coincidence that only a few days before the last

Lodestar flight into Jurby HRH Crown Prince Olaf of Norway arrived on 6th September 1944. He left by air to Hendon, Middlesex a few days later. The last flight, a single Lodestar with 15 Norwegians on board landed on 17th October 1944, ending Operation 'Sonnie', which had flown in 1,402 suspected collaborators.

The Allied build-up for the invasion of Europe was gaining momentum by May 1944 and it was obvious that the RAF's Douglas Dakota transports would be heavily involved in the operation. As a temporary measure, the Ansons of the AN&BS would be employed in the south of England for short-range transport duties in place of the 46 Group Dakotas. On 11th May, the school received a signal from HQ Flying Training Command stating that the AN&BS was to provide a detachment of personnel to operate 50 Ansons from Watchfield in Berkshire. On 15th May, an advance party left, followed on 22nd May by the main detachment of 50 aircraft, including 50 officers and nearly 400 airmen. This left the school very quiet and several officers and airmen left at Jurby were sent on detachments to other airfields in the group while the Ansons were away.

The mountain rescue team continued its work unabated, attending two American air crashes during the AN&BS detachment. Jurby received information on 9th June 1944 that B-24 Liberator 42-51202 of the 311th FYS (Ferrying Squadron) had crashed into the summit of Snaefell. The Liberator was on a ferry flight from Langford Lodge in Northern Ireland to the mainland when the accident occurred, and the pilot, 1st Lt W L Lenox, and three other crew were found dead in the wreckage. The second American crash, and one of the most serious on the island during the Second World War, occurred on 4th July 1944. Martin B-26 Marauder 41-35791 being ferried from Langford Lodge to the mainland crashed into Cronk Ny Arree Laa, with eight crew on board. The mountain rescue team found six crew dead, including the pilot, Mjr H M Scull, with two others seriously injured. The twin-engined bomber was destined for the 449th BS of the 322nd BG, based at Andrewsfield in Essex.

The large Watchfield detachment returned to Jurby on 11th July on a high, feeling that they had contributed to Operation Overlord. The flying hours rose to an average monthly total of 3,000 and the accidents were down. An increasing number of Wellingtons from bomber OTUs were using Jurby as part of their cross-country exercises. One particular aircraft, Wellington III Z1667, from 27 OTU at Lichfield in Staffordshire, experienced engine problems over the Irish Sea on 5th August 1944. While cruising at 4,000 ft, the port engine failed and the pilot, Flt Sgt J G Fleming RAAF, ordered four of his crew to bail out. Fleming brought Z1667 into Jurby for a successful wheels-up landing without injury to himself but the bomber would never fly again. Meanwhile, three of his crew had landed safely on dry land but a fourth came down in the sea, approximately 600 yards off shore. Without hesitation, Cpl H Davies from the Armament Section, seeing the airman in difficulties, swam the distance with ease and rescued him.

After a succession of overshoot accidents at Jurby, a decision was made on 7th September 1944 to extend the main runway. It was hoped to have the work completed by the end of November and in time for the new aircraft destined to arrive for the AN&BS. The first Wellington X for the AN&BS arrived slightly earlier than expected, on 15th October. Air Transport Auxiliary pilots ferried in the bombers and eventually nine would be on strength with the school. A Wellington Conversion Flight (WCF) was formed within the AN&BS to convert pilots from the Anson to the twin-engined bomber. Five Wellington IIIs were ferried in from 20 OTU at Lossiemouth in Morayshire on 19th October, giving the flight sufficient aircraft to begin training. By the end of November, the WCF was averaging nearly 300 hours flying time per month. As part of the additional work being carried out an extra dispersal was constructed for the WCF. Over 250 tons of hard core and 70 tons of cinders were laid as part of the construction.

Considering the war in Europe was drawing to a close, the training programme continued at a good pace with 3,146 hours of flying time logged by the AN&BS in March 1945. A thanksgiving service was held in the station theatre on 13th May to commemorate hostilities ending. The service was conducted by Revd Attwater and Revd Gamble and was attended by 740 personnel. The same day, 43 airmen, including ten pipers and drummers, joined in the VE celebrations in Douglas.

In the early hours of 20th May 1945, Short Sunderland III NJ186 of 423 Squadron took off from Castle Archdale in Northern Ireland for a patrol over the Irish Sea. A combination of poor weather and bad navigation found the large flying boat heading straight for the Mourne Mountains. At approximately 08:00hrs, the Sunderland clipped the top of one of the mountains, seriously damaging the hull, wing tip and aileron and ripping off the starboard float. The pilot, Flt Lt Allen, deciding that the crew would have more chance of survival landing on 'terra firma' rather than the sea, called his home base, requesting directions to a diversion airfield. Other complications caused by the collision with the ground meant that the bomb doors were jammed and

The unexpected arrival of a Sunderland on 20th May 1945 caused considerable damage to the airfield, including this F Type hangar. The blast from the aircraft's depth charges seriously damaged several hangars, while the Wellingtons of AN&BS in the foreground appear unscathed. (PRO Air 29/545)

the fuel jettison pipe was ruptured, making it impossible to jettison either. Allen brought the crippled flying boat into Jurby for a faultless force-landing with only two of the eleven crew injured. The crew ran as fast as they could from the wreck, which had eight live depth charges still on board and a considerable amount of fuel. The Sunderland was now on fire, with Jurby's fire crews desperately trying to control the blaze. Moments after the firemen withdrew from the Sunderland, the depth charges exploded causing more damage to the airfield than the Luftwaffe ever achieved. The damage to the control tower, hangars and buildings throughout the airfield was extensive and it took over two months to repair the damage caused; the station commander was quoted as 'not being amused by the incident'.

The AN&BS was redesignated again on 31st May 1945, becoming No 5 Air Navigation School (ANS). The WCF was also disbanded, as sufficient aircrew had by now been converted to the Wellington, but the main aircraft type on strength was the Avro Anson. The Empire training schools had now been disbanded and the need for basic

Jurby's control tower took the full force of the blast from the Sunderland. (PRO Air 29/545)

observer training had returned to the United Kingdom; 5 ANS was one of these schools.

Royalty passed through Jurby again, with the arrival of the King and Queen in a Douglas Dakota on 5th July 1945. The following day the royal couple left Jurby but not before a parade of 500 personnel from the station and Andreas was organised. An additional RAF guard of honour of 100 personnel, under the command of Flt Lt B Paterson, and a WAAF guard of honour of 30 personnel, under the command of Plt Off. J M Spencer, was inspected by the King and Queen. After the parade the station commander called for three cheers and their Majesties left in the Dakota piloted by Sqn Ldr Millington.

The last occasion that Jurby was used as a diversion airfield was on 4th September 1945. Halifax III NA279 of the EANS was on a flight from Iceland to Shawbury in Shropshire. It was delivering mail when one of the bomber's four engines failed. At 20:30hrs the bomber came into land but on touchdown the bomber swung, overshot the runway, careered through several hedges and ended up in a field with a broken back. The crew were uninjured but suffering from shock and all the mail on board was undamaged.

119

In celebration of Battle of Britain day an air show was arranged at Jurby. On 14th September several aircraft arrived, including a Mosquito, an Oxford, a Harvard, a Typhoon, a Lancaster and a Barracuda. On 15th September, a successful air show was held, with several aircraft flying, supported by many ground displays.

With so many internees being held on the Isle of Man, Jurby received several unusual visitors before the year was out. On 16th October, a French delegation arrived in a Siebel, a small twin-engined communications aircraft, from Croydon to carry out several interviews with internees on the island. This was followed by several flights out of the airfield with witnesses for the many war crimes trials that took place in late 1945 and early 1946.

The Fleet Air Arm (FAA) made a brief appearance at Jurby from 15th August 1946. A detachment of 772 Squadron from Anthorn equipped with the PR.XVI, B.25 and PR.34 flew from the airfield until returning to their Cumbrian home on 21st December 1946. 5 ANS departed from Jurby to Topcliffe in North Yorkshire on 17th September, to be replaced by 11 Air Gunners' School (AGS) two days later. 11 AGS, equipped with the Wellington, Martinet and Spitfire VII, moved in from Andreas after that airfield was closed down. 11 AGS became the last military flying unit to be in residence at Jurby when it was disbanded on 15th October 1947.

Now under care and maintenance, the airfield was re-opened on 17th April 1950 with the arrival of No 1 Initial Training School (ITS). The ITS was re-formed at Wittering in Northamptonshire to provide basic ground training to aircrew recruits. Split into two wings, No1 at Wittering and No2 at Digby in Lincolnshire, both were amalgamated into one on arrival at Jurby. A reshuffle of units meant that 1 ITS lost its title and was officially disbanded on 10th September 1953. The same day, the Officer Cadet Training Unit at Millom was disbanded and its commitment was transferred to Jurby. The New RAF OCTU was formed at Jurby until it was moved to Feltwell in Norfolk on 1st September 1963.

Early the following year, the Isle of Man Government purchased Jurby from the Air Ministry for a mere £133,000. For the next ten years Jurby acted as a diversion airfield if Ronaldsway became fog bound, which it often did.

Today the airfield is virtually intact, although now the runways are mainly used as a motorbike circuit. The control tower, hangars and innumerable buildings still stand, many being made use of by light industry and a hotel.

12
KINGSTOWN
(Carlisle)

The early 1930s was a vibrant period for civilian aviation and virtually every major town and city throughout the country was looking at the advantages of having an airport to its name. Carlisle was quick to act, becoming one of the first cities to have access to a municipal airport. The site was at Kingstown, easily accessed on the northern edge of the city.

Opened in late 1931, the small grass airfield, with just a few wooden huts and a single hangar, had to wait until 23rd March 1933 for the first commercial aircraft to land. Another twelve months passed before regular scheduled services began, the bulk of which were to and from Hall Caine and Ronaldsway, both on the Isle of Man.

Locals had the chance to learn to fly for a relatively modest fee when the Border Flying Club was formed at Kingstown in June 1935. The club's aircraft were mainly the ubiquitous de Havilland Moth and Tiger Moth, which together dominated the civilian aviation market in the 1930s. On 1st July, the first military unit was formed on the airfield. No 38 Elementary and Reserve Flying Training School (ERFTS) was one of over 50 civilian-run flying schools formed since 1935 to train potential pilots for the expanding RAF. 38 ERTFS was operated by the Border Flying Club and flew the Tiger Moth, Hawker Audax and Hawker Hind. The airfield's facilities were expanded in response to the new arrival with hangars and technical buildings, some accommodation and a concrete hard-standing. The total useable area of the airfield was still only 90 acres.

Six Hawker Henley target tugs from No1 Anti-Aircraft Cooperation Unit (AACU) from Farnborough in Hampshire arrived in the summer

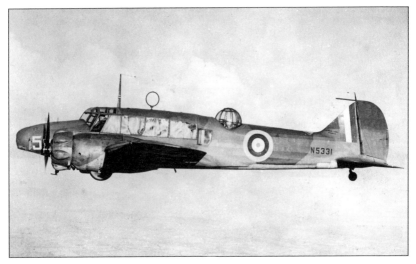

Among the first military aircraft to arrive at Kingstown were the Ansons of 3 Air Observer & Navigator School in November 1939.

of 1939. Two flights took part in local army exercises in July and August, providing valuable target practice for anti-aircraft crews against towed targets.

With the outbreak of the Second World War on 3rd September 1939, all civilian operated flying schools were immediately closed, including 38 ERFTS. The airfield fell silent, with only the movement of civilian aircraft which had been pressed into RAF service. Activity returned on 24th November 1939 with the arrival of twelve Avro Ansons of No3 Air Observer and Navigator School (AONS) from Desford in Leicestershire. Only one aircraft from 3 AONS was involved in an incident while at Kingstown. Anson I N4940 had an engine cut on approach on 7th May 1940, resulting in the aircraft landing short and crashing through a hedge.

A reshuffle of units meant that 3 AONS was moved to Weston-Super-Mare in Somerset on 3rd June 1940. Space was need at Kingstown for another training unit.

The south-east of England in May 1940 was not an ideal location for an Elementary Flying Training School (EFTS) to operate. 15 EFTS, based at Redhill in Surrey, with virtually no notice was ordered to move to the relatively safe skies of north Cumbria. The Chief Instructor, Wg Cdr F S Homersham, the officer commanding 15 EFTS, was summoned without any warning to HQ Flying Training Command and was instructed to move, complete with all civilian staff, to Kingstown and told that a fighter command unit would take over Redhill on 3rd June.

In a somewhat dazed condition, the course of 40 pupils was sent by train, under three officers and two ground instructors, to reach Kingstown on 2nd June with instructions to start work on lectures on Monday morning at Kingstown, which they duly did without losing any training time whatsoever. On Sunday, 24 hours early, the Westland Lysanders of the incoming 16 Squadron began to arrive at Redhill. Fortunately, Monday was a fine day and the fleet of 40 Magisters for elementary training, with the exception of one under repair, flew up with the remaining instructors and the senior course of pupils, who had had only just over four weeks' training.

Affectionately known as the 'Maggie' to both air and ground crew, the Miles Magister was responsible for training thousands of RAF pilots to fly. It was the first monoplane training aircraft to enter service with the RAF on its arrival at the Central Flying School in September 1937. The Magister was fully aerobatic, with a top speed of 142 mph, but had a safe landing speed of only 42 mph, which made it an excellent introduction to flying training. By 1941, 1,230 had been built, the majority serving with EFTSs.

The trip to Kingstown was made in three flights, line astern, with a

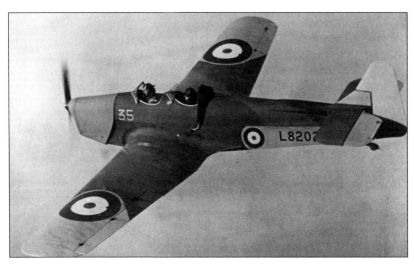

A Miles Magister from 15 EFTS makes a low pass over Kingstown.

stop at Shawbury for lunch and refuelling. In the meantime enough engineers had been sent by train to keep the Magisters serviceable for a time and neither a day's flying nor ground training was lost at any period in spite of the short notice of the move. Almost all of the civilian staff moved up with the school voluntarily, which was fortunate as Carlisle proved to be an area where increased war activity had left no spare labour, skilled or unskilled, unattached to one of the new war developments in the area.

On the unit's arrival at Kingstown, all stores and records had to be moved up from Redhill. New defence schemes and regulations had to be prepared and conditions were made very difficult by the fact that the buildings had been laid out for a different type of flying school and were not adequate or suitably arranged for 15 EFTS. Departing 3 AONS, with half the number of pupils, had already complained that the buildings were inadequate for them. This overcrowding included the fact that the army were sleeping in what should have been the airmen's and pupils' recreation rooms. There was no sergeants' mess and no officers' ante-room amongst other shortages. The cooking apparatus might have been sufficient for approximately 100, had the stove been in a satisfactory condition.

There were no forced-landing or auxiliary landing grounds, though the use of the new aerodrome at Kirkbride was soon obtained for the temporary Polish Flight.

To complicate the matter still further, the English courses were suddenly reduced from eight to seven weeks and the Polish course from three to two weeks with the same amount of flying per course as previously asked for in each case. The instructors flew approx 80 hours per month on average and had less than one day off in seven. The civilian staff worked even harder in dealing with the increase in routine work due to the shorter courses and the enormous amount of extra work caused by the transfer from Redhill. 15 EFTS's old home was commandeered from British Air Transport Ltd. Shortly after reaching Kingstown, the Polish course, which had been slowing down as the supply of Polish airmen in England reduced, suddenly accelerated and the school started courses of 30 pilots each for a fortnight's course instead of the preceding 20 pilots on a three week course. This was due to the influx of Polish airmen from France who were now to follow on through the same 'testing and grading' course at 15 EFTS.

A new Relief Landing Ground (RLG) became available at Burnfoot on 5th July, taking considerable pressure off Kingstown's small landing ground. Because of the clay sub-soil, drainage was a major problem at Kingstown and any alternative airfield was being viewed at the time. A second RLG was made available to 15 EFTS at Kirkpatrick, which improved the situation, especially for the staff constantly repairing the runways at Kingstown.

In July 1940, the first station defence officers arrived and the RAF ground personnel was increased to 120. The lack of buildings and accommodation became worse than ever. Congested accommodation, however, was alleviated by evacuating the small hangar for sleeping accommodation and by the provision of tents. The arrival of the guard was very welcome, as they enabled the pupils to be taken off defence duties at a period when the almost nightly visits of German aircraft had made the calling out of certain pupils necessary every night for defence purposes in view of the possibility of parachute attack. This period of awakening the pupils at night corresponded with a two-week period during which there was an average of an accident per day, making a very black mark on the school's previous, reasonable accident record, there having been only one notifiable accident during June 1940. The first serious flying accident occurred on 2nd July 1940 when the pupil pilot of Miles Magister I R1969 undershot his approach and hit the ground hard enough to virtually wreck the aircraft. A second 'Maggie' was written off on 26th July when L8336 stalled and, on landing, likewise hit the ground hard enough to warrant a 'damaged beyond repair'.

The first three months at Kingstown were spent trying to re-establish the school's original standard of discipline and training under the new and difficult conditions. On 26th August 1940 all pupils were billeted out in the Carlisle area, although not without a considerable amount of friction being caused with the local billeting authorities. This movement of pupils enabled the guard to be moved from the hangar and tents for sleeping purposes but in no way helped the cooking facilities, which were still exactly the same as when the school first arrived. Fortunately, however, the civilian caterers providing the food were able to cook and prepare most of it in Carlisle and bring it out, and the standard of food was described as not bad.

On 26th August, the length of the elementary flying training course was reduced by a further five weeks and at the same time a special request was received to hurry the testing and grading of Polish pilots to maximum capacity

Up until the morning of 26th October 1940, the accident rate of 15 EFTS had been considerably low. Five Magisters, all with frost on their wings, failed to get airborne and crashed at various locations around the airfield boundary. Magister R1850 struck a hangar; R1904 hit a house and two others force landed in neighbouring fields. A fifth aircraft tragically struck a tent containing three members of the ground defence force. AC2 G R Heckler, AC2 L Harrod and AC2 N F Knight were killed instantly in the collision.

By the end of October, the aircraft included 54 Magisters for the English courses, nine Magisters for the Polish courses and 14 Fairey Battles. At this time there were two English courses with 45 pupils on each and a single Polish course with an average of 30 pupils. The station defence force was a healthy 132 personnel, nine of whom were administration staff. Flying times steadily rose, with an average of 2,714 hours between June and October 1940.

All hopes of maintaining the high safety standards that had been set in pre-war days were rapidly disappearing from December 1940 onwards. In the first three months of 1941 alone, the EFTS had lost ten 'Maggies' in a variety of accidents, the majority on or near the airfield. One particular accident, which did not endear the unit to the local population, occurred on 14th April. Cpl Dzierbicki had an engine failure after take off in Magister I R1967. His unavoidable forced-landing resulted in the death of two civilians on Houghton Road, Carlisle.

Every EFTS operating during the Second World War was given a classification according to its size. On arrival at Kingstown, the airfield was given a 'C' classification, which meant that its EFTS had a pupil population of no fewer than 60, two flights of aircraft and at least 36 machines on charge. This rose to a Class 'B' in January 1941, followed by a Class 'A' in May. Class 'A+1' was attained in June, followed by the ultimate, Class 'A+2', in August 1941. This equated to a pupil population of no fewer than 180, and six flights, totalling at least 108 aircraft. 15 EFTS had literally trebled in size, whereas Kingstown had not, making conditions on camp rather restricted at the best of times.

A detachment from 6 Anti-Aircraft Cooperation Unit (AACU), based at Ringway in Cheshire, made Kingstown its home from 1st March 1941 to April 1942. The AACU brought a variety of aircraft to Kingstown, mainly to work with the 213th Light Anti-Aircraft Training Regiment (LAATR). The first aircraft did not officially arrive until 7th June in the shape of de Havilland Leopard Moth AV985. Regular rotations of aircraft and pilots, saw Magisters, Lysanders and Tiger Moths also contribute to the detachment.

The de Havilland Tiger Moth was steadily introduced into the inventory of 15 EFTS from February 1941. Embarrassingly though, the first Tiger Moth to arrive, T7055, with Plt Off. S P Richards at the controls, overturned on landing in snowy conditions after running into one of many soft spots on the airfield.

The Tiger Moth is undoubtedly one of the world's most famous training aircraft and it remained in RAF service for over 15 years. Originally a development of the DH.60 Gipsy Moth, the first Tiger took to the air on 26th October 1931. Designed as a fully aerobatic trainer, the little biplane was an instant success with many civilian owners and operators. The Tiger Moth Mk.Is were powered by a 120 hp Gipsy Major engine but later on the main production version, the Tiger Mk.II had a 130 hp Gipsy Major fitted. The following year, the first of many were ordered by the RAF. Production reached over 1,000 by the outbreak of the Second World War. During the war, the majority of RAF pilots were trained on the Tiger Moth and final British production totalled 4,668 aircraft.

Although the airfield was always small, larger RAF aircraft types would often visit, including Armstrong Whitworth Whitley K8974, which flew into Kingstown on 24th June. The twin-engined bomber stayed slightly longer than planned because, on 25th June, instructor Sgt A G Sadler taxied his Magister into the side of it! The average accident rate was increasing rapidly by August 1941. The unit lost ten more 'Maggies' in a variety of flying accidents: a multiple seagull strike over the Solway Firth, several pupils getting lost and the usual selection of over and undershot landings carried out at Kingstown, Burnfoot and Kirkpatrick RLGs. The month was also blighted by the loss of two Spitfires from 3 FPP based at Hawarden in Flintshire. Plt Off. J Marcinisk, in X4834, and Sgt K Wunschi, both Polish, collided over the airfield on 15th August 1941.

Ground accidents were also commonplace. With so many aircraft on such a small aerodrome it was inevitable that inexperienced airmen would make mistakes. LAC C M Parsons in Magister I N5432 and LAC K Potts in Tiger Moth T6498 taxied straight into each other on 17th September, injuring neither pilot but adding a black mark to their logbooks. Contact with the ground or water was another hazard, which LAC E Sluszkiewicz was lucky to survive on 22nd September. While practising low flying Sluszkiewicz cut it a bit fine when he struck the surface of the Solway Firth, virtually removing the undercarriage but still maintaining control of the aircraft. He returned to Kingstown and performed a safe force-landing, for which he was commended; however, he was also criticised for firstly risking the aircraft and secondly himself!

During November 1941, 15 EFTS had 120 English and 29 Polish pupil pilots who were being instructed by 27 English and two Polish officer flying instructors and a further 23 NCO instructors. The unit was also supported by a further 17 officers and 253 other ranks, all accommodated within the confines of this small airfield. The accommodation situation became even tighter by February 1942 with the arrival of a small detachment from 32 MU at St Athan plus a more substantial influx from 2822 Defence Squadron. The defence squadron relieved all permanent staff from guard duties at Kingstown. The unit consisted of seven officers, including a single army officer, plus 272 airmen, whose presence applied more pressure on the rapidly dwindling accommodation.

A small amount of space was created on 8th May 1942 when the 6 AACU detachment ended. The party, comprising a single aircraft, one officer and ten airmen returned to their parent unit at Ringway.

The Magister's time with 15 EFTS was almost at an end by May 1942. On 31st May the first of many ferrying flights was flown from Kingstown, via Clyffe Pyard in Wiltshire, Peterborough in Northamptonshire and back to Kingstown. Magisters were flown out of the airfield and Tiger Moths were returned in their place. The last Magisters were still operating out of Kingstown throughout June 1942. Magister I R1851 was the unit's last casualty, on 11th June. Plt Off. Bramley and LAC C S M Webb were flying a searchlight exercise, when control was lost and they crashed into the ground near Gaitsgill, south of Carlisle, sadly killing both crew.

An example of the dispensability of trainee aircrew and, to a lesser extent, the instructors was reflected in a comment after Tiger Moth II T6559 crashed on 8th October 1942. The instructor, Plt Off. C Berry, and pupil, LAC S J Ribbands, were performing aerobatics when a wing collapsed, killing them both instantly. Their loss was unfortunately recorded in the following way, 'Both instructor and pupil were killed and struck off the strength of the RAF'.

Harry Wappler, the crewman of a Heinkel He111, and Heinz Schnabel, who were among over 80 pilots shot down in September 1940, were both being held in Camp 13 at Shap Fells Hotel in Penrith (locally known as the 'U-Boat Hotel' because of the number of German naval officers held). On 13th November 1942 they managed to escape from the camp by hiding in laundry baskets and then successfully stowed away on a train heading for Carlisle. Posing as Dutch airmen, without difficulty they gained access to Kingstown airfield and with even less trouble persuaded a pair of civilian groundcrew to start a Magister for them.

The intrepid duo flew south with the intention of refuelling at an airfield in East Anglia and continuing to the Continent. It is rumoured that Wappler and Schnabel landed at Hucknall in Nottinghamshire, but, wherever it was, they managed to persuade another unsuspecting group of groundcrew to refuel them and send them on their way. On the next leg, bad weather closed in and the German airmen became lost. Low on fuel, they landed in a meadow five miles north of Norwich. Despite their escape being successfully concealed at Camp 13, news of the missing 15 EFTS Magister was sent around the country and all airfields in Norfolk were on the lookout. Still claiming to be Dutch airmen, Wappler and Schnabel were apprehended by personnel from Horsham St Faith, near Norwich, and eventually returned to a POW camp. The RAF officer fraternity, who were all encouraged to escape if caught by the enemy, thought the German pair had put on a 'jolly good show'. However this did little to detract from the embarrassment caused to the CO of 15 EFTS and the staff involved in 'handing over' the aircraft.

By early 1943, an internal reorganisation of the way the EFTS trained its pupils was implemented. The unit had originally offered a full 'ab initio' training programme, which effectively taught the student the very basics of flying an aircraft. This method was scrapped in favour of a grading system where the pupil pilot was given a mere eight hours of flying instruction. If the pupil went solo within that time or showed a promising ability to do so he would be sent to an overseas training school to continue the course. From 8th January the unit also began to receive pre-Advance Flying Unit (AFU) pupils on attachment.

Kingstown provided a safe haven for another 55 OTU Hurricane, which was in trouble on 1st February. Plt Off. J L Flinterman, a Dutchman, suffered an engine failure in Hurricane X AG174. Flinterman managed to successfully belly-land the crippled fighter without injuring himself or significantly damaging the aircraft. AG174 spent its entire flying career with 55 OTU before finally being retired in May 1944. Only three days later, another Hurricane from 55 OTU unexpectedly arrived. Sgt Balhatchet in Hurricane I Z4575 also suffered an engine failure, forcing him to make a hurried emergency landing at Kingstown. The Hurricane overshot the airfield but suffered little damage in the process. Z4575 had a busy career, firstly with

1423 Flt and 182 Squadron, before being dispatched out to the Far East; it survived until December 1944.

While the EFTS continued to lose Tiger Moths on an almost daily basis, the job of the 'prop-swinger' could be as dangerous as the flying. The Tiger Moth was usually started with the pilot in the cockpit, a second person swinging the propeller to start the engine. With so many aircraft on the EFTS, the 'prop-swinger' was a full-time job and sadly several accidents occurred at Kingstown. At the beginning of March 1943, civilian James Nugent was seriously injured but a more serious incident happened on 13th April. A pupil in Tiger Moth DE378 was preparing for a night exercise when he gave the engine too much throttle. The aircraft jumped over its chocks, severing the arm of Mr Jenkins, the prop-swinger. Sadly Mr Jenkins died in hospital the next day.

The biggest aircraft to arrive at Kingstown landed on 18th May 1943. An Avro Lancaster III from 467 Squadron, based at Bottesford in Leicestershire, had no difficulty landing at the small grass airfield. The all-Australian crew brought the bomber to show pupil pilots, many of whom would go on to fly the Lancaster operationally.

In keeping with the theme of heavy bomber operations, during the summer of 1943 several instructors from 15 EFTS were attached to operational units for experience. 78 Squadron at Breighton in North Yorkshire was the main host. The squadron was flying the Handley Page Halifax II at the time on almost daily raids over Germany. These attachments continued into early 1944, with 76 Squadron at Linton-on-Ouse also receiving instructors from Kingstown for operational experience. 76 Squadron also flew the Halifax II and, like 78 Squadron, suffered high losses at the hands of enemy night fighters and flak. Luckily no instructors from Kingstown were lost on operations. 53 Squadron at St Eval in Cornwall also received several instructors from the unit for experience. This Coastal Command squadron operated the Consolidated Liberator VA successfully in the anti-submarine role. Operational experience attachments continued until at least June 1944, bringing valuable teaching information back to Kingstown.

The Tiger Moths of 15 EFTS provided the aerial element to exercise 'Hare' on 26th March 1944. The exercise lasted from 05:00hrs to 13:30hrs and also involved the Royal Army Signals Corps Unit and the 1st Battalion of the Cumberland HQ. The outcome of the exercise is unknown but it would have provided valuable experience for the pupils of 15 EFTS cooperating with a ground unit.

With the Allied invasion of Europe on 6th June 1944, the need for pilots was greater than ever. The war was still far from being won and at any one time at least 80 Tiger Moths could be seen on the airfield during the summer of 1944. The hard work that the EFTS had been putting in was recognised by a senior visitor on 7th September 1944. The Air Officer Commanding (AOC) Flying Training Command, Sir Philip Babbington KSC, MC, AFC, and the AOC of 51 Group Flying Training Command, Air Comm D. Iron CBE, inspected the unit and airfield and both were more than happy with the work being carried out by 15 EFTS.

At the beginning of 1945, the strength of the unit had peaked, with 108 aircraft being flown by over 70 flying instructors. With the war in Europe at an end, the throughput of pupil pilots began to decline and so did the size of the EFTS, while still maintaining a high standard of training. By 15th August 1945, the unit had been reduced to 45 aircraft.

Accidents were still happening, although they involved mainly visiting aircraft. An unusual visitor for Kingstown was a North American Mustang from Digby in Lincolnshire. The American-built fighter made an emergency landing with engine trouble on 26th May 1945 but crashed on landing. The pilot was unhurt.

Kingstown Station Sick Quarters (SSQ) became responsible for personnel from Great Orton from 28th May. Great Orton was now occupied by 247 Maintenance Unit (MU), the airfield's sick quarters having been closed down when the airfield was placed under care and maintenance back in June 1945. Kingstown was visited several times by Wg Cdr Bruce the Senior Medical Officer of 42 Group Maintenance Command while medical care was being provided for 247 MU. Kingstown SSQ also became responsible for the recovery of all medical stores from the RAF unit at Greymoor Hill and both RLGs at Burnfoot and Kirkpatrick, which had now closed to flying.

A new unit was officially opened at Kingstown in July 1945 by Air Marshal Sir E L Gossage KCB, CVO, DSO, MC. No 189 Gliding School (GS), which was formed the previous month, operated Slingsby Cadet I and II gliders until its disbandment in October 1947. The school provided glider training for RAF personnel and local ATC squadrons. It also received an attachment of two officers and 23 NCOs from the Glider Pilot Regiment on 12th January 1946.

An Avro Anson from 11 Air Gunners School (AGS) at Andreas made a spectacular arrival in foggy weather on 28th December 1945. Anson I DJ441 with Plt Off. Onions at the controls and four passengers on board overshot the landing and ploughed through a barbed wire

No189 Gliding School was formed at Kingstown in the summer of 1945. The unit's main aircraft was the Slingsby Cadet.

fence into a surrounding field. The Anson, which had served with four previous training units, was a total wreck but all on board escaped without injury.

The neighbouring unit of 14 MU moved all of its medical staff and stores into the Kingstown SSQ during April 1946, pending the closure of its own SSQ. This was the first indication that eventually 14 MU would take over the airfield at Kingstown in its entirety.

By June 1946, the strength of 15 EFTS was reduced still further, with only 45 flying instructors teaching a group of 35 pupil pilots. Despite this, an official 15 EFTS badge was approved by His Majesty The King and registered with the Inspector of RAF Badges on 16th August. A parade was held a few weeks later for its presentation to the unit.

After almost seven years as officer commanding and the unit's chief flying instructor, Wg Cdr C M Homersham AFC, MM was posted on 1st April 1947. Wg Cdr T M Scott AFC, who was seconded from the RAF for duty with British Air Transport Ltd, replaced him. 15 EFTS underwent an administrative change on 21st April when all personnel were posted from the control of 50 Group to 23 Group at Oxenden House in Leighton Buzzard in Bedfordshire. 50 Group, which had

Despite having been established since 1939, it was not until August 1946 that 15 EFTS received an official badge.

controlled all of the RAF EFTSs since February 1939, was disbanded a few weeks later

By October the unit had a mere 30 aircraft on strength and the last full flying course to pass through Kingstown began on 13th October 1947, with four Burmese and two Iraqi officers and two Belgian NCOs attending. A refresher course commenced on 12th November, with eight RAF officers attending, but this was completed at Kirton-in-Lindsey in Lincolnshire.

The remarkable history of 15 EFTS came to an end on 31st December 1947 when the unit was disbanded. Since its formation at Redhill, the unit had flown a total of over 270,000 flying hours and trained more than 12,000 pupil pilots, but not without cost. The EFTS lost 84 'Maggies' and 31 Tiger Moths in a variety of flying accidents at Kingstown and the supporting RLGs. This still equates to an excellent safety record of one accident for every 235 flying hours. The unit was re-formed a few months later, at its original home at Redhill, as 15 Reserve Flying School (RFS), still flying the Tiger Moth. Converting to the de Havilland Chipmunk in 1952, the RFS was finally disbanded on 20th June 1954.

Kingstown came under the complete control of 14 MU Carlisle on 20th April 1948, transferring from 23 Group to 40 Group Maintenance Command, whose HQ was at Bicester in Oxfordshire. 14 MU made use of the airfield until 24th June, when all key buildings situated on the airfield were handed over to Carlisle Corporation.

A limited amount of civilian aviation returned to the airfield during the post-war years. Manx Airlines, flying the de Havilland Rapide, flew a limited service to the Isle of Man until the airfield's closure in 1957. Airlines were expanding, aircraft were getting bigger and

Kingstown was simply not big enough to cope. It was impossible to extend the airfield because of the vast 14 MU site to the north and a railway line running down the western side.

Sadly, today nothing remains of this once active training airfield. It has been swallowed up by the demand for industrial estates, and it's a shame that the local council has not named a road or two Magister Close or Tiger Moth Drive in its memory.

13
KIRKBRIDE

It had been envisaged in senior circles many months before the beginning of the Second World War that areas would be needed for the storage of large quantities of aircraft. Two locations for new airfields were simultaneously surveyed in early 1938, one at Silloth and the other at Kirkbride, only seven miles separating the two locations. Thousands of aircraft would pass through Kirkbride and many more would end their flying careers at this remote airfield during the post-war years.

Work began in June 1938 on the airfield with the intention of it being open on 1st May 1939. The site extended south-west from the road junction at Powhill, less than half a mile south of Kirkbride village. A minor road bordered the airfield on the northern and western sides and this was unofficially incorporated into the airfield design without actually closing it to the public.

With considerable work still to do, Sqn Ldr A Connock was posted in to command the airfield in April 1939. Not a single building on the airfield was close to completion when the opening date arrived and it was postponed to 5th June. With much of the airfield still looking like a building site, the airfield was officially opened and 12 Maintenance Unit (MU), under 41 (Maintenance) Group's command, was formed as a civilian-manned Aircraft Storage Unit (ASU). A small group of RAF personnel under Sqn Ldr Connock's command formed the nucleus of the unit, which would eventually be manned by mainly civilian staff. Sqn Ldr Connock was also in command of 22 MU at Silloth and initially 12 MU was administered by its neighbour.

By 31st July, the first of six E Type hangars was completed and occupied, and Military Transport (MT) vehicles and ground equipment began to arrive. More buildings were being completed as the war drew closer, with particular emphasis on hangars. Kirkbride was very well equipped in this department, eventually a whole array

Four Avro Tutors were the first aircraft to arrive at Kirkbride, only two days after war was declared. Part dismantled, the 1930s trainers arrived by road from 24 MU at Ternhill.

of hangars would complement the E Types, including four D Types, one C Type, four L Types and 23 Robin Blister hangars.

The day after Great Britain and France declared war on Germany, a large recruitment drive of local civilian personnel was instigated to bring the strength of 12 MU to war establishment. A sense of urgency now hung over the contractors still working on the airfield; however, the landing ground was still in no fit state to receive aircraft. Four Avro Tutors did arrive on 5th September from 24 MU at Ternhill in Shropshire, minus wings, although it was a rather subdued affair which was carried out by rail and then road to Kirkbride. Two Hawker Harts followed on 9th September, also from 24 MU, and ten days later the landing ground was finally cleared for 'restricted use', although it was still only 60 per cent complete. Miles Magister N3927 became the first aircraft to land at Kirkbride on 21st September 1939. Delivered from 5 MU at Kemble in Gloucestershire, the Magister was allocated as the station's communication aircraft, a role it performed until replaced by a Tiger Moth in 1942.

With his work done at Kirkbride, Sqn Ldr Connock relinquished command of 12 MU to Sqn Ldr R N Riddell. Connock left on 20th September for a familiar posting at 22 MU at Silloth.

October began with two Fairey Seafoxes arriving by road from

36 MU at Sealand in Cheshire. On 10th October, Hawker Audax K7429 was received from 10 MU at Hullavington in Wiltshire. The Audax was delivered for use on an air mail service between various airfields in the north-west. The same day though, Sqn Ldr Riddell flew the inaugural air mail flight in Magister N3927; the Audax would continue the service in company with a second Audax which was delivered a few days later.

Aircraft were now being received, brand new, direct from the manufacturers. The first of these, a pair of Fairey Battles, arrived by air from the makers at Stockport in Lancashire on 19th October. They were followed on 27th October by the first of many Avro Ansons from A V Roe Ltd in Manchester.

Whilst all efforts on the ground were going into making Kirkbride a usable ASU, airfield defence had been totally overlooked until a signal was received from HQ 41 Group, based in Caldicott House in Abingdon, Oxfordshire, on 2nd November. The signal warned of the possibility of attacks by parachute troops or aircraft landing troops. 12 MU responded by withdrawing two Lewis machine guns from stores, complete with 12 magazines of ammunition. Two machine gun posts were erected on the edge of the main technical area, giving the defender a good field of fire across the landing ground area. A few days later, several temporary rifle posts were considered around the

A Hawker Audax was employed by 12 MU for a local air mail service between airfields located in the north-west of England.

137

edge of the airfield pending the arrival of a Light Anti-Aircraft Detachment.

Attrocious weather throughout December 1939 brought work on the station to a virtual halt and continous rain turned the still incomplete grass runway into an unusable quagmire. Despite the conditions, ten aircraft still managed to arrive by air, with some oddments by rail and road as well. Official figures stated that the landing ground was 48 per cent complete – half of the hangars were built, no brick buildings had been started as yet and a mere 10 per cent of the many roads and aprons needed had been completed.

To handle the anticipated large quantities of aircraft, Kirkbride would need concrete runways; so, in January 1940, Sir Robert MacApline Ltd swiftly began the necessary work. Three runways were laid in traditional triangular pattern, a design which meant that at least one runway would always be pointing into the wind. The runways were 1,400, 1,250 and 1,000 yards respectively, all interlinked by a concrete and tarmac perimeter track.

Additional security precautions were put into place on the 7th February for a different kind of enemy. The Irish Republican Army (IRA) were unaffected by world events and were still prepared to attack British forces at home or on the mainland. In response to this, more RAF personnel were posted in for airfield defence and security.

Kirkbride's runways were now sufficiently serviceable to be of use to 15 EFTS, which had arrived at Kingstown, near Carlisle. The school's 'Temporary Polish Flight' also known as the Polish Grading and Testing Flight, flying Fairey Battles and Miles Magisters made use of the airfield from 19th June 1940 until such time as Kingstown's own Relief Landing Grounds were completed. However, the Polish flight was absorbed into 1 (Polish) Service Flying Training School on 30th November 1940, moving to Hucknall in Nottinghamshire.

Delays in the completion of its own airfield at Chivenor resulted in the airfield being used by Wellingtons and Whitleys of 3 (Coastal) OTU as well. The unit moved to Kinloss earlier in the year and then operated from Silloth and Kirkbride until it moved to Cranwell on 29th July 1941.

Delivery of a large variety of aircraft was gaining pace during June 1940. The landing ground was almost complete, the hangars were now all available and additional areas of land available for dispersal were being inspected. Aircraft that passed through the unit during the month included the Avro Anson, Fairey Battle TT, Blackburn Botha, Handley Page Hampden, Supermarine Spitfire,

All four D Type hangars not only survive on the airfield but are still in daily use by local companies. (Author)

Lockheed Hudson, Gloster Gauntlet, de Havilland Queen Bee, Blackburn Roc and Fairey Swordfish.

A misjudged approach by a Bristol Beaufort on 13th July resulted in the aircraft crash-landing short of the runway. L4473 from 1 (Coastal) OTU, based at neighbouring Silloth was a total write-off, but the crew walked away unharmed.

18 MU, stationed at Dumfries, was the next unit to express an interest in Kirkbride. Sqn Ldr Crowther from 18 MU visited on 18th July with a request to use the airfield during daylight hours, as Dumfries was unserviceable. The first aircraft, Bristol Beaufort I N1088, took off from Dumfries on 25th July with Plt Off. R A D Smith RAFVR at the controls for the short hop over the Solway Firth to Kirkbride. Sadly, Smith never made it, his Beaufort force-landed two miles from Dumfries with fatal consequences.

Wg Cdr Shaw from HQ 41 Group arrived on the first of two visits to Kirkbride on 2nd August 1940. His objective was to inspect the surrounding fields for possible new and more scattered dispersal areas than were presently being used. He returned again on 28th August and by the end of his second visit had selected 20 different sites for consideration. Work began almost immediately on new, dispersed areas to the north and west of the airfield. The new northern site

Although obsolete in appearance the Fairey Swordfish, affectionately known as the 'Stringbag', was a very effective aircraft. 12 MU handled several of these torpedo bombers during the early years of the war.

extended almost to the edge of Kirkbride village and, if it had not been for a railway line, without doubt would have been extended still further.

The accommodation at Kirkbride was not of a particularly high standard and was rather limited. No officers' or sergeants' mess was built, purely because it was presumed that the unit would be manned by civilians. Billets for 236 airmen were constructed on site but as the year crept on and winter approached the unit's administration officer started to travel the area looking for suitable accommodation. He inspected parish halls at Oulton, Aikton and Bowness on Solway as possible billets during the winter months. Whether or not these were found to be suitable is unknown, but on 27th September 54 airmen from Kirkbride were billeted in Wigton and continued to use accommodation in the small town throughout the winter and for the duration of the war.

Sixty miles north-west of Kirkbride a new unit was being formed at Prestwick in Ayrshire during September. No 4 Ferry Pilots' Pool (FPP), Air Transport Auxiliary (ATA) was one of 16 pools being created up and down the country. Each main FPP had a sub-pool located within reasonable flying range. 4 FPP's sub-pool was located at Kirkbride and generally operated the Avro Anson I, Fairchild Argus I & II as well as the occasional visit by a de Havilland Puss Moth.

The first Vickers Wellington arrived on station on 29th September. The biggest aircraft to arrived at Kirkbride so far did nothing to ease the pressure on the dispersal areas. Ansons, Bothas, Battles and Hudsons continued to arrive at a steady pace and both Spitfire Is and IIs kept the civilian workforce busy.

12 MU gained a new commanding officer with the arrival of Wg Cdr J W Mitchell, who took over from Wg Cdr Riddell on 3rd November. Although a healthy number of aircraft were passing through Kirkbride, Mitchell took over an airfield that still resembled a building site. The new dispersal areas were far from complete and the runways were still being finished off, although a few days later, a manager from Sir Robert McAlpine announced that their work was finally complete.

With all three runways fully serviceable, No1 (Coastal) OTU from Silloth wasted no time in making Kirkbride a Relief Landing Ground. From November 1940 through to July 1941, the unit's Hudsons, Beauforts and Whitleys used the airfield for circuits both day and night.

Mother Nature played an unexpected part in creating more space at Kirkbride, when on 21st November a 100 mph gale blew through the area in the early hours of the morning. Five aircraft were seriously damaged; three of them were Bothas, which were damaged way beyond repair. Five days later, Flg Off. Greenhow, a salvage officer from 83 MU at Woolsington, collected the remains for scrapping.

12 MU were beginning to become desperate for additional dispersal space. Work had already begun on two new Satellite Landing Grounds at Wath Head and Brayton Park, but neither would be available until early 1941. The CO looked elsewhere for a short term resolution to the problem and on 2nd December 1940, Wg Cdr Mitchell held a meeting with the commanding officers of 14 MU and 15 EFTS, located side by side on the north-west edge of Carlisle. Plans were put into place for the movement of aircraft, but by the time the event was organised both SLGs became available for use.

December 1940 was a month filled with inspections and visits as Kirkbride started to look more purposeful and organised. These included the Inspector General of the RAF, Air Marshal William Mitchell KCB, CBE, DSO, MC, AFC, who inspected the unit on 8th December, followed by the Marshal of the RAF, Sir Edward L Ellington GCB, CMG, CBE, who visited on 27th December on liaison duties, both were satisfied with what they found at Kirkbride.

Considering the number of aircraft coming and going from the airfield, the accident rate up until now had been exceptionally low. This record was tarnished on 25th January 1941 when, at 15:00hrs, a pair of Wellingtons departed from Kirkbride for 20 OTU, based at Lossiemouth. All seemed well until about an hour into the flight when the weather deteriorated and the two aircraft lost contact with each other. Wellington Ic R1164, being flown by Flg Off. J F M Millar, the sole occupant, was killed when the bomber smashed into Box Law, approximately 3 miles east-north-east of Largs in Ayrshire. One of the recommendations from the obligatory court of enquiry that followed was that, in future, all delivery flights would be carried out with a wireless operator on board.

The first of three visits by representatives of locally based fighter OTUs arrived on 31st January 1941. The first was by Air Commodore Vincent DFC of HQ 81 Group and Wg Cdr I R A Jones, OC 59 OTU. 59 OTU had been formed only the previous month and was still assembling at Turnhouse, pending the opening of its new home at Crosby-on-Eden. The reason for their visit to Kirkbride was to ask permission to use the airfield to land their Hurricanes, effectively using it as a satellite airfield. This was denied and the more conveniently located Longtown was used for this purpose instead.

A similar request and visit came on 19th March 1941 when Gp Capt. Price and Sqn Ldr Gough of 55 OTU, accompanied by Sqn Ldr Augois, arrived from Usworth. A flight of Hurricanes had been at Usworth only since 12th February, with the main unit arriving on 14th March. Kirkbride was viewed as a potential alternative home for all of the unit's 68 Hurricanes, 21 Masters and various support aircraft! The move never happened. 55 OTU remained at Usworth until April 1942, when they moved to Annan.

Pressure on Kirkbride's own dispersal areas was finally relieved in April when No10 SLG opened at Wath Head. Hampdens and Bothas were the first aircraft to make the short flight to the SLG. It would be many more months before the unit's second SLG, at Brayton Park, became available.

A third and final visit to investigate the suitability of the airfield to accommodate a fighter OTU was carried out by Gp Capt. C L Lea-Cox and Wg Cdr R M Gough on 16th May. Once again, either the airfield was deemed unsuitable or a better alternative was found.

At the beginning of July 1941, 4 FPP sub-pool began expanding in preparation for becoming 16 FPP, an autonomous unit still based at Kirkbride. Very little changed, although new accommodation and support buildings were constructed for the pool's use. This work was inspected by Gp Capt. Hanson-Abbott and Wg Cdr Riddell, both from HQ 50 Wing as well as Capt. White ATA, OC HQ Service Ferry Squadron, based at Dumfries, on 12th July. More ATA officers visited over the following days, culminating on 23rd July with the arrival of Gp Capt. Daly and Commander d'Elanger, the ATA's most senior officer. 16 FPP was officially formed on 28th July. Its main task was the ferrying of 12 MU aircraft direct from Kirkbride and the supporting SLGs, a task it carried out with great efficiency beyond the war's end.

12 MU took its first four-engined aircraft on charge during July with the arrival of the first of many Handley Page Halifaxes. The Halifax was by far the largest aircraft to arrive at Kirkbride to date. The first aircraft was flown in by one of the resident test pilots, who landed with ease on the airfield's main runway with plenty of room to spare.

Considering the number of aircraft movements by 12 MU in and out of Kirkbride, virtually no accidents or incidents worthy of note were recorded up until October 1941. The statistics were tarnished on 20th October when Hampden I P2127 crashed on approach to the airfield at Little Brampton. The pilot, Sgt A Raw, had taken the twin-engine bomber for an air test with A Robson, a civilian fitter on board. The Hampden caught fire after crash-landing and sadly, both Raw and Robson were beyond help before the emergency services arrived.

In early November 1941, the first American-built aircraft arrived at Kirkbride. The Bell P-39 Airacobra was a unique design when it first flew in 1939. It was one of the first fighters to have a tricycle undercarriage and its Allison engine was mounted centrally in the fuselage behind the pilot's seat. The aircraft the RAF received were originally intended for the French Air Force and in total an order for 675 aircraft was placed with the Bell Aircraft Corporation, whose home was in Buffalo, New York. Only 50 aircraft were actually received. Known in RAF service as the Airacobra I, it served only with 601 Squadron and it was quickly realised that its perfomance was totally inadequate for anything other than ground attack operations. The Airacobra was an alien aircraft to the workers of 12 MU and several visits by representatives of the Allison Engineering Company and Bell aircraft were made during the short period when the American fighter was at Kirkbride. Problems were also experienced by the local ferry pilots, culminating in the loss of Airacobra I AH598 on 15th November. Capt. W L Hanley ATA was killed when his aircraft crashed out of control near Fingland, 2 miles east of the airfield.

Sqn Ldr Field-Richards, an RAF test pilot, visited Kirkbride on 21st November to discuss the potential arrival of another large four-

The Bell P-39 Airacobra was the first American-built aircraft type to arrive at Kirkbride.

engined bomber. The Consolidated Liberator was another American design. It shared the same tricycle undercarriage layout of the Airacobra and was the first American heavy bomber to do so. 2,181 aircraft went on to serve with Bomber Transport and particularly successfully with Coastal Command. With the latter, the Liberator was developed into a very efficient submarine hunter. Field-Richards suggested that the airfield's runways be extended to safely accommodate the bomber. The following day, Field-Richards landed a Liberator and after several test take-offs and landings reiterated his comments of the day before. While the Halifax was of similar dimensions, its all-up weight was less than that of the Liberator, which was far too close to its safety margins to clear for operations from Kirkbride. Wg Cdr Riddell and a Section Officer from the Air Ministry Works Department (AMWD) held a conference at Kirkbride on 5th December to discuss the runway extensions and improvements of the perimeter track and hard standings. However, with more important commitments elsewhere, the airfield would have to wait nearly 18 months before any new work was carried out.

The arrival of the Consolidated Liberator warranted extension work to both the runways and the perimeter tracks.

Kirkbride managed to avoid the personal attentions of the Luftwaffe for the entire duration of the war. The nearest it came was when the air raid warning 'Red' was sounded on 29th December 1941, followed by two more, on 10th January and 9th February 1942. A very effective blackout was implemented on all three occasions, resulting in the enemy passing over Kirkbride to concentrate on another target of opportunity.

The wait for the opening of 39 SLG at Brayton was proving to be a painfully slow experience. As a temporary measure, 9 SLG at Hornby Hall was made available from January until May 1942 for the dispersal of Wellingtons. Wg Cdr Mitchell had already inspected the SLG the previous year, with an obvious element of foresight should Brayton still not be ready.

The Newton Arlosh to Powhill road bordered the northern edge of the airfield. A rather relaxed policy of opening and closing the road to allow aircraft to be towed to the northern dispersal site was in place by early 1942. On 17th February a Spitfire, being towed by a 12 MU tractor was crossing the road when it was struck by a Cumberland County Council ambulance. No one was injured but all parties concerned had to attend the local police court in Wigton for an enquiry. It is not known whether the ambulance was on a call or not, but, unfortunately for the driver, he was convicted of careless driving.

Potential sabotage was being taken very seriously in the whole area, with particular focus on aircraft on the more remote dispersal areas and SLGs. On 12 MU's SLGs, dedicated anti-sabotage units had been formed, but as yet no such group had been initiated at Kirkbride. Throughout February 1942, several reports had been received from workers inspecting dispersed aircraft that damage had been inflicted on the airframes. None of it was serious, but it still took up valuable time to repair and was viewed as local pranksters at work rather than an attempt by enemy agents to immobilize the aircraft. On 18th February, Superintendent Graham of the Cumberland County Constabulary Wigton Division visited Wg Cdr Mitchell to discuss the sabotage problem. A further visit on 1st April was made by the local police, who conducted several interviews with potential witnesses and, in some cases, suspects, but came to no conclusion. The following day, Wg Cdr Mitchell invited the Provost Marshal from Carlisle to investigate the suspected sabotage cases. A conference was held, which included the local police, but frustratingly nothing came to light in the police reports and no culprit was ever found. The police probably came very close to the offender, as there were no more reports of sabotage at Kirkbride.

Kirkbride was rapidly reaching capacity, specifically with regard to the storage of Wellingtons. 8 SLG at Hutton-in-the-Forest became available for 12 MU's use and, from March, Wellingtons were flown the short distance, once again relieving the pressure on Kirkbride.

The ferrying of aircraft was potentially as dangerous as any other training or operational sortie flown by the RAF. The local changeable weather claimed many victims throughout the war and 16 FPP suffered a double blow on 15th March 1942. A pair of Spitfire Vbs were being ferried to an RAF airfield further north when they both flew into cloud and crashed into high ground. AD296 came down near High Lochenbreck and AD395 struck ground at Breconside Farm, north-west of Thornhill, both locations in Dumfriesshire. Sadly, both ATA pilots were killed; their funerals on 19th March were attended by personnel from 16 FPP and 12 MU.

ATA operations increased slightly at Kirkbride with the forming of the Air Transport Auxiliary Movements Flight at White Waltham in Berkshire. The flight was formed to carry urgent spares between the country's four main ASUs, located at Aston Down, Cosford, Hawarden and Kirkbride. The flight offered scheduled services between these airfields and operated the Anson I, Proctor III, Argus and Dominie until it was disbanded in August 1945.

The morning of 13th April did not start well for a pair of 59 OTU Hurricanes who were practising formation-flying high above Kirkbride. Hurricane I Z7150, being flown by Sgt Taylor RCAF, collided with Hurricane I Z4103, piloted by Sgt Ross. Taylor stood no chance and his Hurricane crashed one mile south of the airfield, spreading itself over a wide area. Sgt Ross, with his aircraft badly damaged and without a propeller, skilfully performed a high-speed glide approach into Kirkbride.

A few moments later, a considerably less impressive display of flying occurred with the arrival of a Hudson from 1 OTU. N7322 was obviously carrying a lot of speed and, having approached from a westerly direction, it was inevitable that the aircraft would overshoot across the Kirkbride to Wigton road. This would have not been a problem if a civilian lorry had not been travelling down the road at the time. The resulting collision injured two civilians in the lorry and the two occupants on board the Hudson, and both the vehicle and aircraft were written off. The wreckage was very difficult to remove and, much to the annoyance of the local population, the road remained closed until 17:00hrs.

Defence exercises on RAF stations were a common event leading up to the allied invasion in June 1944. They were also taken very seriously and Kirkbride's first major exercise occurred on the 29th April 1942. It was, however, very difficult to take this particular exercise seriously, because not even blank ammunition was made available to the defenders or the attackers! It was virtually impossible to decide whether or not the 'enemy' forces were successfully repelled or the airfield overrun! Several useful 'in house' events included exercising the civilian staff in first aid and simulating the demolition of dispersed aircraft if ever the airfield was taken over by enemy forces. 16 FPP staff were also supposed to be participating in the exercise, but their contribution was described as 'singularly inefficient and the CO's attention has been drawn to their slackness'.

The issue of dispersal space at Kirkbride reared its head again in May, specifically the increasing number of Wellingtons and Halifaxes. Wg Cdr Mitchell had already visited other SLGs in the area the previous month, looking for additional space. After a visit to 9 SLG at Hornby Hall on 27th April, Wg Cdr Mitchell contacted OC HQ 50 Wg to arrange that the SLG, which belonged to 22 MU at Silloth, should be temporarily handed over for use by 12 MU. On 4th May the first Wellingtons were moved from Kirkbride to Hornby Hall, but frustratingly the SLG was found to be unsuitable for operating the

Halifax. A meeting followed on 11th May with OC 50 Wg, as Kirkbride approached bursting point with an influx of Halifaxes which could not be effectively dispersed around the airfield. A decision was made that all Halifaxes would be dispersed at 10 SLG at Wath Head, and when, the following day, the first aircraft made the short flight to the SLG, the pressure was relieved yet again.

While the age of health and safety was decades away, strict safety precautions were always in place when working on aircraft, especially inside hangars. However, a stray spark on 28th May tested the airfield's fire section to the limit. At 15:45hrs, the fire alarm sounded in a B2 hangar on the airfield. Wg Cdr Mitchell and the Station Executive Officer (SEO) arrived promptly on the scene to discover Hudson IIIA FH344 well ablaze inside the hangar. Civilian workers were quickly moving aircraft away from the hangar but the intensity of the flames, fanned by a high wind, meant that no aircraft could be towed clear from inside the hangar. The firemen managed to fight the fire successfully and their efforts saved two other aircraft and several aircraft engines in the hangar.

The increasingly cramped conditions of the dispersed aircraft at Kirkbride was again relieved slightly on 29th May 1942. The long overdue opening of 39 SLG at Brayton Park finally arrived and immediately several Wellingtons were flown out for dispersal.

By June 1942 the main technical site at Kirkbride was well established and difficult to camouflage, especially from the air. A visit from the local Camouflage Officer on 15th June did note several improvements had been put into place since his last visit. He did point out the importance of camouflaging the main site hangars with scrim-netting to break up their outline and eliminate shadows. This comment obviously upset Wg Cdr Mitchell quite a bit, resulting in the following comment in the station diary 'This brilliant discovery has on many previous occasions been submitted by the CO with little or no results!'

The same day, Sgt D E W Garvan from 55 OTU at Annan crashed Hurricane I W9119 on the airfield. With a failed engine, Garvan attempted to force-land on the main runway but instead overshot between two dispersal areas; luckily only the fighter's undercarriage was damaged.

The first North American B-25 Mitchell arrived at Kirkbride on 26th June 1942. This twin-engined medium bomber was to become a common sight at Kirkbride throughout the remainder of the war. Named after Brig. Gen. William 'Billy' Mitchell, the B-25 was very popular with its crews, performing well in almost every theatre during the Second World War. Its tricycle undercarriage warranted a conversion course for the 12 MU pilots. These were instructed by Plt Off. Eastwood from 20 MU at Aston Down in Gloucestershire on the 1st July. All of the local test pilots were successfully checked over a five day period. Known in RAF service simply as the Mitchell, the first to reach the service were 23 B-25Bs, which were designated Mitchell I. These were assigned to 111 OTU, based in the Bahamas. The first operational B-25s to serve with the RAF were B-25Cs and Ds, which were designated Mitchell II by the RAF, and it was these that were first to arrive at Kirkbride. A total of 93 Mitchell Is and IIs had been delivered to the RAF by the end of 1942. Several aircraft prepared by 12 MU took part in the first RAF operation with the Mitchell II, which took place on 22nd January 1943, when six aircraft from 98 and 180 squadrons attacked oil installations at Ghent. The RAF was allocated 316 B-25Js, which were designated the Mitchell III. Deliveries began from August 1944 until August 1945; however, only about 240 of aircraft reached Britain. A total of 910 B-25s went to Britain under the Lend-Lease scheme (theoretically still belonging to the United States) and only a few were actually returned to the USA at the end of the war.

HQ 41 Group allocated another American-built aircraft to 12 MU in July 1942. The Boeing B-17 Flying Fortress, known as the Fortress I, had an inauspicious entry into RAF service with Bomber Command in early 1941 and was quickly withdrawn. The Fortress II and later III were allocated for service with Coastal Command, where they were successfully operated throughout the war. Kirkbride's main runway was still only 1,400 yards long and Wg Cdr Mitchell was dubious about whether a Fortress could be landed there. After contacting HQ 41 Group, he was assured that the runways were suitable but Wg Cdr Mitchell then went onto explain that none of his test pilots were converted on type. The single Fortress that was planned to arrive was diverted elsewhere and an immediate conference was held to discuss extensions to the runways and perimeter tracks.

Another American-built aircraft, which had no problem getting into Kirkbride, was the Lockheed Ventura. Intended as a successor to the Hudson, the Ventura looked similar but was slightly larger, heavier and more powerful. Never as popular as the Hudson, it suffered high losses on operations with Bomber Command and by 1943 the majority of remaining Venturas were serving with Coastal Command.

No 18 Bomb Disposal Squadron (BDS), under the command of Plt Off. A Langley, had been stationed at Kirkbride for a few months.

They were often called out to assist rescue teams at local air crashes, one of which occurred near Kelsick, five miles south of the airfield, on 7th July 1942. A Miles Master from Annan had crashed into boggy ground; one of the two occupants, Flt Lt Rockel, managed to bail out successfully but the pilot, Sgt Triester, stayed with the aircraft and was killed. The BDS unit travelled to the scene of the crash at 22:00hrs and worked flat out until 01:00hrs the next morning in an effort to recover Sgt Triester's body, which was thought to be deeply embedded inside the aircraft in a peat bog. Work continued virtually non-stop, all the next day. The squadron experienced continuous problems with the collapsing bog and quicksand. The recovery continued and pumps had to be brought in, as the hole the BDS had made was constantly filling with water. Finally, on 10th July, traces of the dead pilot were found and efforts continued to remove his body from the wreckage until 16:00hrs. By this time, the inaccessibility of the body, the inflow of water, the pressure building on the sides of the excavation and unsatisfactory timber available made further efforts dangerous. Work was therefore discontinued by order of the OC 12 MU, who notified the officer commanding Annan and the county coroner. The following day Wg Cdr Mitchell placed on record his appreciation of the untiring efforts of 18 BDS in attempting to extricate the body of the dead NCO in the crashed Miles Master. His main comment read, 'Every member of the Squadron from the Officer in Charge downwards refused to give in until the situation became hopeless'. Much to the annoyance of the OC 12 MU, the Bomb Disposal Group was later reorganised and with much bad grace 18 BDS was disbanded on 21st April 1943.

The throughput of aircraft at Kirkbride by August 1942 consisted of the Hampden, Wellington, Spitfire, Boston, Mustang and Havoc. Other, unusual aircraft which passed through the unit included the Sikorsky Kingfisher I, which was used by the FAA as an observation floatplane, but it could also be fitted with wheels. A few Stinson Vigilants were prepared by 12 MU, but only a few of these high-wing single-engined liaison and observation aircraft ever entered service with the RAF.

A typical short-notice task for the staff of 12 MU was received on 5th September. A special assignment was received by the unit at 16:30hrs for the conversion of five Spitfires from 30 gallon to 90 gallon fuel tanks and the fitting of new wireless sets. The requirement was needed by 18:00hrs the following day but was actually completed by 14:30hrs. These hastily implemented modifications were the 'bread and butter' work for maintenance units and quite often, much to the

Seen here in its landplane configuration, the Sikorsky Kingfisher served as a floatplane with the Royal Navy.

frustration of the workforce, tasks would be cancelled or changed to completely different criteria.

Wg Cdr J W Mitchell's hard work at Kirkbride was rewarded on 3rd October 1942 by his promotion to Group Captain and a posting to 50 Wing HQ. Sqn Ldr T V Nelson assumed temporary command on 5th October, pending the arrival of the new OC, Wg Cdr H Bassett Collins, who arrived on 19th October.

Because of a high work load, contractors who had attended the conference to discuss extensions to the airfield, finally arrived on 27th October. An inspection of the airfield was carried out and all proposed work on the runways and perimeter track was approved. A 'hastening action' was placed on the work by the Air Ministry but the Ministry of Aircraft Production (MAP) said they would undertake the work if the ministry was unable to do so. Considering all this was being put into place specifically for the arrival of the Fortress, the type still managed to arrive during the month without any trouble. It was also joined by an influx of Halifax bombers and yet another American-built type, the Martin Baltimore. A development of the Maryland, which also served with the RAF, the Baltimore served with all of the Commonwealth air forces.

Daily aircraft movements, when the weather would allow, were constant and, considering this, the accident rate was actually much

The Stinson Vigilant was used by the RAF for liaison and observation duties and several passed through Kirkbride.

lower than expected. Occasionally though, there were days when things did not go according to plan. Over a three day period, 16 FPP lost or damaged four aircraft. The first was a Spitfire, on 13th November, which overshot the runway and overturned, not injuring the pilot. The following day started with the departure of a Hudson returning from Silloth. Unfortunately, the bomber swung during take-off and careered into a stationary Spitfire belonging to 16 FPP, which was parked on the edge of the airfield. The crew on the Hudson were uninjured but both the Hudson and Spitfire were written off. During the afternoon a Grumman Martlet fighter, which was using Kirkbride as a stop over, spun into the ground after take-off. The wing tip and engine cowling were seriously damaged and the undercarriage collapsed. The ATA pilot from 16 FPP was unhurt. On 15th November, 16 FPP's trusty Percival Proctor spun on take-off and tipped on its nose, damaging the propeller.

Kirkbride became the last resting place for a Lancaster from 97 Squadron, based at Woodhall Spa in Lincolnshire. Lancaster I W4356, with Sgt A A Johnson RNZAF at the controls, was on a training exercise when the bomber started to develop engine trouble. Whilst on approach to the airfield all seemed well until a multiple engine failure occurred and the Lancaster crashed short of the runway. No one on board was injured. W4356 had only been delivered to the squadron on 22nd November and, with only 9 hours' total flying time to its name, the Lancaster was destined never to perform a single operation.

From 31st December 1942, 12 MU was able to offer test pilots from other units conversion courses on the Wellington and Hudson. Firstly this saved other instructor test pilots from having to travel to the area. Secondly, it meant a valuable facility was in the neigbourhood for pilots from 22 MU at Silloth and 18 MU at Dumfries, who would benefit the most.

As Kirkbride had rapidly become the busiest airfield in Cumbria by the beginning of 1943 it was blessed with some senior attention. The Marshal of the RAF, Sir Edward L Ellington, returned to find the airfield considerably more active than on his last visit in December 1940. He returned again in February, with regard to local arrangements for the 'Wings of Victory' week, which, like so many other units, 12 MU was supporting. Sir Ellington visited Kirkbride in May as well, possibly highlighting how important the unit's work had become.

Despite having its own dispersal areas and SLGs, aircraft were still parked very close to the runways simply because of the lack of space. This meant that, if an aircraft was to leave the runway during take-off or landing, collisions were inevitable. This is exactly what happened on 3rd February 1943 when Hudson I N7257 from the FTU had an engine cut on take-off. The bomber swung violently off the runway, crashing into Spitfire PR.V X4411 of 16 FPP first; then colliding with Havoc I AX911 of 12 MU. Both the Havoc and Spitfire had served with great distinction operationally only to be destroyed by mechanical failure on another aircraft.

Another new type to arrive at Kirkbride was the Brewster Bermuda, the first of which was received on 11th June 1943. The Bermuda was a two-seat dive-bomber, which after its first flight in 1940 was supplied in numbers to the USAAF and the USN. The RAF ordered 750 Bermuda Is but only 226 arrived, which, in hindsight, was not such a bad thing, as none of them entered operational service. In fact all but three remained in storage and all had been scrapped by April 1945, many of them at Kirkbride.

12 MU lost its only Mitchell in a flying accident on 30th June. Mitchell II FV492 was flying an air test when, for an unknown reason, the bomber crashed after take-off near the airfield and was destroyed by fire.

A silent visitor descended upon Kirkbride on 31st July. An Airspeed Horsa glider which had obviously been towed to within the vicinity of airfield landed safely. It is not known whether 12 MU actually handled this type in any great quantity. It would be surprising if it did, as, even by this stage of the war, plans were being drawn for the invasion of Europe and every available glider was being stored in the open on airfields in the south of the country.

The runway extension work was finally completed in August 1943. Although the work was initially proposed for the Boeing Fortress, it was the American bomber's main rival during the Second World War that took advantage of the longer runway. The Consolidated Liberator could now pass through the unit and the first arrived only days after the extention was cleared for operations.

Sir Edward Ellington paid another informal visit to Kirkbride on 16th September. He was accompanied by Air Vice Marshall R Collishaw CB, DSO, DSC, DFC, the famous Canadian First World War fighter pilot. Collishaw had shot down a remarkable 60 enemy aircraft during the First World War and his distinguished career with the RAF had recently ended in July 1943. Rather disgruntled at 'being retired' he took the job of a regional air liaison officer, which was his capacity during his brief visit to Kirkbride.

Kirkbride became a satellite for 6 OTU at Silloth from October 1943. The unit's various marks of Wellington caused little disruption to the operation of the airfield because the bulk of their flying was carried out at night. It was just another airfield for the monotonous rounds of circuits and bumps that 6 OTU carried out until at least the beginning of 1945.

A final change of officer commanding during the war years occurred on 21st October 1943 when Wg Cdr Bassett Collins was posted overseas. Sqn Ldr J S Steele took over command of 12 MU until the arrival of Wg Cdr H L Macro DFC, AFC on 3rd November.

The only Brewster Bermuda to be lost on British soil crashed on 6th November 1943. On flight test in the hands of a 12 MU test pilot, Bermuda I FF437 was returning to the airfield when the pilot discovered that the undercarriage was jammed. Unable to lower it, he was advised by radio that he stood a better chance of survival by abandoning the aircraft to its fate. The pilot parachuted to safety and the torpedo bomber plunged into marshy ground near Newtonholme, only one and half miles north-west of the airfield.

The Vultee Vengeance was the next new type of aircraft to be received by 12 MU. The first of these American-built twin-seat dive-bombers, arrived on 1st February 1944. The Vengeance was by this time obsolete and virtually all of these aircraft that remained in service were resigned to target tug duties. The Vengeance was unique when it entered service with the RAF in mid 1942. It was the only aircraft designed specifically as a dive-bomber, in close support of Army operations, to enter the RAF.

At the same time the unit prepared to receive the Airspeed Oxford in bulk. It was a very common aircraft during the Second World War but only a few had ever passed through Kirkbride before.

The protracted work that was being carried out on Kirkbride's dispersal areas was finally coming to an end. Several extra dispersals, which were mainly filled with Mitchells, were brought into use, including one on Lowthers Farm, from February 1944.

Throughout early 1944, 16 FP (now renamed Ferry Pool) was heavily engaged in ferrying the Handley Page Hampden, of which many were passing through the airfield. The Hampden first entered RAF service back in August 1938 and its career with Bomber Command ended in September 1942. Many aircraft were given a new lease of life as torpedo bombers, serving with 144, 415, 455 and 489 Squadrons with distinction until they were replaced by the highly capable Beaufighter. It was the torpedo variant which was being ferried into storage, following its departure from front line duties in December 1943. It seems ironic that on 29th February 1944 Hampden I P1160 of 16 FP managed to collide while taxiing with Beaufighter X NE590. NE590 survived the encounter, going on to serve with 16 South African Air Force (SAAF) Squadron until it was shot down by flak and ditched near Cape Malea, Greece, in June 1944.

Kirkbride had received several visits by local Air Training Corp (ATC) squadrons from 1942. The commandant of ATC HQ for the north-west of England, Air Comm W T Y Guilfyle OBE, MC was touring all of the area's RAF stations that were receiving visits by squadrons. He arrived at Kirkbride on 6th March 1944, accompanied by Flt Lt Carr, commanding officer of the ATC at Wigton, with the intention of making personal contact with OC 12 MU, Wg Cdr Macro. The main topic of conversation was what facilities were being afforded to the ATC by the unit. The air commodore was especially pleased to note that flying experience was being obtained by the cadets. Whenever an ATC camp was on station, the unit's test pilots would usually make room for a cadet or two on an air test.

The daily routine of 16 FP operations was disrupted again on 13th May. Beaufort IIA ML610 was rolling down Kirkbride's main runway, when suddenly the torpedo bomber swung off the runway and ground-looped, followed by the undercarriage collapsing as the aircraft slumped back to terra firma. The ATA pilot was unhurt and ML610, although seriously damaged, was eventually transferred to the Admiralty on 10th September.

The main aircraft type passing through 12 MU during the summer of 1944 was the Mitchell. A delay in production on 12th August caused many headaches to the senior staff on the unit. The main problem was the hold-up in the supply of GEE modification parts for the Mitchell II. Another issue was that the majority of aircraft held by the unit were either old aircraft or still required the fitment of the FN.64 ventral gun turret, which was unique to RAF Mitchells. Mitchell III production was disrupted as well because the exact modifications required for each aircraft was unknown. In many cases, no leaflets or drawings were available. Often only the modification title was known – this was usually a completely meaningless reference number. Other problems arose when aircraft that were being withdrawn from long-term storage would require a lot more work to prepare for operations.

The Armstrong Whitworth Albemarle became the last aircraft type to pass through the unit in any quantity during the Second World War. Originally designed as reconnaissance and light bomber, the Albemarle was quickly relegated to the second line, perfoming such duties as glider towing and transport. First flown on 20th March 1940, the Albemarle was the first tricycle undercarriage aircraft to enter RAF service; it was powered by a pair of Bristol Hercules radials. The aircraft took part in both the D-Day landings and the less successful Operation Market over Arnhem. Many of the aircraft which had survived these operations were stored and later prepped for more squadron service at Kirkbride; the first began to arrive at the beginning of October 1944. An extra C Type hangar was brought into use to help with the production of the Albemarle.

A veteran de Havilland Mosquito being ferried by a pilot of 3 FPP from Hawarden in Flintshire made a dramatic arrival on 27th November. Mosquito VI NT147, which had served with distinction with 107 Squadron from Swanton Morley in Norfolk, swung and crashed after a single-engined overshoot. The tricky manoeuvre resulted in the Mosquito hitting the ground hard but the civilian ferry pilot escaped injury.

There had not been a major fire on the ground at Kirkbride since the Hudson III back in May 1942. Only the second such incident to occur during wartime happened on 24th January 1945 when Vengeance IV FD321 caught fire during practical maintenance. After the alarm was sounded the crash crew with a fire engine was on the scene in less than

90 seconds! Despite their speed the aircraft was burnt out and only good for scrap.

Mitchell III KJ562, piloted by 12 MU test pilot, Flt Lt A L Davis became the last wartime flying accident at Kirkbride on 25th April 1945. The bomber's undercarriage would not lower after an air test; so Davis skilfully performed a wheels-up landing on the grass without injury to himself or the passengers on board. KJ562 never saw operational service and the aircraft, which had flown only a few hours, was scrapped a few weeks later.

Personnel strength of 12 MU during April 1945 was 16 officers, 66 airmen and 733 civilians. By June, a large proportion of this workforce was preparing aircraft for long-term storage, a less demanding task but still one that required a large number of skilled workmen. With the war now at an end, retaining this workforce was becoming more difficult. For example, in July 1945, the actual tradesmen strength of the unit had an establishment of 366 but only 246 were available for 12 MU. One of the colossal jobs carried out that month was the removal of the main planes from 320 aircraft!

16 FP, ATA was officially disbanded on 31st August 1945 and authority was given immediately for 12 MU to take over their buildings. The closure of the ATA unit slightly improved the manpower position regarding tradesmen, mainly because the airmen attached to 16 FP were internally posted to 12 MU. Despite this, personnel were being released at an alarming rate, which was being strenuously opposed by the senior staff at Kirkbride.

The closure of 39 SLG at Brayton brought about an influx of Wellingtons, which continued until its closure in December. The total stock holding of aircraft had risen rapidly to over 1,000 aircraft by September 1945. Aircraft or their component parts were covering literally every available piece of dispersal or grass area. By November, aircraft still held on the unit were the Albemarle I, II, V and VI, Boston IIIA and IV, Martinet TTI, Mitchell II and III, Oxford I and II, Tiger Moth II and Vengeance I and II, which came to a grand total of 1,206 aircraft.

Crucial staff were now being posted on a regular basis and this included 12 MU's only Electrical Engineering Officer on 16th November. A mass re-organisation of the dispersal areas was implemented to cope with all the aircraft that were still arriving. Aircraft engines were still being maintained in running order up to this time as well. Over 400 were still being periodically tuned up in December 1945.

L Type hangars were dispersed all around the airfield and virtually all are intact and in use. This particular one is on the southern dispersal area at the edge of the Wedholme Flow South Solway Mosses Nature Reserve. (Author)

During peacetime, 12 MU adopted the role of a long-term storage unit and eventually a disposal unit. Hundreds, if not thousands, of aircraft were scrapped at Kirkbride, although, unlike many of the wartime aircraft, the majority of the post-war machines did actually see squadron service.

Not all the aircraft to pass through the unit ended their days by being scrapped. Several Mitchells were refurbished for the Netherlands and a large number of Tiger Moths survived to be flown on the civilian register as well. Many Douglas Dakotas and Avro Yorks were also prepped and returned to military duties. But the final memory for many who served at 12 MU was the sad sight of hundreds of Gloster Meteor jet fighters waiting to be scrapped. 12 MU was officially closed on 30th June 1960.

From an aviation point of view, the airfield is still very active today and the main runways, perimeter tack and dispersal areas are still virtually complete. Many hangars, technical buildings and the control

Many original buildings still survive and virtually all are occupied, including the airfield's main guardroom at the entrance to the technical site. (Author)

tower still stand as a fitting tribute to one of the busiest airfields in Cumbria and possibly the country.

The main runway is the only one in use today and, at 1,280 metres in length, is more than capable of handling all traffic from microlights to jets. Microlights and more unusually gyroplanes are the most common sight around the airfield today. Resident today are the Kirkbride Aero Club, Solway Microlights and RS Gyroplanes.

14
LONGTOWN

The layout of Longtown gives the impression that, when construction began, the contractors were working from plans for a bomber airfield and when they had finished a fighter station was the result. Located 1.5 miles east of Longtown, eight miles north of Carlisle off the A6071 near Brisco Hill, work began on the airfield in the middle of 1940. Three runways were laid in a typical triangular pattern; the main runway was a generous 2,000 yards long with the shorter subsidiary runways measuring in at 1,380 and 1,150 yards respectively. Dispersals consisted of five loop type for bombers and 28 small fighter hardstandings, giving the whole airfield a 'mish-mash' feel. Hangarage was a meagre, single Type T-2 hangar and a pair of Blisters but there was room for so much more.

The airfield was ready for its first unit by July 1941. Longtown had been allocated to Crosby as its satellite many months before completion and so, on 14th July 1941, 'D' Flight of Hurricanes from 59 Operational Training Unit (OTU) became the first residents. The flight was commanded by up-and-coming Flt Lt Bobby Oxspring, who had served in the Battle of Britain and would go on to become the commander of 24 Wing flying Spitfires before the war's end.

It was not long before the first of many accidents involving the Hurricane occurred at Longtown. Six days after 'D' Flight's arrival, Hurricane I W9110 made an emergency belly-landing on the airfield after the engine cut. Not repaired, the aircraft was eventually struck off charge five months later. Despite the reputation that preceded fighter OTUs, 1941 was a relatively uneventful year, with one more Hurricane accident recorded on 23rd October. Hurricane I V7245 had enjoyed a trouble free career, having served with 303, 229, 315 and 303 Squadrons, only to suffer at the hands of a trainee pilot who overturned it after landing.

The Hawker Hurricanes of 59 OTU were the first aircraft to take over Longtown.

From 30th March 1942, all Hurricanes operating from Longtown had the luxury of a VHF (very high frequency) RT (radio transmitter) fitted. A ground station was set up in the control tower, which had an aircraft set installed. The flight commander on duty was usually responsible for its use and it meant that a direct link to a more experienced pilot on the ground was always available. At the same time, 59 OTU became associated with the Catterick Sector for reinforcing in the event of an invasion and whenever an aircraft was airborne from Longtown.

Another Hurricane unit shared Longtown with 59 OTU from May 1942. 55 OTU was also a dedicated single-seat fighter training unit, first formed at Aston Down in Gloucestershire in November 1940. The unit moved north to Usworth, County Durham in March 1941, followed by Annan in Dumfriesshire in April 1942. A satellite airfield was needed quickly so that Annan would not become congested with aircraft. 'C' and 'D' Flights of 55 OTU first occupied Longtown on 13th May and advanced training operations began immediately with the most senior course of pupil pilots.

Lockheed Hudsons from 1 (Coastal) OTU stationed at Silloth made use of the airfield from 7th July 1942. It was used mainly for night circuit training, which continued into early 1943.

A combination of inexperienced pilots and tired aircraft resulted in

All fighter OTUs during the early years of the Second World had several Miles Masters on strength. This is a Master III of 55 OTU, which operated from Longtown in 1942/43.

an above-average accident rate in 55 OTU. From May to August 1942, the unit lost 12 Hurricanes and a single Miles Master. Many losses were caused by mechanical failure, although this was not the case when Hurricane I Z7077 and Hurricane X AG125 collided over Drumburgh on 8th July. A split-second lapse in concentration during formation flying tragically cut short the flying careers of two potential fighter pilots. The previous day Miles Master I T8411 was described by eyewitnesses 'to be flying in a spirited manner' when the port wing broke off over Abbey Town.

The one and only occasion that the airfield hosted a fully operational squadron was on 1st August 1942, when 41 Squadron arrived from Debden in Essex. Equipped with the Supermarine Spitfire Vb, the squadron stayed only until 11th August, departing for Llanbedr. During their brief stay, much lively discussion was conducted on whether the Hurricane or Spitfire was the better aircraft, with neither side yielding to the other's argument.

With the completion of Milfield and its satellite at Brunton, both in Northumberland, the decision to move 59 OTU was made. The unit's main ground and air parties, consisting of 17 Hurricanes, left Longtown for Brunton on 4th August. The last aircraft were a pair of Miles Masters, which left for Brunton on 9th August.

The loss of an aircraft was never good for morale, especially when it happened over your own airfield. Sgt D R S Dixon RNZAF was carrying out dog fighting practice on 14th August in Hurricane I V6857

162

of 55 OTU. Several ground crew were watching the exercise as, after a high speed aileron turn, the Hurricane was seen to pull out at 4,000 ft, roll on its back and quickly enter an unrecoverable spin. It is presumed that Dixon had blacked out; the fighter crashed into Jean Syke Wood on the edge of the airfield.

The movement of 59 OTU created space for another major training unit to move into Crosby and in turn Longtown, once again as the satellite airfield. 9 (Coastal) OTU was first formed at Aldergrove in Northern Ireland in June 1942 to train long-range fighter crews for Coastal Command. 9 OTU arrived at Longtown on 6th September 1942, bringing the Bristol Beaufighter and Bristol Beaufort plus several support aircraft, which included the Airspeed Oxford and Avro Anson. Many of the Beauforts employed by the unit were fitted with dual controls, which made flight training considerably easier. There was no such luxury in the cockpit of a Beaufighter. It was Beaufort I L4478, which became the unit's first casualty on the airfield on 26th September. An engine cut on take-off, the aircraft crash-landing at the end of the runway and skidding out of the airfield boundary.

Flying by 9 OTU from Longtown was brought to a halt from early November 1942. Wg Cdr Woodruff, the Officer Commanding 9 OTU, was not happy with the runway safety margins at Longtown and, on 11th November, Thornaby in North Yorkshire was brought in as a temporary satellite while the airfield was modified. It was also decided that Longtown should be used mainly for night flying training, possibly because of the amount of 55 OTU movements during the day. The unit began using the airfield again on 3rd December, with more emphasis on nocturnal operations.

55 OTU's operations continued unabated with a steadily growing casualty list as another aerial collision happened on 28th December. Night flying was being increasingly introduced into the unit's syllabus and it was whilst on approach that Hurricane X AG150, piloted by Sgt G H Walsh, collided with Hurricane I W9233 being flown by Sgt A V Marshall. The two airmen had no chance, AG150 came down near Brisco Hill, west of Longtown, and W9233 crashed in flames on Tan Hill Farm.

Night flying courses were being successfully completed from February 1943 onwards by 9 OTU. The night flying unit was known as 'N' Squadron and was under the command of Plt Off. Nelson. An instructors' squadron with 9 OTU, under the command of Sqn Ldr Harrison, was formed at Longtown in March, providing useful refresher courses for current instructors and sourcing new potential candidates as well. 'A' Squadron moved from Crosby to Longtown in April, combining two existing squadrons specifically for Beaufort conversion and night flying training; it was also under Sqn Ldr Harrison's command.

The majority of accidents involving 9 OTU aircraft were not particularly serious. Several aircraft had been written off at Longtown but up until the end of August none had been fatal. It was quite common for local Air Training Corp (ATC) squadrons to visit RAF stations to experience what the real air force was like. The resident units were always very keen to take cadets flying and on 27th August two cadets were lucky enough to get a flight in a Beaufort. Sadly the aircraft was lost in the Solway Firth with the loss of all on board. A few days later, Sgt Grant was carrying out conversion training on Beaufort I DX132. After a heavy landing, the starboard propeller struck the runway sending the aircraft crashing off the edge of the runway and killing the pilot instantly.

The AOC of 17 Group (Training) Coastal Command, Air Vice Marshal Smart, visited Longtown on the October 1943 to discuss 9 OTU's future. Plans were in place to turn Longtown in a Heavy Conversion Unit (HCU), so all units on the airfield would have to be moved. 9 OTU's move to Crosby to join the main unit was carried out with great efficiency only two days later.

The advance party of No 1674 HCU arrived from Thornaby, despite the main unit being located at Aldergrove, where it first formed in October 1943. Thornaby was the home of 1 (Coastal) OTU, whose role had changed to the training of Coastal Command crews on the Boeing Fortress, Handley Page Halifax and Consolidated Liberator. A pair of Halifaxes were the first aircraft to arrive on 18th October, supported by 23 officers and 30 NCOs. Wg Cdr T W T McComb, the CO, arrived the same day and the main party arrived from Aldergrove on 19th October with 29 Officers, 86 NCOs and 512 Airmen, who all arrived by rail. A single Fortress, a Halifax and an Oxford also arrived. The Liberator flight which was also originally part of 1 OTU remained at Aldergrove as a detachment, from where operational Liberator squadrons were already flying.

Another unit which had become part of 1674 HCU was No 1 (Coastal) Engine Control Demonstration Unit, which was formed at Longtown on 19th October. Equipped with the Vickers Wellington, the unit moved to Great Orton on 17th November through lack of space at Longtown.

55 OTU also had to find a new home and, with no room at the parent

Serving with 1674 HCU, the Consolidated Liberator was a regular sight at Longtown up until the summer of 1944.

airfield at Annan, a new satellite had to be found. On 20th October, 'E' and 'F' Flights of 55 OTU, with only a total of 8 Hurricanes and 1 Miles Master on strength, made the short flight to Great Orton. During their stay at Longtown, 55 OTU had lost 38 Hurricanes in a variety of accidents, plus five Miles Masters. The cost of training was high on aircrew and aircraft.

To add to the mix of October 1943, Longtown became the satellite airfield of 6 OTU, based at Silloth. The airfield was used by the unit's Wellingtons from 16th October, although the airfield was officially handed over to Silloth's control on 27th October 1943.

1674 HCU began its training programme on 30th October with the commencement of No 1 Fortress Course and the continuation of No 3 Halifax Course, which had started at Thornaby. On 3rd November, Wg Cdr McComb was posted to 7 (Coastal) OTU at Limavady in Northern Ireland. His replacement was the highly experienced Wg Cdr R D Williams, posted in from 86 Squadron, who were flying the Liberator from Ballykelly in Northern Ireland, at the time.

Just as 1674 HCU was beginning to settle in at Longtown, Wg Cdr Williams received a visit from Gp Capt. Carr DFC, CO of Silloth and

Gp Capt. Brown, the CO of Crosby. Longtown was to be handed back to Crosby as its satellite in the new year.

On 5th January 1944, Longtown became the home of 9 OTU again and 6 OTU ceased to use the airfield as a satellite. 1674 HCU began to make plans for a return to Aldergrove and on 15th January four Fortresses and 55 personnel left Longtown. A further 60 personnel left by rail the following day, including the CO, followed by the unit's headquarters, which left for Aldergrove on 1st February 1944. Several Halifax remained and were officially designated the Longtown detachment, later the Halifax flight, under the command of Sqn Ldr Massey. One of these aircraft, Halifax II BB278, was lost on 14th February in sea off Silloth, with the loss of all on board. Another crew was lost on 12th April when Halifax II BB310 crashed into Great Dun Fell, ten miles east of Penrith. Eight pupils and their instructor were killed. The following day, Halifax II BB276 swung on take-off, immediately followed by the inevitable undercarriage collapse, and then burst into flames. Luckily all seven of the pupil aircrew and their instructor escaped with minor burns.

Longtown was used by several aircraft from the parent unit at Aldergrove for navigation exercises and, on several occasions, Fortresses and Liberators visited the airfield. 1674 HCUs time at Longtown came to an end on 6th July 1944 when five aircraft from Aldergrove collected the remaining groundcrew and equipment. However, records show that the unit's Fortresses used Longtown to at least 17th August for various transit flights.

Another change of role occurred on 11th August 1944 when both the parent unit at Crosby and Longtown were transferred to 44 Group Transport Command. No 1332 Conversion Unit (CU) was formed at Longtown on 5th September 1944 with the intention of training transport crews. Several senior staff arrived the same day, including the Chief Flying Instructor, Wg Cdr R N Stidolph DFC, Sqn Ldr F Heppell, the Chief Ground Instructor, plus three flight commanders. Over the next two days, 15 Short Stirlings, four Liberators and four Avro Yorks arrived at Longtown but unfortunately the airfield was found to have insufficient facilities to support such a unit. An alternative home was quickly found and on 6th October an advance left for Nutts Corner in Northern Ireland.

The airfield was reduced to a state of care and maintenance in November 1944, with a skeleton staff of airmen attached from Crosby, which was still the parent unit. It was not until 20th October 1945 that Longtown was to receive another unit. No1521 Beam Approach

The Stirling IV along with other aircraft belonging to 1332 CU made a brief appearance at Longtown.

Training Flight (BATF), under the command of Sqn Ldr J H A Wells, arrived from Wymeswold in Leicestershire. As with the majority of these flights, the main equipment was the Airspeed Oxford, of which 1521 BATF had at least eight on strength.

The flight was joined by the Dakotas of No1383 (Transport) Conversion Unit, based at Crosby. The unit had adopted Longtown as its satellite from 15th November 1945 to 30th March 1946 but, with plenty of room at Crosby, the airfield's use was limited.

Despite several attempts to work with staff at Crosby, 1521 BATF found itself detaching training courses to Snaith and Pocklington, both in North Yorkshire. This it continued to do until the unit was disbanded on 1st April 1946, bringing Longtown's flying days to a close.

Today only large sections of the runways and perimeter track remain. The few buildings that had been there were demolished long ago and generally the entire site has returned to agriculture.

15
MILLOM
(Haverigg)

During the Second World War this windswept airfield was located at Cumbria's most southerly point, its isolation lending itself perfectly to the training of thousands of bomb aimers and air gunners.

Work began on a new airfield on the coast at Haverigg Point, between the villages of Kirkstanton and Haverigg, in late 1939. Officially named Millom by the Air Ministry, it was known locally as Haverigg airfield and still is by many today.

It was built as an advanced fighter station under the control of 9 Group Fighter Command, stationed at Barton Hall near Preston in Lancashire. By the time the airfield was completed in early 1941, the fighter defence of the north-west of England was a lesser priority.

Being built to a fighter specification meant that the three runways were only 1,000 yards long but narrow extensions at the end of each meant that they could possibly be lengthened in the future. Good hangarage was provided, with six Bellman Type hangars in a group on the technical site plus 13 Extra Over Blisters scattered around the edge of the airfield. Accommodation was typically of the temporary type, Nissen and Maycrete huts, which provided homes for up to 2,350 officers and airmen, although very few of these were ready when the first of many personnel began to arrive on 7th January 1941.

Millom was now under the control of 25 Group, Flying Training Command, whose headquarters were located at Buntingsdale Hall near Market Drayton in Shropshire. The first aircraft to arrive was Blackburn Botha I L6169, which was delivered on 14th January from 48 Maintenance Unit at Hawarden in Flintshire. The airfield's first unit, No 2 Bombing and Gunnery School (B&GS), was formed at Millom on 20th January 1941 in accordance with the 'Opening up Programme', being implemented by Flying Training Command at the time. Millom was temporarily under the command of Wg Cdr C C O'Grady, who was the most senior officer on the airfield at the time. He had actually been posted in to serve as the school's chief instructor. An opening up party was detailed to arrive on the same day, this being made up of personnel who had already been posted onto the airfield.

As with virtually all new airfields built during wartime, 2 B&GS found the technical and domestic areas far from complete. In particular, only a handful of airmen's accommodation huts were ready

Aerial view of Millom in 1945, clearly showing the three runways, perimeter track and seven hangars. It is now the location of Haverigg Prison. (RAF Millom Aircraft & Military Museum)

for use and neither sergeants' nor officers' messes were ready for occupation. All of the roads on the airfield were described as being in poor condition and the ground was generally badly waterlogged. The contractors had also had problems laying the deeper parts of the sewerage and drainage system and a time scale of a further six weeks was given for the completion of the airmen's facilities.

Essential stores were also lacking at Millom, including mattresses and beds. Airmen were making do with blankets and sleeping on dining tables or improvising with the builders' materials which littered the airfield. Officers were billeted in the town of Millom and at various houses in the surrounding countryside, causing immediate friction with the locals. Most of the spare accommodation at that time had been taken up by workmen from the local ironworks and mines and those employed actually constructing the airfield.

On 21st January, Gp Capt. A M Wray MC, DFC, AFC arrived to assume command of Millom, releasing Wg Cdr O'Grady to his intended flying duties. By the end of the month a further 16 Bothas arrived at Millom, all delivered from Maintenance Units, which included 22 MU at Silloth, 12 MU at Kirkbride and 18 MU at Dumfries. The Botha was to be the school's main aircraft type, with nearly 70 on strength by May 1941.

The Blackburn Botha was one of three types of new aircraft that were chosen to re-equip the RAF's maritime squadrons before the outbreak of the Second World War. The other aircraft were the Saro Lerwick and the Bristol Beaufort; the latter was the only one that performed well, with both the Lerwick and Botha withdrawn from front-line service after a short period of time. The Botha was designed to operate as a general reconnaissance or torpedo-bomber, although it only went on to serve with 608 Squadron, based at Thornaby in North Yorkshire. In hindsight, it was a quite remarkable decision that the aircraft was ordered direct from the drawing board without any consideration for its potential failings, which were many. Its main weakness was lack of power; its two Bristol Perseus engines were totally inadequate, and the design of the aircraft exposed serious visibility problems, especially downward and laterally. The Perseus engines suffered particularly at Millom because of its position next to the sea. Sand from the neighbouring dunes blew across the airfield on a regular basis, causing engine wear which resulted in a high number of engine changes.

Personnel strength at Millom was rising rapidly and, by 31st January 1941, 28 officers and 458 other ranks were resident. Now

The Blackburn Botha was an unpopular aircraft with its crews. It was not the most reliable of aircraft and this was aggravated at Millom by drifting sand from the nearby beaches, which caused excessive wear to the Perseus engines.

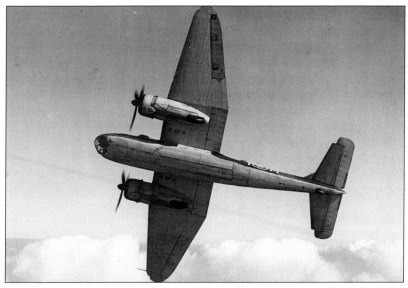

2 OAS struggled on with the Botha until it was finally phased out in favour of the Avro Anson in mid 1942.

with sufficient staff, Millom and the B&GS were divided into three wings. Training Wing consisted of a bombing squadron, gunnery squadron and the station squadron, made up of the Target Towing Flight (TTF) and Station Flight. Each of these squadrons had an instructional and flying flight attached to it. Maintenance Wing was made up of the Maintenance Squadron, Servicing Squadron and Station Workshops. The third wing was Administration Wing, which comprised all other services not encompassed by the previous wings. Millom was now in a position to begin flying training and the first task was to familiarise all those pilots who had not flown the Botha before.

The first of 18 Fairey Battles arrived on 1st February; they were immediately allocated to the TTF and air-to-air firing practice could now commence. The opening up programme continued through February, stage V commencing on 3rd February. A further 311 airmen arrived that day and the acquisition of essential stores was still proving to be a problem. Difficulties in securing supplies of essential furniture and the continued lack of mattresses were the main headaches. A 'special hastening action' was implemented for the mattresses and 1,000 arrived just in time to allow for a rapid increase in personnel strength. The local MP heard about the difficulties that Millom was encountering, possibly from the mouths of a few disgruntled airmen. He voiced his concerns in the House of Commons regarding the conditions airmen were living under. Despite a large element of truth in his allegations, the Air Ministry dismissed them as baseless.

2 B&GS had hardly begun its training programme when Gp Capt.

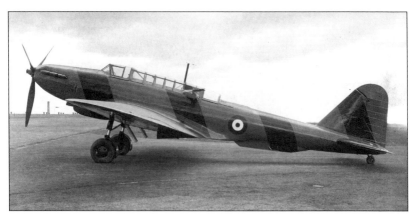

Target towing for 2 B&GS was originally carried out by converted Fairey Battle light bombers.

Wray and Wg Cdr O'Grady were called to attend a conference at HQ, Flying Training Command. The main topic of the meeting was the potential conversion of 2 B&GS into a Bombing and Gunnery and Air Observer Navigation School. The conference came to the conclusion that Millom would not make a good location for a combined school and that only Air Observers should be trained there. No 1 Air Observers Course, with 40 pupils attending, commenced on 25th February, many months before the school was officially redesignated as an Air Observers School. The same day, six meteorological officers arrived for a short navigation course as well.

The Central Flying School (CFS) Flight, equipped with the Fairey Battle, was transferred to Millom from Manby in Lincolnshire on 11th February 1941. The first three aircraft were flown in by Flg Off. L E Duke, Flg Off. A J Holderness and Flg Off. J A Gordon, with more following throughout the month.

One of only a few Bristol Blenheims to serve at Millom arrived on 21st February. Blenheim I L6736 saw action with 25 Squadron during the Battle of Britain before spending a long career with various training schools and it survived long enough to become an instructional airframe in February 1943. The same day, 2 B&GS had its first flying accident, which involved Botha I L6487. The Botha, which had only been delivered on 3rd February, swung off the runway and crashed into an obstruction, luckily with no injuries to those on board. This was the first of many incidents involving the Botha. The first fatal accident occurred on the 24th February. Plt Off. S G Rudd, in Botha I L6262 with three crew, was on a cross-country exercise to Detling in Kent. For no apparent reason, the Botha dived out of control into the ground near Tonbridge in Kent, killing all on board.

Station defence was given a boost on 6th March with the completion of four anti-aircraft gun posts around the perimeter of the airfield. A few days later, 100 .303 rifles were delivered for the use of the airfield's ground defence force. A further four pillboxes were ready for occupation on 7th May 1941. These were to be manned 24 hours per day, and each pillbox was fitted with a pair of Lewis machine guns.

Botha engine failures and the number of man-hours being used for their servicing and replacement was becoming a major problem by May 1941. Its seriousness was highlighted when the Station Engineering Officer (SEO), Sqn Ldr Christmas, attended a meeting at the Ministry of Aircraft Production (MAP) in London in May. A presentation named 'The technical aspects of operating conditions for aircraft stationed at Squires Gate and Millom and the failures of the

Perseus XA engines in Botha aircraft' attempted to address the problems being experienced by 2 B&GS. That very day a further ten engines were being replaced owing to excessive oil consumption caused by the action of sand. It appears that the only useful advice gleaned from this meeting was that filters should be fitted over the Perseus engine carburettor intakes.

The filters seemed to have had little or no effect and, on 29th May, a complete re-organisation of personnel was made to provide a full maintenance wing organisation. Servicing personnel who had been attached to flights were now centralised and placed directly under the control of the SEO. During May 1941 alone, 21 failures and defect reports were declared during the month for aircraft engines. Fourteen of the failures were attributable to sand. To alleviate the workload, an additional 24 airmen from 32 MU at St Athan in Glamorganshire arrived in June to help with the replacing of engines and the fitting of air filters. They continued this task until the end of August 1941.

Despite several Air Observer courses having passed through Millom already, it was not until June 1941 that 2 B&GS became 2 Air Observers' School (AOS). 2 AOS was originally formed on 15th November 1938 from 7 Air Training Station (ATS) at Acklington in Northumberland. It was dissolved into 10 AOS at Warmwell in Dorset on the outbreak of the Second World War before being resurrected at Millom. Their equipment remained the same, the main type being the Botha with a few Avro Ansons and Airspeed Oxfords in support.

The training programme was now beginning to suffer because of the increasingly unreliable Botha. Gp Capt. Wray and Sqn Ldr Christmas travelled by air on 21st June to HQ 25 Group and then later in the day to HQ Flying Training Command. Botha serviceability was discussed and a decision was made to supply 2 AOS with an additional 18 Avro Ansons to keep training at Millom on track. The majority of the Ansons were transferred from 6 Service Flying Training School (SFTS) at Little Rissington in Gloucestershire and 12 SFTS at Grantham in Lincolnshire, both were converting to the Airspeed Oxford as their main aircraft type.

The Botha engine failure rate continued to rise to a point in June 1941 when 21 out of 26 engine failures and defects were attributable to sand. It was now becoming more practicable to dispatch damaged engines to another unit for servicing and in turn receive a refurbished unit in its place. Engines were dispatched by rail from Millom railway station from 1st July onwards. Two Perseus XAs and a single Merlin II from a Battle were dispatched by rail to the Bristol Aircraft Company

In contrast to its predecessor, the Avro Anson brought reliability to Millom and remained on the airfield until 2(O)AFUs disbandment in January 1945.

and Sunbeam Talbot. Seven more Perseuses were dispatched to Bristol's and three refurbished units were received from 12 MU at Kirkbride. This coming and going of engines continued for many months, especially while the Botha continued to operate from Millom.

Plt Off. J. Spychala and his four crew had a lucky escape from their Botha on 15th August. After take-off, an engine cut on Spychala's Botha I L6354, and, unable to maintain height on a single engine, he ditched into the Irish Sea two miles south-west of the airfield. The crew scrambled onto the top of the aircraft, which was perched on a sand dune with the tide at a fairly low point. The Barrow lifeboat rescued the crew, who were all uninjured.

An influx of Airspeed Oxfords began on 26th August 1941. Several arrived from the de Havilland Aircraft Company at Hatfield in Hertfordshire with others from the Standard Motor Company at Ansty in Warwickshire. Little use was made of them because, within days, they were traded for Ansons from 1 Beam Approach School at Watchfield in Berkshire. However, the Oxford along with the Anson, was used by 2 AOS in great numbers, much to the relief of the ground engineers, their reliability being greatly welcomed.

The Hawker Henley and Boulton Paul Defiant target tugs of 'R' Flight, 1 Anti-Aircraft Cooperation Unit (AACU) was the next unit to arrive at Millom, on 13th September 1941. Formed at Farnborough in Hampshire in June 1941, the flight moved north to Squires Gate in Lancashire at the beginning of September. Squires Gate was still a long distance from the anti-aircraft units that the flight would be working with, so they moved again to Millom. 'R' Flight remained at Millom until January 1942, when they moved a short distance to Cark in Lancashire only to disband later that year owing to a lack of aircraft.

Each Air Observers course at Millom had 40 pupils and the average pass rate was quite high, at 90 per cent. A typical course, which terminated on 19th September 1941, achieved 37 out of 40 pupils going on to continue their training. The next stage was a bomber Operational Training Unit (OTU); from this course 17 were posted to 15 OTU at Harwell in Berkshire, three to 13 OTU at Bicester in Oxfordshire, six to 42 OTU at Andover in Hampshire and eleven to 2 (Coastal) OTU at Catfoss in North Yorkshire. Of the three pupils who did not complete the course, two were injured in flying accidents and a third was killed.

A Defiant of 2(O)AFU with air and groundcrew at Millom. (RAF Millom Aircraft & Military Museum)

Gp Capt. Wray's tour of duty came to an end at Millom on 18th October 1941. He was posted to Goxhill in Lincolnshire; his replacement, Gp Capt. A W Franklyn MC, arrived from Stormy Down in Glamorganshire.

From November 1941, the Fairey Battle target tugs were being steadily replaced by factory-fresh Westland Lysanders, all specifically converted for target towing. The last Battle departed for 2 Air Gunners' School (AGS) at Dalcross, Invernesshire on 13th February 1942. The first Lysander TT.III R9003, which was more affectionately known as the 'Lizzie', arrived on 16th November from the Servicing Aircraft Section at Abingdon in Oxfordshire. Several more arrived over the next few weeks, many from Westland's home at Yeovil in Somerset.

The new year began with the spectacular arrival of Wellington III X3605 on 13th January 1942. The ex 9 Squadron bomber, destined for Kirkbride, was being delivered by an ATA pilot of 3 Ferry Pilots Pool, based at Hawarden in Cheshire. Poor weather meant a diversion to Millom and, on landing, the wing tip struck the ground, swinging the bomber off the runway. The resulting crash meant that X3605 would never fly again.

Twelve Fairey Swordfish of 822 Squadron used Millom as a

A Lysander IIIA Target Tug of 2(O)AFU makes a great back drop for this cheerful bunch of ground crew. (RAF Millom Aircraft & Military Museum)

177

stepping-stone on 25th January 1942. The biplane torpedo bombers were flying from Gosport in Hampshire to Hatston in the Orkney Islands, more commonly known to the Fleet Air Arm as HMS *Sparrowhawk*. Poor weather delayed their departure until 27th January.

More talk of 2 AOS changing its role again resulted in Gp Capt. Franklyn attending a conference at HQ 25 Group. It was suggested at the conference that 2 AOS should be converted to an (Observers') Advanced Flying Unit (O)AFU. The plan was for the existing Air observer course to be transferred to other AOSs, with Millom's new (O)AFU tasked with training aircrew which had already been Dominion trained, i.e. already been put through schools in Canada, South Africa, Australia or the USA. The plan was for each intake to contain an average of 240 officers and sergeants, remaining at Millom for a six week course.

Before 2 AOS was redesignated, on 7th February 1942, Millom received a visit from the Air Member for Training, Air Marshal A G R Garrod CB, OBE, MC, DFC, Air Vice Marshall R A Cochrane CBE, AFC, the Director for Flying Training, Air Vice Marshall R Leckie DSO, DSC, DFC, the officer in charge of Air Training Scheme Canada plus a large number of Dominion and Allied representatives. The high-ranking group inspected all aspects of training given by the unit and 'great satisfaction was expressed by all members of the conference'.

2 AOS became 2 (O)AFU on 18th February 1942, still under 25 Group control. The only change was the slow phasing out of the Botha in favour of the Anson. Botha I L6224 & L6169 became the last of their type to leave the airfield on 29th March.

While drifting sand continued to make life uncomfortable for those working on the airfield, the ability of the Anson to cope with it was a valuable compromise. The loss rate was not reduced though; between May and July 1942, the unit lost six Ansons, a Lysander from the TTF and a de Havilland DH.60 Moth, which was part of the station flight. In addition, several aircraft from other units crashed in the local area and were given assistance by personnel from Millom. With this in mind, senior staff thought, because of Millom's location on the southern edge of the Lake District, it would make a good location for a Mountain Rescue Unit (MRU). Gp Capt. Franklyn agreed that this would be a good idea but was under the impression that personnel would be posted in to run the unit. However, for almost 18 months, Millom had to provide the personnel (locally known as the MRP (Mountain Rescue Party) before a proper MRU was officially recognised at the airfield. Skilled personnel were diverted from their own tasks and, as a result, the training programme and maintenance schedules of the unit's aircraft began to suffer.

The only enemy attack on Millom occurred at 12:20hrs on 14th August 1942. A single enemy aircraft, thought to be a Junkers Ju 88, shot up the airfield with cannon fire. Millom was lucky – the airfield escaped with no casualties or damage and there were no more enemy raids for the remainder of the war.

An American unit was briefly attached to the unit on 26th September 1942 with the arrival of seven North American P-38 Lightnings. These big fighters were actually at Millom for bombing practice, staying a week before returning to their home airfield. At this time 2 (O)AFU had three bombing ranges at its disposal, all near to Millom. Ranges were located at Duddon, two miles north of Millom town; Silecroft, literally a walk from the airfield, on the coast; and Askam, positioned north of Askam in Furness in Lancashire. Because of manpower shortages, all personnel working on the ranges were ordered to return to Millom. From 1st October, ranges were attended only for maintenance as necessary. This eased the depleted personnel situation at Millom, caused by the continuous allocation of rescue parties.

By December 1942, 2 (O)AFU had 47 Ansons, 15 Defiants and six Lysander target tugs on strength. The Defiant target tugs were phased out in February 1943, with the Lysanders carrying the load throughout the rest of the year.

A typical day and night's work for the MRP occurred on 27th December 1942. The rescue party was called out to search for a missing Fairey Swordfish which was believed to have crashed in the Duddon Estuary. Whilst searching for the Swordfish, the MRP were split into two parties to search for Lysander III T1674 from 10 Air Gunners School (AGS) at Walney in Lancashire. The Lysander became lost in fog and crashed near Beck Farm on Low Scales, two miles northwest of the town of Millom, with only slight injuries to the crew.

A long-term detachment from 776 Squadron, based at Speke in Merseyside (now John Lennon Airport), arrived with a variety of aircraft on 30th December 1942. Aircraft types included the Dominie I, the Vought-Sikorsky Chesapeke I and the Blackburn Skua II, the latter being the most common type to be seen at Millom. Many more aircraft types followed during their stay at Millom. Whilst carrying out their own FAA tasks, the aircraft of 776 Squadron provided additional support with Air Sea Rescue duties and the MRP.

Despite the MRP having been unofficially formed many months

The Vought-Sikorsky Chesapeake was a rare 'bird', operated by 776 Squadron at Millom.

earlier, their first recorded 'mountain' rescue occurred on 8th August 1943. An aircraft from 18 MU at Dumfries crashed on the Scawfell Mountains, which includes Scafell Pike, the highest peak in England, at 3,210 ft. The following day, the rescue team were tested again when four Ansons, three of them from 10 OAFU at Dumfries and another from 3 OAFU at Bobbington, later named Halfpenny Green, in the West Midlands, crashed at various locations within the surrounding peaks.

The MRP's first major Mountain Rescue Exercise was held on 9th September 1943. The task was to tackle the 1,690 ft summit of Black Combe, located five miles north-west of the airfield. A 4x4 Humber ambulance remained at base whilst a Bren Gun Carrier accompanied by the American built 'Willys' Jeep attempted the climb. Unfortunately, the jeep quickly got into difficulties and had to turn back while the Bren Gun Carrier made easy work of the ascent. The carrier overcame the difficulties of steep gradients and stony or boggy ground. A new transmitter and receiver in the ambulance also proved a success with good contact being made with the team using walkie-talkie type radios.

Many of the MRP tasks involved the grisly task of recovering the bodies of crewmen, as very few airmen survived crashes in such a

Millom's Mountain Rescue Team was officially recognised during the post war period.
(RAF Millom Aircraft & Military Museum)

hostile unforgiving terrain. The MRP was called to a Boeing B-17G Flying Fortress 42-39913 crash at High Low Scale near Millom on 23rd November. The only saving grace was the fact that the bomber was without a full crew and only the pilot, 2nd Lt Ronald L Garkie, and co-pilot, 2nd Lt Sullivan, were killed. The MRP was generally led by the Station Medical Officer (SMO), Sqn Ldr Bowes, who travelled in the Willys Jeep, closely followed by the Humber ambulance.

A more encouraging event occurred on 19th December when a Martinet target tug crashed near Ravenglass. Mountain rescue vehicles and equipment were dispatched to the scene to find the Tow Target Operator (TTO), LAC Hudson, patiently waiting by the crashed aircraft. The pilot, Sgt Valentine, who was also uninjured, decided to set off on foot to a local army unit.

Another call out, on 11th January 1944, resulted in the MRP's jeep getting stuck, again searching for a missing Beaufighter. The Beaufighter VI KW152 of 301 FTU (Ferry Training Unit) from Lyneham in Wiltshire crashed near Bootle, five miles north of Millom. The boggy ground caused the jeep to get stuck twice, much to the frustration of the rescue team who would have preferred their efforts to be concentrated on the missing fighter. Sadly, when the crash site was finally reached, the pilot, Flt Lt H S Ray, and his navigator, Plt Off. Angold, were found dead in the wreckage. As a result of the jeep getting bogged down, it was arranged for the vehicle to carry timber baulks in future.

The following day, Millom's own rescue party was officially recognised as an MRU, the second to be formed in the United Kingdom following the unit at Llandwrog which covered Snowdonia and much of Wales. Sqn Ldr Bowes was relieved of his command of the new MRU, the officer commanding Flying Squadron taking charge of the unit. With its change in status, the MRU was suddenly presented with new equipment to test, much of which stayed with the unit at Millom. An American built DUKW amphibian was tested on 19th January and it impressed the trials team so much that a single example was immediately allocated to the MRU. It went into action for the first time on 20th January when a Skua from 776 Squadron crashed on Haverigg Beach. The crew, Sub Lt W Mogridge and Plt Off. J Bennett, were rescued safely by the DUKW. In May, a full-scale trial was held for a Snow Weasel tractor vehicle in front of senior officers on nearby hills. Once again, an example was delivered to the MRU for rescue duties to replace the old Bren Gun Carrier, which had performed sterling work. The Snow Weasel was the predecessor of the Snow Cat which remained in service well into the 1980s with the British Army.

By the beginning of 1944, the Lysander target tugs had been phased out and replaced by the purpose-built Miles Martinet. The Martinet was developed from the Master II, becoming the RAF's first aircraft specifically designed and built as a target tug. The dual controls were removed from the rear cockpit, the canopy was modified to facilitate the operation of a side-mounted winch for flag or sleeve drogue targets stowed in the rear fuselage and the front fuselage was lengthened. The type was first flown in April 1942 and a further 1,722 were delivered to RAF and FAA units, the last leaving the production line in early 1945.

The sortie rate by the Ansons of 2 (O)AFU was modified from 15th June 1944. 20 day sorties were flown and, with more emphasis on nocturnal operations, two details of 20 sorties each were carried out at night. The accident rate at night rose markedly but the valuable experience gained by pupils was seen as an acceptable trade-off.

It was while the second night detail of 20 Ansons was returning to Millom on 7th October that a request was made to divert a further 13 Ansons from Dumfries. At 05:00hrs the duty control officer successfully guided 33 aircraft into Millom without incident.

The DUKW amphibian helped again on 17th October 1944 when a Halifax got into trouble over the county. At 21:05hrs, the pilot of the bomber ordered his crew to bail out at 11,000 ft; the last position given by the pilot was near Ullswater. The MRU was dispatched to the area and in a short time found the pilot of the Halifax, safe and well, near to the lake. The duty flying control officer ordered the DUKW to follow the MRU to Ullswater, enter the lake and search the water with all its headlights on. As a result, all of the crew of seven were found unharmed around the edge of the lake.

Five days later, another Halifax crashed near Coniston, followed by a second at Little Langdale, four miles west of Ambleside, on 23rd October. Together, they resulted in a total loss of 16 aircrew, all recovered by Millom's MRU.

The 776 Squadron, which had gone from Millom back to its home station at Lee-on-Solent in Hampshire in April 1944, returned for a second and final tour at Millom on 27th October 1944. The squadron was now equipped with the Blenheim IV, Defiant TT.III and Swordfish II. It would remain at Millom until 4th January 1945 when it was moved to Walney Island in Lancashire for a final detachment before eventually disbanding at Burscough in Lancashire on 30th October 1945.

The training programme of 2 (O)AFU began to thin down from November 1944 onwards. With sufficient (O)AFUs providing the necessary amount of personnel needed during this period, it was only a matter of time before 2 (O)AFU was disbanded. The day came four months before the end of hostilities in Europe, on 9th January 1945.

The MRU carried out its last rescue from Millom on 8th January 1945. Anson EF935 from Wigtown in Dumfries and Galloway crashed on hills north of Millom, injuring three crew and killing a fourth. The MRU was in the process of moving to Cark in Lancashire at the time, but still managed to carry out a successful rescue without much of its proper equipment.

Millom's flying days were now over and the airfield was reduced to care and maintenance until June 1945, with Sqn Ldr O F Kennedy in charge, plus two officers and an attachment 60 airmen and WAAFs from 10 AGS at Walney. The airfield was taken over by No 14 Aircrew Holding Unit (AHU) at 16:00hrs on 14th June 1945. The unit was temporarily under the command of Plt Off. Price who received a message that the unit should be ready to receive 1,000 Royal Australian Air Force (RAAF) personnel on 21st June.

Plt Off. Price was relieved of his position when Wg Cdr R A Norman DFC, RAAF took over the unit on 19th June. Wg Cdr Norman found the new unit completely unprepared for its task of repatriating Australian air crew. With the war in Europe now at an end, there was a distinct lack of permanent officers and airmen being posted in to run the unit.

Millom was described as a 'forgotten unit', reflecting the fact that the AHU was relying on the intakes of Australians to actually run the unit. A draft of 615 NCOs arrived via the light cruiser HMS *Orion* on 13th November, becoming the last intake for 14 AHU.

Despite being closed to flying, Millom provided an emergency landing strip for a Supermarine Seafire on 23rd November 1945. Lost in bad weather, the Seafire made a hurried approach, crashing onto the main runway and ripping off the undercarriage and damaging the propeller and wing. Luckily, the pilot was uninjured.

Similarly, Millom provided a safehaven for a Mitchell which was flying to Kirkbride for scrapping on 6th December. With Flg Off. Jukes at the controls, the Mitchell landed with a fire in the port engine. The fire was put out by the aircraft's own extinguisher without further damage to the aircraft or injury to the crew. The Mitchell was later unceremoniously scrapped at Millom instead.

14 AHU closed down on 15th December 1945, its task completed

under difficult circumstances. Wg Cdr Norman handed over command of Millom to Flg Off. J Chisholme, who was in charge of the second care and maintenance party to arrive at the airfield. Wg Cdr Norman made the final comment in the operational records book (ORB): 'It cannot be said that many personnel were sorry to leave Millom as the Unit was so isolated, the surrounding towns being, in the Staff's opinion, not worth visiting!'

Millom was placed in the hands of the War Department on 24th September 1946 and remained dormant until 1952. The Officer Cadet Training Unit (OCTU) was formed at Millom on 1st September 1952 as an additional unit to the OCTU at Spittlegate near Grantham, Lincolnshire. The OCTU did not last long at Millom; it was disbanded on 10th September 1953, with its personnel transferred to the RAF OCTU at Jurby on the Isle of Man.

The airfield was used briefly as the home of several Army regiments before being sold off. The airfield was taken over in 1967, the technical site becoming Haverigg Prison. Although all of the hangars were dismantled, several of the Maycrete huts were taken over by the prison, many of which remain in place today. The airfield itself is

The RAF Millom Aircraft and Military Museum is crammed with exhibits relating to the airfield and a host of other military subjects. (Author)

The museum uses several original wartime buildings, and larger exhibits, such as a Whirlwind helicopter and these engines, are displayed outside. (Author)

virtually complete with the bulk of all three runways still in place; the perimeter track is still complete. The land now belongs to Hempland Farm and has returned to agriculture. The site also supports a cluster of wind turbines.

Formed in 1992, the Millom Aviation and Military Museum is well worth a visit. The museum uses several original wartime buildings and all are jammed packed with a vast range of exhibits. Independently funded, the museum is partnered by the Lancashire Aircraft Investigation Team, South Lancashire Aviation Research and the Peak District Air Crash Research Groups. Aviation and military history is represented for Cumbria, Merseyside, Greater Manchester, North Cheshire, North Wales and the Peak District.

16
RONALDSWAY

Boasting a throughput of over 700,000 passengers per year, the Isle of Man's Ronaldsway Airport is a great asset to the island. The airport has a host of regional and international routes, supported by airlines such as British Airways, Eastern Airways, EuroManx, Emerald Airways, Flybe and Manx Regional to name a few. Aircraft of all shapes and sizes use the airport, from general aviation types to regional jets, medium-sized airliners to military aircraft.

Situated one mile north-east of Castletown, Ronaldsway was

Handley Page HP.27 Hampstead G-EBLE of Imperial Airways landed in a field owned by Ronaldsway Farm in 1928.

Sir Alan Cobham's famous DH.50J G-EBFO, which landed near to the future Ronaldsway airfield in 1929.

unofficially recognised as a landing ground in 1926 and it was listed as an Automobile Association Landing Ground not long after that. *The Motor Cycle* journal was obviously popular on the island in 1928 because of the T.T. races. Copies amounting to over a ton in weight were delivered by Handley Page HP.27 Hampstead G-EBLE of Imperial Airways, landing in a field owned by Ronaldsway Farm. Sir Alan Cobham visited the island in 1929, landing his de Havilland DH.50J G-EAFO on or near the location of the landing ground. Cobham became a great supporter of the idea of a larger airfield at Ronaldsway. The Tynwald (the Isle of Man parliament) had been considering the question of a 'public aerodrome' on the island since 1920. A lengthy and expensive method of finding the site for an airfield, by calling for a plethora of 'expert reports', achieved no further progress. The Tynwald continued the search until 1935, by which time Ronaldsway was already established and Hall Caine was operating in competition.

Blackpool and West Coast Services acquired the small airfield and began services on 8th April 1933, flying the de Havilland DH.84 Dragon. The company's regular route was via Blackpool's new municipal airport at Stanley Park and Squires Gate, both in Lancashire. The following year, Capt. G P Olley, who had already formed Olley Air Services on the mainland, saw the potential in Ronaldsway and formed Isle of Man Air Services Ltd. Olley acquired the landing rights and looked at expanding the landing ground into the island's main airport.

In 1935, after more land was purchased, the site totalled 88 acres and, by the end of the year, more suitable runways had been marked out on the grass. A hangar was constructed plus a few ancillary buildings, including a booking office and a wooden terminal building. These buildings struggled to cope as the novelty of flying to the Isle of Man attracted over 8,000 passengers in 1936. Despite spirited backing by some major airlines of the day, Hall Caine Manx Airport could not compete and its scheduled services were lost to Ronaldsway in 1937.

As the number of flights increased, a wireless station was built on the airfield. Larger-capacity aircraft started to use Ronaldsway, raising the annual passenger figure to over 12,000. Routes opened up to Dublin, Belfast, Leeds, Glasgow and Carlisle by fledgling airlines such as Aer Lingus and Manx Airlines. Manx was a branch of Railway Air Services, which flew the DH.84 Dragon on a regular Barton, Blackpool and Isle of Man run. It originally considered using the larger four-engined DH.86, but Ronaldsway was still too small to operate the aircraft safely. A smaller Dragon proved the point on 1st July 1935 when it crashed on take-off.

An unexpected visit from the RAF took place Ronaldsway on 10th June 1938. Blenheim I L1157 of 110 Squadron from Wattisham in Suffolk overshot its landing and crashed into a wall. The crew were uninjured but L1157 was sufficiently damaged for it not to fly again.

The land the airport occupied was on lease from the Ronaldsway Estate. When the owner died in 1938, the trustees granted a twelve-year lease of the land at £220 a year, with the option of extending the airfield up to 150 acres. Further expansion continued until the beginning of the Second World War.

Unlike the rest of the country, the island was allowed to continue civilian aviation and a comparatively limited service was in place. Operated by the Isle of Man Air Service, the route was maintained under an agreement with the Joint Air Service Committee. This was not frowned upon either when several Air Ministry officials arrived at Ronaldsway in April 1940. The RAF requisitioned Ronaldsway in May and began a limited amount of construction on the airfield. A temporary canvas Bessonneau hangar of First World War vintage plus three Blister hangars were constructed around the edge of the airfield.

Accommodation huts were also built plus the usual array of technical buildings associated with a military airfield of the period.

The first unit to arrive at the airfield was No 1 Ground Defence Gunners' School (GDGS) from North Coates in Lincolnshire, on 1st July 1940. Formed at North Coates on 20th November 1939, the GDGS was under the control of 25 Group, whose HQ was at Buntingsdale Hall, Market Drayton in Shropshire. As the unit's name implies it was tasked with training new recruits in all aspects of ground defence training and the use of large weapons.

Under the command of Wg Cdr T M Abraham, the GDGS operated its own Target Towing Flight (TTF), which was made up of twelve Westland Wallaces and five Hawker Harts, which were later replaced by the Gloster Gauntlet – hardly cutting edge technology but all they were required to do was tow a banner over a range so the trainees could practice their ground-to-air firing skills.

Training commenced on 3rd July when 32 airmen reported for No 23 Two Gun Course. Other courses run by the GDGS included Cannon, Three Gun, Lewis Gun, Musketry practice, Vickers Gun, Hispano Cannon as well as Instructors' and Officers' ground training courses. The average course lasted for 14 days, three of which were taken up by drill and discipline.

1 GDGS employed several Gloster Gauntlets for cine gun practice. This aircraft is in pre-war colours; wartime examples would be camouflaged.

The majority of aircrew who flew the target tugs were from Poland and virtually all new arrivals were posted in from 15 EFTS at Kingstown. There was nothing more frustrating for a Pole than being posted onto a training unit. They flew the obsolete GDGS aircraft very hard and there were several cases of Polish aircrew at Ronaldsway being disciplined for their aerial antics.

To cater for a shortfall of accommodation at Ronaldsway, additional properties were requisitioned in Castletown on 30th September 1940. They included No 6 and 7 The Promenade, 23, 25 and 27 Arbory Street and Bridge House. The intake of pupils had increased to over 450 per month and the unit was struggling to cope. A new GDGS establishment was implemented on 1st November; it consisted of 62 officers, 1,313 other ranks, including 24 civilians. The numbers under instruction at any one time rose again to a maximum of 30 officers and 870 airmen.

Wg Cdr Abraham was posted to 10 B&GS at Dumfries on 6th January 1941. Wg Cdr T Moss OBE, whose first major task was to receive a visit from the Air Officer Commanding (AOC) 25 Group, Air Vice Marshal Champion de Crespigney on 25th February, replaced him. Several senior staff, including Air Vice Marshal Don and the chief engineer, both from Flying Training Command, accompanied the AOC. They were very impressed with the organisation of the GDGS and the high throughput of trainees. All the military airfields being constructed throughout Great Britain were in need of ground defence personnel. Many had to rely on skilled tradesmen who were needed to keep aircraft in the air, not to be tied down by guard duties.

The accident rate at Ronaldsway was very good and even the exuberant Polish pilots had not wrecked any of the TTF aircraft. Many of the Poles had managed to get themselves posted onto front-line units, finally unleashing their venom against the enemy. Several visiting aircraft crash-landed on the airfield, including, on 2nd February 1942, Blenheim IV L9408 from 254 Squadron at Dyce in Aberdeenshire. The twin-engine bomber crashed on landing in poor weather but was later repaired, remaining in RAF service until August 1946 and becoming one of the longest-serving examples.

The first accident to involve a TTF aircraft occurred in spectacular style on 14th February. Flt Lt Dunphy was on approach to the airfield in Gauntlet II K5335 when he collided with an Isle of Man road services bus. Remarkably, no one was hurt on the bus and Dunphy walked away uninjured from the wreck of his biplane. K5335 was first delivered to 65 Squadron at Hornchurch in Essex back in July 1936. It was then passed on to five different units before arriving at Ronaldsway on 4th February 1941. The hard working little biplane fighter was struck off RAF charge three weeks later and scrapped.

The RAF Regiment was formed on 15th February 1942 and the GDGS and No 1 Ground Gunners School (GGS) were also formed from the main unit. The GDGS was transferred to Technical Training Command, whose HQ was Shinfield Park near Reading, Berkshire. This now placed the new GGS within 20 Group, which, like 25 Group, was also based at Buntingsdale Hall.

The first of several navy courses began to pass through the unit on 20th February, followed by the first Royal Marine officers' ground training course in March. Facilities available to the GGS were rapidly expanded, additional ranges being constructed on the coast near the airfield. Others were located at Langness Point, Fort Island and Spanish Head and all were in daily use. A locally modified anti-aircraft Lewis gun mount was designed by Capt. Peacock and was fitted to a seaplane tender. It was accepted into service and was used to fire at targets being towed by another boat.

The social scene appeared to be quite active at the time. Regular RAF dances were organised at Collinson's restaurant in Douglas and the Oddfellows Hall in Castletown. The first of several RAF concerts was also held at the Villa Marina from March 1942.

The Douglas High School Air Cadet Squadron (ATC) worked very closely with the GGS during their time at Ronaldsway. The cadets even took part in exercises and written examinations for some of the GGS equipment, including the Lewis gun. At every opportunity the TTF took cadets up for experience flights, which was always encouraged. On 24th March, Wallace IIs K6064 and K8695, each with cadets on-board, took off from Ronaldsway for air experience flights. On their return to the airfield, whilst in formation, the two aircraft collided and K8695 crashed into Quayle's Orchard, Grenaby Farm, two miles north of Ballasalla. The pilot, Sgt A G McGill, and his passenger, ATC Cadet P E Wolton, were killed. K6064, although damaged, managed to land safely at Ronaldsway.

2nd April 1942 was a busy day for the ground crews at Ronaldsway, with three flying accidents on the airfield. Wallace II K3568, piloted by Sgt Adey, tipped onto its nose after landing, followed by Anson I L9165, which had to force-land, as the weather had deteriorated. Fairey Battle I P6727 force-landed in similar circumstances moments later.

Ronaldsway, like all other airfields at that time, had its own ground defence squadron. 2796 (Defence) Squadron under the command of

Sqn Ldr E H Bellingham was a shining example of how such a unit should operate. Having all trained at Ronaldsway, the unit was actually incorporated into the GGS training programme to show new recruits the kind of duties they would be carrying out. Lt Col Baker of 20 Group inspected the squadron on 8th April. Baker witnessed the unit training and then proceeded on to the ranges at Langness to see a demonstration of firing using G28 Camera Guns against dummy parachutists.

A meeting at Ronaldsway on 6th May 1942 decided that a new RAF Regiment Recruits Weapon Training Wing would be instituted at a military camp on the outskirts of Douglas. This was the first indication that the GGS might be moved to a more suitable location. The following day, instructions were also received regarding the possibility of laying out one 25-yard and two 300-yard rifle ranges in the vicinity of Douglas. These ranges would be required to meet the commitment of 2,000 recruits for the RAF Weapon Training Wing. The site for these ranges was decided on at Douglas Head and HQ Technical Training Command was informed of this decision.

The GGS designation was changed to No 3 RAF Regiment School on 14th May and was actually formed at the site near Douglas. The TTF flying section of the school would continue to operate from Ronaldsway and support the training of the RAF regiment. By this time, the TTF had lost its Hawker Harts, but still maintained several Wallaces, Gauntlets and at least one Wellington was on strength as well.

Cine Gun Camera training was a particularly efficient way of honing the skills of ground defence gunners. Cine guns were positioned on the top of Creggans's Hill near Castletown while the Gauntlets dived down at the gunners as they fired the cameras. The Gauntlets continued this role well into the Second World War, but, with their mid-1930s performance, they were hardly a good representation of a German fighter or even bomber. The officers and ratings of HMS *Radiant* made use of a G28 Gun Camera onboard ship under the guidance of instructors from the Regiment School on 20th June. A Gauntlet from the TTF carried out an attack on the ship. HMS *Altair* carried out a similar exercise on 4th July.

In August 1942, the airfield was brought to the attention of the Admiralty as a potential home for a Torpedo Training Squadron and several front line squadrons. An incredibly in-depth report of Ronaldsway was produced, covering the current site and the possibilities for its expansion. At the time of the report, the landing ground was owned by the Crookhall Estates, represented by J F Garside, who resided at Talbot Chambers, 18 Athol Street, Douglas. The airfield had slowly increased to 120 acres in size and was being held on requisition by the Air Ministry from Isle of Man Air Services. The airline was still operating a civilian route to Speke and the Admiralty was not happy about this. The report looked at the feasibility of acquiring more land, which would have to total at least 300 acres, at a cost of no less than £70 per acre. Four farmers would be affected as well as King William's College. Despite a lengthy list of disadvantages presented by the report, the following advantages made Ronaldsway the only option available to the Admiralty: a suitable area for torpedo dropping was available, placed with port facilities nearby at Douglas; no air congestion; preliminary work on surveys had been completed and represented a fair start as against the other option of selecting and surveying an alternative site, three other sites being surveyed – Anthorn, Kirkandrews and Cruden Bay – being considered unsuitable for torpedo work and no further sites suitable having been offered by the Air Ministry. By October 1942, Ronaldsway's future was sealed but it would be several months before the airfield was handed over.

At 14:00hrs on 2nd October 1942, the coastguard received information that a fishing boat had been observed approximately five miles south-south-west of Spanish Head, towing a wreck. This was the beginning of a five-day operation to recover Anson I L7960 of 5 AOS, which had successfully ditched in the Irish Sea. The crew escaped unharmed, took to their dinghy and where rescued by Fishing Boat CT.34, owned by Mr Woodsworth of Port Erin. A seaplane tender went out to meet the fishing boat and at 15:30hrs took over the towing of L7960, which refused to sink. By 18:30 hours, the tender had made slow progress and at a point two miles east of Langness Point, a second seaplane tender arrived to help. By 19:50hrs, the two boats had towed the Anson to within 400 yards of the shore abreast of the Station Sick Quarters (SSQ), which was located on the south side of the airfield, just over the sea bank. The following day, the combined effort of several airmen from Ronaldsway Anti-Aircraft Flight and the Gunnery School managed to beach the Anson high and dry close to the sea bank. The Anson was stripped of as many heavy components as possible and incredibly the whole aircraft was manhandled over the sea bank onto the airfield on 5th October. L7960 was one of a batch of 67 Ansons built by Avro at Chadderton, Greater Manchester and delivered in August 1938. L7960 served only with training units, including 10 ERFTS,

12 FTS, 1 AOS and finally 5 AOS, where this hard working aircraft's career ended.

The same beach caused the evacuation of the SSQ on 22nd December 1942 after a mine was washed up and later defused by a No 63 Bomb Disposal unit, based at Jurby.

The advance party of No 1 GDGS left the airfield for Filey in North Yorkshire on 18th January 1943. Four days later the advance party of the Target Towing Flight departed for Hutton Cranswick, also in North Yorkshire, and was redesignated 1634 Flight. Hutton Cranswick was 20 miles away from the main unit and was the only airfield then available in the area. At the time and for the remainder of the war, Yorkshire airfields were heavily committed to Bomber Command and its squadrons.

The main flying party and remainder of the GDGS had left the airfield by 15th February, the last RAF aircraft departing on 28th March. Three days later, Ronaldsway was officially handed over to the Admiralty and RAF personnel vacated all buildings and accommodation. A new chapter in the airfield's history was about to begin.

What followed was a massive and lengthy reconstruction of the airfield and the requisitioning of nearly 500 acres of additional land including several playing fields from King William's College.

The original torpedo storage huts still stand, complete with a Second World War recovery plant in the foreground. (Jarrod Cotter-www.flypast.co.uk)

Expansion also included the laying of four tarmac runways, the longest at 1,500 yards, with the remainder at 1,000 yards long, and all electrically lit. The Royal Navy required runway widths of only 30 yards to conform to carrier flight decks as against the 50 yards width required by the RAF larger 'A' Class airfields. Additional hangars, three large concrete aprons and additional accommodation for up to 1,644 officers, chiefs, petty officers and ratings plus 480 WRNS was also built.

While the construction was still going on, the airfield still managed to provide a safe haven for at least three different aircraft in trouble. Hudson V AM798 from 1 (Coastal) OTU at Silloth overshot on landing, hit a wall and caught fire on 26th August 1942. Wellington IV Z1339 of 104 (Transport) OTU, based at Nutts Corner in Northern Ireland, followed on 21st January 1944. The bomber was landing on a single engine but swung badly after touchdown and the undercarriage collapsed. The final aircraft to land at Ronaldsway during its 'closed' period was Mosquito II DD733, on 5th June 1944. The night fighter from 60 OTU at High Ercall in Shropshire crash-landed on one of the new runways after an engine failed over the Irish Sea.

The new airfield, almost unrecognisable compared to its layout in

A typical three-storey Royal Navy control tower at Ronaldsway is still serving the modern airport. (Jarrod Cotter-www.flypast.co.uk)

1942, was completed in late spring 1944. On 21st June 1944, HMS *Urley* (Manx Gaelic for 'eagle'), RNAS Ronaldsway, was officially commissioned. The airfield would now support the basic and operational training of torpedo, reconnaissance, dive bomber air crew and anti-submarine training under the guise of No 1 Naval OTU.

Before the first Fleet Air Arm (FAA) unit arrived, a Consolidated B-24 Liberator became the first aircraft to make proper use of the new runways, on 4th July. The four-engined American bomber was being ferried from Meeks Field in Iceland to Valley in Anglesey when it ran short of fuel.

747 Squadron was the first FAA unit to arrive on 14th July 1944. The squadron was formed at Fearn in Ross-shire in March 1943 as a Torpedo Bomber Reconnaissance (TBR) Pool Squadron. The squadron developed into an Operational Training Unit and, after several moves, arrived at Ronaldsway equipped with the Fairey Barracuda II, under the command of Lt Cdr T M Bassett RNZNVR.

747 Squadron was joined by 713 Squadron on 12th August, under the command of Lt Cdr A G McWilliam RNVR. The squadron was

The most common type to be seen at Ronaldsway after the Admiralty took control of the airfield was the Fairey Barracuda II.

197

re-formed at Ronaldsway as a TBR training squadron with the Barracuda II and later the III as well. 'A' Flight of the squadron operated an anti-submarine course and 'B' Flight acted as the Squadron Commanders' Attack School, with a short course on dive bombings. It also provided the final stage of training of the TBR course.

The next unit was 710 Squadron, which also re-formed after originally serving as a Supermarine Walrus squadron from August 1939 to October 1943. The squadron was reborn at Ronaldsway on 7th October 1944, under the command of Lt Cdr D R Conner RNVR, as a Torpedo Training Squadron operating within 1 Naval OTU. 710 Squadron's main equipment was the Barracuda II and III plus several Fairey Swordfish Is and IIs. The squadron also provided training for the TBR course alongside 747 Squadron.

Air-to-air firing was also required as part of the Navy's training programme and a detachment from 725 Squadron provided this. The squadron provided four Miles Martinet TT1s; the detachment lasting from August to November 1944, when they were moved to Ballyhalbert in Northern Ireland.

A squadron without any aircraft staged through Ronaldsway on 15th November. 822 Squadron, commanded by Lt Cdr L C Watson DSC, RNVR, had been fighting the Japanese as part of the Eastern Fleet, operating the Barracuda II. The dive bomber did not perform well in the tropical climate and the squadron returned to Britain aboard the escort carrier HMS *Rajah* without its aircraft. The personnel of 822 Squadron left Ronaldsway on 18th November for Lee-on-Solent in Hampshire.

A common visitor, the Fairey Swordfish, also served at Ronaldsway until at least June 1945.

Corsair IIIs of 772 Squadron [B Flt] made regular appearances during the unit's detachment in 1945.

Swordfish from the Merchant Aircraft Carrier MV *Empire MacRae* passed through the airfield on 23rd December 1944. The Swordfish Is and IIs from 'A' Flight, 836 Squadron continued to Maydown in Northern Ireland three days later. 'U' Flight, also of 836 Squadron, made a similar transit journey through Ronaldsway on 16th January 1945.

The first of two detachments from 'B' Flight of 772 Squadron arrived from Ayr on 5th January 1945. The unit flew a vast array of aircraft, including the Hurricane IIC, Vought Corsair III, Stinson Reliant I, Swordfish II, Martinet TT1, Douglas Boston III and Fairey Firefly I. 'B' Flight left on 17th April but returned for a second detachment on 6th September 1945, leaving for a final time on 10th January 1946.

The last squadron to be re-formed at Ronaldsway was 705 Squadron, on 7th March 1945, commanded by Lt Cdr S M P Walsh DSC and Bar, RNVR. The squadron took the role of a Replacement Crew Training Unit, equipped with the Swordfish III. The unit was tasked with operating an anti-submarine course. However, with the end of hostilities in Europe on 8th May 1945, this training was no longer needed and the squadron was disbanded on 24th June 1945.

Following the victory over Japan and the end of the Second World War on 15th August 1945, the training of torpedo bomber crews at Ronaldsway became superfluous. Many FAA crews trained at

Ronaldsway is the home of the Manx Aviation Preservation Society, which uses a pair of the original wartime buildings. (Jarrod Cotter-www.flypast.co.uk)

Ronaldsway had seen action, virtually all in the Far East. 747 Squadron departed for Crail, Fife on 15th November; 'B' Flight, flying the Anson, remained. On 20th December 1945, all training ended with the combined disbandment of 710 and 713 Squadrons and 'B' Flight of 747 Squadron.

By 1946, the Royal Navy had left Ronaldsway, and the Isle of Man Government purchased the airfield in 1948. Civilian services were quickly resumed and the airport was continually improved and modified. The original narrow naval runways were widened and lengthened in 1957 to cater for the increasing number of larger airliners.

The modern terminal building, which was refurbished and extended between 1998 and 2000, has removed many of the wartime buildings. However, the control tower built by the Royal Navy in 1943 is still in daily use. The Tynwald, who granted more funding for the airport in March 2006, has approved more extensions and additional departure gates. As the Isle of Man's main airport, it could be safely said that Ronaldsway's future is very secure.

Worthy of a visit is the Manx Aviation Preservation Society (MAPS), which first opened in November 2000. On display in the museum are a variety of exhibits representing military, civil, and wartime aviation on the Isle of Man. The museum is located on the western side of the airport and utilises several wartime buildings.

17
SILLOTH

With surprising forethought, a site for a new airfield was selected east of the small seaside town of Silloth on the edge of the Solway Firth in early 1938. Many airfields were built as a 'knee jerk' reaction after the beginning of the Second World War. Maintenance Command appeared to be more organised and it knew it would need large airfields for its maintenance units (MU) when, by this time, the inevitable war was fast approaching.

Work began in late 1938, and, like all Maintenance Command airfields, it was built to a high standard with many technical buildings, including a vast selection of hangars. Once work was completed, Silloth could boast three C Type, four D Type, six E Type, four L Type, one A1, one Bellman, thirteen Robin Blisters and five Super Robin

As at its sister airfield at Kirkbride, virtually all of Silloth's original wartime hangars still stand. (Author)

Blister hangars. A huge array of dispersal areas was also constructed, including 38 pans 100 ft in diameter and at least 43 others of varying sizes. The main runway was 1,580 yards long with two others at 1,130 and 1,090 yards in length, making the airfield capable of receiving all of the main aircraft types of the day and, potentially, of becoming a diversion airfield later on in the war. Initially, they were grass but were later replaced by more durable concrete. Silloth also had a pair of Q decoy airfields constructed at Pelutho and West Newton, both south of Silloth on the Aspatria road. These were meant to attract enemy bombers away from the main airfield.

The unit that would occupy Silloth for many years to come was formed on the same day as the airfield's official opening date, 5th June 1939. 22 MU was a civilian-manned aircraft storage unit (ASU) under the control of 41 (Maintenance) Group. As its name implies, the unit's main task was the storage and preparation of aircraft for front-line operations. 22 MU's first commanding officer, Sqn Ldr A Connock, was posted to Silloth back in April but he later relinquished command to Gp Capt. J W B Grigson DSO, DFC on 3rd September 1939.

The first aircraft to arrive at 22 MU was a de Havilland Dragon, on 14th September. This was followed by a multitude of different aircraft including the Airspeed Oxford, Blackburn Skua, Supermarine Spitfire, Hawker Hurricane, de Havilland Gipsy Moth, Hawker Audax, Miles Mentor, Avro Anson, Vickers Wellington, Percival Vega Gull, Lockheed Hudson, Vickers Vildebeest and North American Harvard before the year was out.

A variety of aircraft flooded into Silloth including several obsolete types such as this Vickers Vildebeest.

Fleet Air Arm types were also catered for, such as the Blackburn Shark.

When war was declared, all civilian-operated aircraft were either grounded or impressed into military service. Several Percival Vega Gulls were prepped by 22 MU for service with the RAF.

Several Wellington Is from 215 Squadron arrived on detachment from Basingbourn in Cambridgeshire from September through to November 1939. The bombers were using Silloth as a forward operating airfield for air-to-air firing practice on one of the local ranges. The squadron caused Silloth's first flying accident, on 29th November. Wellington I L4388 swung on landing on wet grass and crashed into Wellington I L4389 from the same squadron. Neither aircraft flew again, L4389 going on to become a ground instructional airframe.

A visit by senior staff from Coastal Command in late September described Silloth as an excellent location for teaching aircrew general reconnaissance techniques. On 1st November 1939, Silloth was transferred to 17 (Training) Group Coastal Command, whose HQ was at Fort Grange, Gosport in Hampshire. This effectively made 22 MU a lodger unit but no less important.

The same day, the Coastal Command Landplane Pilots' Pool was formed to train crews and provide a reservoir of aircraft for front line Coastal Command squadrons. Within a few days of its formation, the pool had ten Ansons, six Hudsons, five Bothas and four Beauforts on strength. The first Hudson Conversion Course began on 7th December, with additional courses before the year's end.

Silloth became one of many outstations for Cunliffe-Owen Aircraft Limited from the end of November 1940. Cunliffe-Owen was one of 43 companies which were working for the newly formed Civilian Repair Organisation (CRO) and they took over one of Silloth's large 'D' Type hangars. This complex organisation was formed at the outbreak of the Second World War to relieve the pressure on RAF units and aircraft manufacturers responsible for aircraft repair work. Scottish Aviation Limited, as part of the CRO network, also used a single hangar at Silloth from the summer of 1941.

The Coastal Command Landplane Pilots' Pool was redesignated No1 (Coastal) Operational Training Unit (OTU) on 1st April 1940. 1 OTU continued the Hudson conversion courses and added similar ones on the Anson, Blenheim and Beaufort. The last three aircraft types were the catalysts for Nos 2, 3 and 5 (Coastal) OTUs, who were yet to form. A bombing range was specifically built at Mawbray Bank for the use of 1 OTU, complete with observation towers and large concrete arrow-shaped markers leading to the targets. During this time of high enemy activity around the coast of Britain, fully armed aircraft were always on standby to support the front-line squadrons. From 1 OTU's formation, a single Avro Anson was permanently bombed-up in case of an emergency. The only time it was called out was on 15th July 1940

The long association between the Lockheed Hudson and Silloth began with the formation of the Coastal Command Landplane Pilots Pool in November 1939.

when the Workington harbour master reported a submarine off the coast. After a lengthy search, the Anson returned to Silloth empty handed.

By the end of May 1940, 22 MU had 271 aircraft on the airfield and eleven hangars were occupied. Personnel strength, both military and civilian, was still too low for such a unit, with only five RAF officers, five airmen and 229 civilians working for 22 MU. The unit sent a signal to HQ 41 Group on 17th May, requesting an additional 36 aircraft fitters, 67 engine fitters, 26 armourers, four wireless mechanics, 24 electrical fitters and ten trained stores personnel. 41 Group responded quickly, recognising the importance of 22 MU by sending 123 civilian personnel just two days later. The remainder of the request was completed by 29th May with the arrival of more civilian staff.

By June 1940, 22 MU aircraft holdings surpassed 300 for the first time. The most common aircraft type to be seen was the Wellington, many of which were parked out in the open around the edge of the airfield. Unusual aircraft continued to arrive, including a Savio-Marchetti in May, a twin-engine Percival Q6 and a de Havilland Flamingo, both in June 1940.

With so many aircraft out in the open it was not long before Silloth drew the unhealthy attentions of the Luftwaffe. On 15th July 1940, just before 01:00hrs, a yellow air raid warning signalled. Approximately 150 bombs were dropped by an enemy aircraft to the south of the airfield. The nearest bomb fell approximately 550 yards from a picketed Wellington. The bombs were described as being of 'heavy calibre' with parachutes attached, which would indicate a marine type mine. The airfield and its aircraft were lucky because only the wing of a Wellington was slightly damaged by splinters. This raid prompted the senior staff of 22 MU to consider dispersing the aircraft over a wider area around the airfield. More fields were requisitioned with more dispersal areas being constructed on the northern and southern sides of the airfield.

During July 1940, enemy activity increased in the area. Air raid warning yellows (subsequently purple) were received by the unit on twelve occasions between 14th and 31st July. Ten of the warnings were at night. Only one, on 15th July, was a red, although no bombs were dropped on Silloth. The work on the new dispersals was being hurried during this period and by 31st July good progress was being made on the hangars on the new 'E' and 'F' dispersal sites. Aircraft out in the open at this time were 38 Wellingtons, 13 Ansons, 11 Bothas and a single Heyford. In response to the enemy activity, a combined Army and RAF guard was introduced on all sites by night and arrangements were put in place to implement a fire picket on each site at night as well. More dispersal areas were chosen on 30th August when Wg Cdr Shaw visited from 41 Group. He selected an even wider area for a further 20 Blister type hangars at a minimum distance of one mile from the airfield. Natural camouflage in the shape of farm buildings and trees helped to disguise these areas.

Another raid by the Luftwaffe was carried out in the early hours of 25th September 1940. At 01:30 hrs an air raid warning yellow was in operation when a pair of high explosive, incendiary and oil bombs were dropped by at least one enemy aircraft in the vicinity of the airfield. The HE bombs were 250 kgs in size and the incendiaries were mainly the magnesium type, weighing in at two or three pounds each. The two HE bombs fell within the perimeter of the aerodrome, one about 150 yards east of the eastern most hangar on 'C' site and the other near hangars on 'B' site. Damage was caused to a farm approximately three-quarters of a mile east of the 'F' site dispersal, otherwise no harm was caused to the unit's personnel or aircraft.

This particular air raid could possibly be blamed on the Royal Aircraft Establishment (RAE), who were experimenting with flares from the airfield. The RAE were looking into various ways of illuminating enemy bombers at night. One method was to fit high powered flares on bomb racks under the wings of a Handley Page Hampden. The Hampden followed a black-painted Whitley bomber (acting as the enemy) but when the RAE operator ignited a flare, the Hampden pilot was blinded by the bright reflection from his own propeller blades. The flare was designed to last for three and half minutes; so the pilot told the Whitley to dive out of the way to avoid a collision. On the very first experiment, the flares emitted so much light that Silloth and the surrounding countryside were highly visible. The enemy bomber was attracted to the scene like a moth to a lamp and the RAE were politely encouraged to experiment over somebody else's airfield!

A detachment from 320 Squadron, based at Leuchars in Fife, arrived at Silloth in October. The squadron was first formed on 1st June 1940 at Pembroke Dock in Pembrokeshire using Fokker T VIIIe/G patrol seaplanes. These were evacuated from the Netherlands when the Germans invaded and sufficient numbers arrived to form 320 Squadron. When spares ran out, the squadron converted to the Avro Anson, which it brought to Silloth in preparation for conversion again to the Lockheed Hudson. Whilst at Silloth, all of the squadron's crews were converted to flying the Hudson, which served with the unit until March 1943. At the end of hostilities, 320 Squadron was transferred to the Royal Netherlands Navy, where it still serves today, flying another Lockheed aircraft, the P-3C Orion.

Silloth's last brush with the enemy came on the morning of 24th October 1940. A yellow air raid warning was already in place when a single enemy aircraft dropped a large bomb, estimated to be 2,000 lbs in size, near to what was known as the 'cemetery' site on the southern side of the airfield. The device, which was possibly attached to a parachute, left a large crater in a nearby field but once again there was no damage to Air Ministry personnel or property.

When the airfield was transferred to Coastal Command, Gp Capt. Grigson became Silloth's station commander, while Sqn Ldr Connock was returned to his original position of OC 22 MU. On 4th November, Sqn Ldr Connock was posted to 29 MU at High Ercall, Shropshire and was replaced by Wg Cdr D W Dean.

1 OTU was reorganised during November 1940, with various detachments and flights being incorporated into other Coastal OTUs. A detachment of seven Hudsons, at Speke was transferred to 2 (Coastal) OTU at Catfoss in North Yorkshire on 1st November.

'B' Flight, which operated a few dual control Beauforts, was transferred to 3 (Coastal) OTU at Chivenor in Devon on 27th November. The following day, 'E' Flight, with six Ansons, was also transferred to Devon. 1 OTU also hosted a training flight of Wellingtons and Whitleys at Silloth from November 1940 through to May 1941. Kirkbride was used as an RLG for this flight, which went on to form part of 3 OTU as well.

One fascinating device that was actually developed at the airfield was the Silloth Trainer. The brainchild of Wg Cdr G B Iles, the device was designed for the training of all members of aircrew and was primarily a type familiarization trainer for learning drills and the handling of malfunctions. As well as the basic flying behaviour, all engine, electric and hydraulic systems were simulated. An instructor's panel was provided to enable monitoring of the crew and for deliberately inserting malfunctions. Many of the parts inside the Silloth

1 (Coastal) OTU operated several types of aircraft, including the Bristol Beaufort, seen here in Coastal Command markings.

Trainer were made from piano parts, and at least fourteen were built specifically for OTUs.

By February 1941, construction work on the airfield was virtually complete. The personnel strength of 22 MU was very healthy, with 11 RAF officers, 19 airmen and 755 civilians (the actual establishment was 802). 210 aircraft were on the airfield and the first of 22 MU's Satellite Landing Grounds (SLG) was nearing completion. No 9 SLG at Hornby Hall received its first aircraft on 17th March 1941. Not only did this relieve the storage pressures at Silloth but it also expanded the dispersal capability of the unit. 22 MU gained a second SLG at Hutton-in-the-Forest on the 1st June. 50 (Maintenance) Wing (Northern) was re-formed at Silloth on 21st April to take over the Northern Region of increasing maintenance units. The wing moved to Hutton Hall on 1st June.

1 OTU was also growing in size; by May 1941, the unit could boast a fleet of nearly 50 Hudsons, eight Ansons, eight Oxfords and five Battle target tugs. The unit was now officially recognised as a dedicated Hudson training unit and the accident rate took a steep upward turn to reflect this. On 3rd May, Hudson I T9361 hit the main runway too hard, the undercarriage collapsed and the aircraft caught fire. The next day Hudson I N7304 stalled and spun into the Solway Firth, not far from the airfield. This last occurrence was so common that the Solway Firth was renamed 'Hudson Bay'!

Col Carr, the commanding officer of the 3rd Cumberland (Carlisle) Home Guard visited Silloth to discuss the potential formation of a new unit. With so many civilians working on the airfield, it was suggested that the new unit be called Silloth Company 3rd Cumberland (Carlisle) Home Guard. Three days later, Wg Cdr Dean lectured all areas of 22 MU about the formation of the new Home Guard unit and appealed for volunteers. The following day, 162 enrolled and by the end of the month the new company had 175 on strength. A 200-yard rifle range at Grune Point was also made available for the new Home Guard unit, which shared the many guard duities around the airfield.

Throughout the summer of 1941, 22 MU prepared a large variety of aircraft for many front-line squadrons. Aircraft included the Hurricane I and II, Wellington Ic, Hudson III and V, Battle, tropicalised versions of the Blenheim IV for the Middle East and several Swordfish. The diversity of the aircraft required specialist sections located at various points around the airfield, almost like autonomous units within the main 22 MU.

22 MU received its first American-built fighter on 21st November

1941. A batch of Bell P-39 Airacobras, known as the Airacobra I, arrived at 22 MU for preparation with 601 County of London Squadron. The 601 Squadron pilots found numerous flaws and weaknesses during their initial work-up with the Airacobra and the Spitfire quickly replaced it. Many of the Airacobras prepped by 22 MU were transferred to the USAAF.

Between November 1941 and March 1942, the accident rate of 1 OTU continued to climb. The unit lost an incredible 17 Hudsons and a single Oxford, three more of the Hudsons crashed into the Solway Firth. One particular accident involved Hudson I T9308 on 31st January. During a low flying exercise, the pilot went too low and crashed into a house at Corby, four miles east of Carlisle. Several Hudsons were lost in take-off and landing accidents, including Hudson II T9383 on 24th February. On landing, the aircraft collided with Hudson N7307 from the same unit and the fire that quickly followed destroyed both aircraft.

Silloth's location meant that it could boast a very good weather record making it a potentially good diversion airfield. Prestwick in Ayrshire was the final destination point for the Atlantic Ferry Organisation and, by the end of the Second World War, over 37,000 aircraft landed at the Scottish airfield. It was envisaged that many of these aircraft would make use of Silloth if the weather was poor at Prestwick. Three B-24 Liberators did land at Silloth on 12th December 1941 and a few months later an American officer visited the airfield to discuss the possibility of many more arriving. However, Prestwick also enjoyed a good weather record and Silloth was only occasionally used for diversions.

22 MU was being prepared for the largest aircraft so far to arrive at Silloth. The American-built Consolidated Liberator transformed Coastal Command's ability to perform long-range patrols over the Atlantic. The first aircraft arrived at the beginning of 1942 and on 11th January, Sqn Ldr P J Field Richards arrived from HQ 41 Group to flight test and demonstrate the aircraft to the pilots of 22 MU. A few weeks later two of the unit's test pilots, Flt Lt R H Ashton and Flt Sgt R M Redy left Silloth for 1427 Flight at Thruxton in Hampshire for a Liberator conversion course. One of the tasks that 22 MU carried out on the Liberator was the installation of gun turrets and their associated weapons. Liberator AL531 was the first aircraft to have this work completed, on 23rd April 1942. It was then dispatched to Scottish Aviation at Prestwick in Ayrshire before joining a front-line squadron.

Another American arrived on 13th May 1942 in the shape of the Lockheed Ventura. The influx of aircraft at this time, which included a new line of Airspeed Oxfords, warranted an extension of overtime hours for the civilian staff. Overtime work on operational and non-operational aircraft, which were about to be allotted, was extended to 21:00hrs.

24 Hudsons from 1 OTU were detached to Thornaby in North Yorkshire on 25th May 1942. Each aircraft was armed with four 250 lb bombs and the plan was for the Hudson to take part in Bomber Command's first 'Thousand-Bomber' raid to Cologne on 30th/31st May 1942. The hopes of gaining operational experience so soon in their flying careers were dashed for the aircrews when their participation in the raid was cancelled and they returned to Silloth. A second detachment of 24 Hudsons returned to Thornaby and, this time, all took part in attacks on coastal targets while the second 'Thousand-Bomber' raid took place over Bremen. One aircraft failed to return, with the loss of all on board.

The civilian strength of 22 MU decreased significantly throughout the summer of 1942 as more of the staff were being called up for military service. This came at a time when more types of aircraft were being flown into Silloth, including the first Boeing Fortress, on 5th June 1942. The RAF's first experience with the Fortress I of Bomber Command was a bad one and they were sceptical about using the type again. By now, the RAF had the Lancaster and Halifax as their strategic bombers and looked at using the new Fortress IIA with Coastal Command. It was a role that suited the aircraft and it became popular with its crews because of its good armament and long range, combined with good reliability.

Liberators began to fill every available piece of dispersal space around the airfield and, in July, unsuccessful flight tests were carried out at the SLGs to see if they were suitable to accept the large bomber. Problems were also being encountered by 22 MU with the preparation of the Ventura. A specialist RAF Aircraft Service Party was brought in on 6th July and an additional civilian working party on 13th July. The party was from Lockheed's factory at Speke on Merseyside and had the specific task of removing the Ventura fuel tanks, which were being sent to Goodyears at Wolverhampton for modification. Problems beyond 22 MU's remit continued and another specialist party from Pratt and Witney arrived to carry out modifications on the Ventura's engines on 31st July. Problems with engines continued into September, when difficulty was experienced actually running the engines. Eventually, all technical difficulties were resolved and several of the Venturas which passed through Silloth went on to see limited front-line service.

The Lockheed Ventura was one of many American built types handled by 22 MU.

Longtown was used by 1 OTU from 7th July for night flying and, by the middle of August 1942, the unit was at its maximum strength. 68 Hudsons, 24 Ansons and Oxfords and eight Lysander target tugs could be seen on the airfield. The number of Hudsons was reduced by two on 20th August when a pair collided over the Solway Firth. Hudson I T9723 and AE646 were carrying out formation practice when they came together with the loss of 12 aircrew.

The first North American Mustang fighter was received by 22 MU on 3rd August 1942, followed by the first Fairchild Argus on 7th September. Both aircraft were straightforward to prepare for front-line service; several of the Mustangs went on to equip home-based squadrons. The Argus was a utility transport and communications aircraft, known as the UC-61 Forwarder in the USA. Under the Lend-Lease scheme, about 670 of these aircraft served with the RAF and the Air Transport Auxiliary (ATA) and many are airworthy today, including a handful in the United Kingdom.

On the evening of 21st September, a fire broke out inside the 'D' Type hangar being used by Cunliffe-Owen. A Hudson was completely destroyed in the fire but negligible damage was caused to the hangar. The airfield's fire section was praised for its prompt action, which prevented several other aircraft from being damaged.

The water tower at Silloth remains in good condition: the water gauge on the outside of the building still registers. (Author)

A signal was received from HQ 41 Group on 1st October 1942 requesting 22 MU to begin conversion of all Hurricanes to tropical standard. The changes to the aircraft were the fitting of a Vokes carburettor intake filter, which slotted under the nose of the fighter, and an additional water tank for cooling, which was fitted behind the cockpit. All marks of Hurricane could be converted, although at the time 22 MU were holding the Hurricane IIB and IIC. For two days, a shop foreman and several aircraft fitters were sent to 48 MU to study the methods involved in carrying out the tropical conversion. A new line specifically for the conversions was set up, and over the next few days several representatives arrived from the Hawker Aircraft Company. On 17th October the first fully converted aircraft, Hurricane IIB HW358, left Silloth for front-line service, followed by many more over the next few months.

The personnel and workforce of Silloth were distracted by the sound of 92 Wright cyclone engines on 23rd October. The engines belonged to 23 Boeing B-17s which were being ferried from Iceland, only to find Prestwick closed because of poor weather. All landed safely, leaving for their final destination later that day. Other diverted American visitors included a Douglas C-54 Skymaster on 3rd July 1943 and 13 Republic P-47 Thunderbolts on 29th October 1943 en route to Warton in Lancashire.

The Air Ministry sent out a memorandum on 31st December 1942 calling up employees between the ages of 18 and 25 for service with the forces. Previously the unit had managed to cope with the initial wave of volunteers but the compulsory call-up would hit 22 MU hard when this group of employees departed. The unit took steps to try and cover the possibility of losing several staff by introducing a scheme for the training of juveniles. On 2nd Januray 1943, 22 MU received the authority from HQ 41 Group to engage personnel for training in aircraft trades to fill established vacancies and to cover the employees most likely to be called to the Services.

The majority of aircraft prepared by the unit left the airfield by air but a rushed instruction from HQ 14 Group on 6th January needed several Hurricances to be despatched by road. After the order was received at 15:00hrs, 14 Hurricane IICs were rapidly dismantled and packed ready for the road journey to 215 MU at Tinwald Downs, Dumfries, prior to their dispatch by sea to India. The staff of 22 MU worked through the night and all of the fighters were ready by 06:00.hrs the following morning. A similar order was received the following day and once again the efficient workforce prepared the Hurricanes in record time.

The first of several new types arrived on the 15th January in the shape of the Hurricane IV. This particular mark of Hurricane had an uprated Merlin XX 24 or 27 engine and additional armour plate and was fitted with 'universal' wings, capable of carrying bombs, cannon or eight rockets.

Stinson Reliants started arriving from 7th February, followed by the very rare Brewster Bermuda on 18th February. Known as the SB2 Buccaneer in service with the US Navy, the Bermuda was a single-engined scout bomber and the RAF took delivery of a few under the terms of the Lend-Lease scheme in 1942. All were relegated to training and target towing duties and several passed through 22 MU.

The flow of trained Hudson aircrews from overseas OTUs was on the increase by early 1943. 1 OTU's role at Silloth and its long association with Silloth was coming to an end. The attrition rate of the unit had been incredibly high: over 60 aircraft had been lost in flying accidents, the vast majority were Hudsons. On 10th August, 1 OTU moved to Thornaby in North Yorkshire and that airfield's main unit, 6 OTU, moved into Silloth. Both units' departure was completed by the next day and Silloth also gained a new station commander, Gp Capt. R Halley DFC, AFC.

6 OTU was originally formed within 11 Group, Fighter Command on 6th March 1940 at Sutton Bridge in Lincolnshire, tasked with the training of fighter pilots. Disbanded on 1st November 1940, it re-formed as a Blenheim unit, only to be absorbed into 42 OTU in July 1941. The following day, the unit re-formed again at Thornaby, initially equipped with Hudsons specialising in training General Reconnaissance crews. The Hudsons gave way to Wellingtons in October 1942 and around the same time the unit absorbed a Polish training flight from 18 OTU and the following month 1429 Czech Flight. These two flights were to provide crews for the two Wellington squadrons within Coastal Command crewed by nationals of the two countries.

6 OTU's occupation of the airfield reduced the available space for the dispersal of 22 MU aircraft to a minimum. The OTU was equipped with six different marks of Wellington. 25 were marks VII, XI and XIII, plus 22 marks IC, III and X, the last being the most prolific variant in RAF service at the time. The unit also had 18 Ansons and Oxfords plus five Lysander target tugs.

22 MU gained a new commanding officer on 14th April 1943 when Wg Cdr Starling was posted to the Air Ministry. His replacement was Wg Cdr N W Law and one of his first tasks was to make 22 MU a specialist in the preparation of the Hurricane and Sea Hurricane. Although aircraft types being held by the unit at the time included the Anson, Botha, Hudson, Mustang and Oxford, the Hurricane was the most prolific, great emphasis being placed on despatching them to overseas locations. By the middle of 1943, 22 MU's holding, including those held on the SLGs, totalled 437 aircraft!

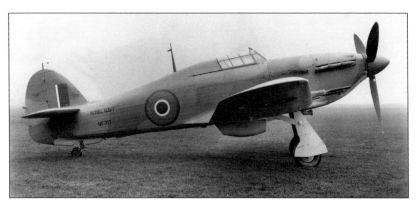

22 MU became a specialist in the Hurricane and Sea Hurricane in April 1943. An example of a Sea Hurricane is pictured.

6 OTU continued the previous unit's tradition of crashing aircraft into the Solway Firth when the unit lost its first aircraft from Silloth on 24th April. The pilot of Wellington X HE496 lost control when the twin-engined bomber caught fire, entered a spin and crashed into the sea. The Czech flight of 6 OTU was disbanded on 31st August 1943. The unit was supplying trained aircrew to 311 (Czech) Squadron, operating the Wellington, but as this unit was re-equipping with the Liberator, the flight was surplus to requirements. The Polish flight was transferred to 3 (Coastal) OTU at Haverfordwest in Pembrokeshire on 5th October, leaving the main unit to concentrate on Leigh light training. The Leigh light was a powerful 22 million candle power searchlight, 24 inches in diameter, fitted to Coastal Command aircraft to help them to spot surfaced German U-boats at night. It was successfully used from June 1942 onwards to attack U-boats recharging their batteries on the surface at night. The aircraft would approach the submarine using its air-to-surface radar, switching on the searchlight at the last moment to catch the submarine stranded on the surface. With no time to dive, the U-Boat was effectively a sitting duck. The Leigh light was so successful that the German submarines were forced to switch to daytime battery charging, giving the crew some time to spot an aircraft approaching. After the introduction of the Leigh light Allied shipping losses caused by U-Boat attacks fell from 600,000 to 200,000 tons per month.

Leigh light training became a prominent part of 6 OTUs training programme as well as training crews for all Wellington GR (ground attack and reconnaissance) squadrons at home and abroad. The unit took over the Leigh light training commitment from 3 (Coastal) OTU on 4th January 1944, making 6 OTU the specialist on this equipment for Wellington crews. More room for training was created when Longtown and Kirkbride were made available for the increasingly busy activities of 6 OTU. Great Orton took over as the unit's satellite airfield in June 1944, remaining in this role until 6 OTU's departure.

By March 1944, 6 OTU had lost 12 aircraft in flying accidents and this reflected the number of aircraft on strength. Ten dual control Wellington ICs, IIIs and Xs, three Wellington XIIIs, 20 Wellington XIIs and XIVs, two Oxfords and five Miles Martinet Target Tugs made up the units serviceable aircraft.

22 MU was no less busy; its aircraft-holding reached a new record on 31st March 1944 with 515 aircraft held at Silloth and the two SLGs. The main reason for this peak in aircraft was the arrival at short notice of 75 P-51D Mustangs from fighter squadrons of the USAAF, all flown in by American pilots. The Mustangs were prepared and transferred to RAF squadrons within a matter of weeks, redesignated the Mustang IV.

The build up to the Allied invasion of Europe was one of the busiest periods of 22 MU's history. During April 1944 alone, 222 types of various aircraft were received and 152 were dispatched. Hangar space was becoming a rare commodity and it became necessary to store wooden aircraft in the open. As a result, these aircraft had to be carefully watched for signs of deterioration and wing covers were placed over the more vulnerable aircraft, particularly the Avro Anson. Many aircraft suffered because of heavy rains followed by frost and thaw. A simple wooden trimmer tab on a Mustang was overlooked on one occasion. The offending tab disintegrated in flight and caused the fighter to force-land; it was later confirmed that moisture in the wood had contributed to the incident.

Such was the large number of aircraft movements at Silloth that the main runway had to undergo emergency repairs in July. The two shorter runways continued to cope with the influx of aircraft; the month still managed to produce a wartime record of 740 aircraft held by 22 MU. Repairs continued into September when the airfield was closed from 23rd September to 1st October. Work on the intersections of the runways did not stop; three aircraft urgently required were still flown out of Silloth to Kirkbride by 22 MU test pilots.

Throughout November 1944 an unusually high amount of rain fell on the area, making maintenance very difficult on Silloth's open dispersals. It was reported that the hard standings at the dispersal points were under as much as three to four inches of water and the surrounding fields were flooded. The floors of the Robin and Super Robin Blister hangars were also covered in two to three inches of water, making working conditions very difficult for the civilian staff.

The work of Scottish Aviation was drawing to a close by the beginning of 1945. The D Type hangar they had occupied since the summer of 1941 was returned to 22 MU for the preparation of aircraft in February 1945. A second C Type hangar, also used by Scottish Aviation, was returned to 22 MU on 21st April 1945, bringing to an end the association between the company and Silloth.

Large numbers of Liberators arrived at Silloth in March. 24 of the four-engined bombers arrived during the month; 14 were stored and ten others were non-effective, awaiting major spares which would probably not arrive before the end of the war. To cope with the influx of Liberators, 6 OTU allocated a spare dispersal to 22 MU to cope with the new arrivals. Once an aircraft arrived, it was immediately towed into a hangar for checking and preparation for storage, which was normally in one of the more distant dispersal areas.

In order to keep on top of the increased workload, a 48-hour working week was introduced from 23rd April 1945. Overtime was worked as necessary and all focus by 22 MU was now on preparing aircraft for storage rather than operational service.

6 OTU's time at Silloth came to an end on 18th July 1945 when the unit moved to Kinloss in Morayshire. The unit left many of its Wellingtons behind at Silloth because 6 OTU's equipment was set to change to the Warwick and eventually the Avro Lancaster. The ex 6 OTU Wellingtons left at Silloth were transferred to 12 MU at Kirkbride and 8 MU at Little Rissington in Gloucestershire; both units were specialists in the type.

A Gloster Meteor became the first jet to land at Silloth on 11th August 1945. It was refuelled under special arrangements and departed later in the day. Later in the month, 22 MU became a specialist holding for the de Havilland Mosquito. The first of many arrived on 20th August.

With 6 OTU's departure, Coastal Command had no more use for Silloth and just as the airfield had been in 1939, it was returned to Maintenance Command with 22 MU as the main unit again. The strength of the unit had been bolstered by the influx of several hundred airmen returning from duty overseas. It was also expected that a high number of civilian staff would apply to leave the unit when the war in the Far East ended. When VJ Day arrived on 15th August the unit celebrated like so many others and public holidays were granted. Several civilian staff did apply to leave 22 MU, but the number was considerably less than expected.

A detachment of four Vultee Vengeance target tugs and three Spitfire LFIXs of 1353 Flight arrived on 1st October 1945. Based at West Freugh in Wigtownshire, the flight worked closely with the RAF Anti-Aircraft Gunnery School at Netheravon in Wiltshire. The flight returned to West Freugh in January 1946.

Peacetime resulted in the disbandment of the Air Transport Auxiliary (ATA), which had dispatched and delivered hundreds of aircraft to and from Silloth. There was still a large amount of ferry work to perform and, to cope with this, the RAF formed their own units. No5 Ferry Pool (FP) was formed at Silloth on 15th October 1945, specifically to work for 22 MU. The pool was under the command of acting Sqn Ldr G R Duffy AFC and the unit flew a variety of aircraft, including the Anson, Argus, Dominie, Proctor, Barracuda, Warwick and Mosquito. Their workload remained sufficiently high for the FP to remain busy for another five years, until its disbandment on 25th May 1950.

The airfield began to steadily shrink in size during the latter part of 1945. Local houses, which had been requisitioned at the beginning of the war, were handed back to their original owners. Various portions

The Motor Transport Pool, just one of many buildings that still survive at this well equipped airfield. (Author)

Aircrew of all nations lie side by side in the cemetery to the south of the airfield. There are 56 graves of airmen who did not make it through their flying training at Silloth. (Author)

of land used for distant dispersal areas were also released to their original owners, who quickly returned them to agriculture.

The bulk of post-war work carried out by 22 MU was the mass scrapping of various aircraft. A few of the aircraft scrapped included the York, Mosquito, Dakota, Lancaster, Twin Pioneer, Chipmunk, various Austers, Attacker, Firebrand, untold Ansons and many more. Aircraft were stripped of all useful components and the bare fuselages were passed on to High-Duty Alloys at Distington for the recovery of aluminium. High-Duty was a shadow factory during the Second World War, producing a variety of aircraft components. 22 MU stored many other aircraft, which were refurbished, and either dispatched to foreign air forces or sold onto the civilian market.

In 1954, a handful of airworthy Lancasters descended upon Silloth for the making of a classic war film. Several scenes from *The Dambusters* starring Richard Todd and Michael Redgrave, were filmed at the airfield. Bristol Type 170 Freighters of Manx Airlines briefly operated from the airfield in 1956 and, in late 1960, the last military flight left the airfield. 22 MU's long history ended at Silloth on 31st December 1960 and despite the end of the war 15 years previously, many of the original civilian staff had remained to the end.

Industry is now the main occupant of Silloth, in the many hangars and buildings that are still in place today. Original surviving buildings include the guardroom, station headquarters, motor pool, stores and many more. All three runways, perimeter tracks and dispersals remain, making the airfield feel as though the RAF's departure was not so long ago.

18
WATH HEAD

With the local maintenance units overflowing with aircraft, the humble Satellite Landing Ground (SLG) was rapidly becoming the most important airfield in northern Cumbria. Wath Head, which was also known as Jenkins Cross, proved itself invaluable for the dispersal of aircraft throughout the Second World War.

Work began in late 1940 on an additional SLG for 12 MU at Kirkbride, just south of the A595, three miles east of Wigton. It was first inspected on 16th December 1940 by the commanding officer of 12 MU, Wg Cdr Mitchell, accompanied by Kirkbride's Senior Engineering Officer (SEO). There was still much more work to be done on the landing ground and Wg Cdr Mitchell and 12 MU's Chief Test Pilot visited again on 15th March 1941. The SLG was still found to be unfit for use, but pressure on local contractors meant that a test take-off and landing could be carried out on 23rd March. Two successful landings were made by a 12 MU test pilot in an Avro Anson. The SLG was pronounced fit for use.

On 7th April 1941, No10 SLG Wath Head was brought into operation for the first time when a handful of Handley Page Hampdens arrived for dispersal. Several others followed and by the end of April, 36 aircraft had arrived at the SLG, creating valuable room at Kirkbride.

Defence of the SLG was the main point of discussion when Air Com. C H Edmonds DSO, OBE and Gp Capt. Rowe of HQ Maintenance Command visited on 16th April. The subject continued to be overlooked throughout 1941, with consideration given only for the siting of a pair of machine gun posts in September. It took until November for Sqn Ldr Edgley from 12 MU to approve the sites.

Between May and September 1941, exactly 300 aircraft passed

The first aircraft to descend upon Wath Head was the Handley Page Hampden.

through Wath Head without incident. Camouflage was always a big problem and, during an aerial inspection by Wg Cdr Mitchell on 1st July, Wath Head's aircraft were easily distinguishable.

Exceptionally heavy rain in October and the failure of the SLG's drainage system resulted in Wath Head closing between 22nd and 29th October. Emergency repair work was swiftly carried out but not before senior staff, including the officer commanding 50 Wing, arrived at the SLG to oversee the work. Gp Capt. Hanson Abbott inspected the runway on 1st November, declaring the SLG open for business once again.

Heavy snow in late January and early February closed the SLG from 1st to 5th February 1942. This was followed by another period of poor weather in early March, which closed Wath Head again. This did not stop Flt Lt Farquharson, a 12 MU test pilot, from carrying out several test take-offs and landings in a Handley Page Halifax in mid February 1942. The SLG was found to be perfectly satisfactory for the dispersal of the big four-engined bomber and a few additional huts were built to accommodate a Halifax maintenance party.

The risk of sabotage was quite high for any unit that had large quantities of aircraft dispersed and limited resources available to protect them. At the time a detachment of men from the 30th Battalion, Manchester Regiment, was responsible for the security of the site. Wath Head was particularly susceptible and a case was reported relating to 'interference with a Wellington aircraft' in early February 1942. In response, a sergeant and corporal from the Provost Marshal Department of the Air Ministry arrived to investigate on 5th February.

The two airmen departed the next day, no wiser as to who the culprit was. The incident was serious enough for Wg Cdr Mitchell to replace both the Officer Commanding and Engineering Officer of the SLG.

After Wg Cdr Mitchell's aerial inspection back in July 1941, he repeated the exercise on 4th May 1942, hoping to see an improvement. Personnel at the SLG had put in a lot of work improving the camouflage of the dispersed aircraft and the effect must have been evident, as Wg Cdr Mitchell praised the work carried out. There was still room for improvement and the task would become even harder when the Halifaxes began to arrive.

The Halifax was now arriving at Kirkbride in large numbers and, with Wath Head full of Wellingtons, an alternative had to found. 9 SLG at Hornby Hall was allocated for use by 12 MU, but this SLG was incapable of handling the larger Halifax. However, it could handle the Wellington and from 9th May they were moved from Wath Head to Hornby Hall to create room for the Halifax. The first Halifax arrived from Kirkbride on 12th May 1942 with additional fire-fighting equipment brought in for the occasion. The usual practice was for the local fire brigade to attend any incident that occurred at an SLG.

Accidents at Wath Head were rare and the first did not happen until 19th May. Flt Sgt I K Arber in Botha I W5051 was at the point of take-off when one of the aircraft's Bristol Perseus engines failed. Arber

Despite its size, the Handley Page Halifax landed at Wath Head without any trouble.

immediately crash-landed the Botha back onto the landing strip, a dry stone wall bringing the aircraft to an abrupt halt. Arber managed to get himself out of the wrecked Botha, escaping with just minor injuries. He was admitted to Fusehill Military Hospital in Carlisle and was pleasantly surprised to receive a visit from Wg Cdr Mitchell that evening.

The risk of fire at dispersed sites was high, particularly those which made use of existing woodland to conceal aircraft. The National Fire Service (NFS) at Carlisle had noted this after a recent inspection. Divisional Officer Williams from Carlisle thought it was essential for the SLG to have an immediate supply of water so as to tackle a fire before the NFS arrived. In response, a 5,000-gallon water tank was erected and in place, ready for use on 30th May 1942. Two weeks later, the chief regional fire officer, J H Fordham, visited the SLG to discuss the new firefighting arrangements. Thankfully, no major outbreak of fire occurred but at least the SLG was better prepared.

Camouflage of the SLG was continually improved throughout 1942. The commanding officer of Kirkbride was still not happy with the SLG's high visibility from the air during yet another aerial inspection on 4th June. It was decided that camouflage hedges should be put in place across the landing strip so as to break up its appearance. This was a very effective method of detracting the eye from the straight lines that can reveal a runway.

On 26th June, the first North American Mitchell arrived at Kirkbride for storage. Wath Head was expected to provide dispersal space for the twin-engine bomber and Plt Off. Heathwood arrived by air from Kirkbride on 4th July to inspect the SLG's suitability. Heathwood found Wath Head to be unsuitable for the tricycle undercarriage of the Mitchell and an alternative location was sought.

Despite the very effective camouflage now in place at Wath Head, a Hurricane from 55 OTU at Annan found the SLG without difficulty. The Hurricane made an emergency landing with suspected engine trouble on 24th August. Engineers at the SLG quickly solved the problem and the fighter returned to its home station without any further problem.

Aircraft dispersed at Wath Head began leaving for Kirkbride from early September 1942. The plan was to clear the SLG for the winter in order to carry out extension work on the runways. This would improve the capability of the SLG, allowing for a more varied selection of aircraft to be dispersed there.

The SLG closed down on 23rd September with only a maintenance

Large numbers of North American Mitchells were dispersed at Wath Head, the first landed there in March 1943.

party in charge and a reduced army detachment for night patrols around the site. The closure was short-lived because 39 SLG at Brayton had become completely water-logged and beyond use. Wath Head was re-opened on 1st November 1942 at 15:00hrs with Flg Off. H G Moss in command. At 15:15hrs, the first aircraft arrived for dispersal and both the landing strips and dispersal areas were dry and in excellent condition, much to the relief of 12 MU.

Responsibility for the security of Wath Head changed hands on 11th November 1942. A detachment of the RAF Regiment made up of two NCOs and 11 other ranks, arrived to take over the patrols and anti-sabotage duties. The detachment of the 30th Battalion, Manchester Regiment left the SLG for the last time on the 16th November.

Plans were being drawn up for several improvements to the SLG when Wg Cdr H Bassett Collins, the new commanding officer of 12 MU, arrived on 19th November. He was accompanied by Sqn Ldr Appleby from the Ministry of Aircraft Production (MAP), who had drawn up a scheme of constructing several hardstandings and access tracks into the dispersal fields. The SLG was also to be provided with concrete anchorage blocks and blast walls, and, for some reason, one of the external dispersal fields was planned for de-requistion. A canteen was planned for construction and a maintenance gang was brought in to improve the surface of the landing strip, which had a large 'bump' in the middle of it which needed levelling. The bulk of this work was carried out through the winter of 1942/43, with only the delivery of a few Halifaxes to disrupt the work to the SLG during this period.

After the improvements were completed, 12 MU again looked at testing a Mitchell at Wath Head. The tests were satisfactory and the first Mitchell landed at the SLG in March 1943. A large number of Mitchells passed through the SLG during 1943, the vast majority were prepared for squadron use and dispatched direct from Wath Head by Air Transport Auxiliary (ATA) pilots.

The problem of camouflage from the air reared its ugly head again during the spring of 1943, but this time it was not the fault of the SLG. An increasingly large number of Coastal Command aircraft were arriving for dispersal and their white and medium grey colours blended in with their local surroundings. They were, however, visible for miles from the air and special measures had to be introduced to conceal them. Literally tons of camouflage netting were delivered to Wath Head and after a liberal covering the brightly coloured aircraft could have been part of the flora and fauna.

1944 began with a change of ownership, 12 MU relinquishing control of Wath Head to 18 MU at Dumfries. The transfer took place on 12th January 1944, and, with Dumfries at bursting point, 43 Wellingtons flew into Wath Head over the next few weeks. Even this influx of aircraft, which was more than equalled at 18 MU's other landing ground, 27 SLG at Lennoxlove in Lothian, was not enough for Wg Cdr W H Dyson, the commanding officer of Dumfries. On 14th May, he put in a request to HQ 50 Wing that the maximum holding of aircraft at Wath Head be increased from 50 to 80. He also demanded an increase in personnel at the SLG to cope with the handling and maintenance of so many aircraft. At this stage of the Second World War, the enemy was perceived as being far away and camouflage of dispersed aircraft was becoming a lower priority. More aircraft were simply picketed out in the open, allowing for more to be crammed into Wath Head.

Poor weather resulted in Wath Head being water-logged and temporarily closed to aircraft on 25th November 1944. This continued through December and aircraft that did manage to leave the SLG caused a great deal of damage to the landing strips and dispersal areas. A similar situation was occurring at Lennoxlove, causing several 'target' orders to be missed by 18 MU.

With the war at an end in Europe and no demand in the Far East for the aircraft that were being stored by 18 MU, plans were put into place to wind down Wath Head. Air Comm. Ludlow, the officer commanding 41 Group Maintenance Command, visited Dumfries on 18th August 1945 to discuss the matter of reducing the aircraft holdings at both Wath Head and Lennoxlove. From 31st August 1945, the Wellingtons began to leave Wath Head and, with only a token maintenance crew left behind, 10 SLG Wath Head was officially closed down on 1st December 1945.

Very little remains at Wath Head today, the most significant building is the original guardroom and watch office, which was disguised as, and still looks like, a small bungalow. A few other rapidly decaying brick buildings are just clinging on. The landing ground and dispersal areas have been returned to agriculture.

19
WINDERMERE

Technically not an airfield, but still worthy of a chapter in this book is the Short Sunderland aircraft shadow-factory, which was constructed on the shoreline of Lake Windermere in mid 1942.

Production of the Sunderland flying boat was already in full swing at Short Brothers Ltd at Rochester in Kent, Belfast in Northern Ireland and the Blackburn Aircraft Company in Dumbarton, Strathclyde. But

35 Short Sunderlands were assembled at the shadow factory at White Cross Bay on the shores of Lake Windermere.

during 1940, these major factories were beginning to attract far too much attention from the Luftwaffe. Short Brothers looked for a remote location, far from enemy eyes, and found it in the heart of the Lake District, at Windermere. The lake, at 12 miles long, one mile wide and 220 ft deep, was more than adequate for the operation of large military flying boats such as the Sunderland.

A proposal for a shore factory was forwarded to Lord Beaverbrook, who, at the time, was the Minister of Aircraft Production. When the news of the factory reached the local population, the highly influential pressure group called 'The Friends of the Lake District' was appalled. The group's secretary, Revd H H Symonds wrote in their Annual Report for 1940 that the suggestion of a factory on the shores of Windermere was 'an abomination … which profanes the sanctuary and makes desolate a famous and frequented part of it'. The group had a century-long record of conserving the region's unspoiled beauty and had protested against seaplanes operating from the lake since before the First World War.

Confirmation of the proposal was sent in a secret letter from Lord Beaverbrook's office to the local MP, Mr Keeling. The main points of the letter read as follows:

My dear Keeling

You will remember coming to see me on deputation to ask that the Ministry should not erect a factory on the shores of Lake Windermere …

The product is a flying boat. A site on the edge of deep water is essential. We had a thorough search made and, indeed, that was resumed after I saw you … We sent a man to investigate at Lytham St Anne's. The mud-flats were our difficulty there.

We have, therefore, had to decide on Windermere. I am sorry. Time, however, is all important.

As leverage, Beaverbrook stated that the factory was being constructed as a temporary building and that when the necessary work, or the war, came to an end it would be completely dismantled. This was reluctantly agreed to by The Friends of the Lake District, enabling Short Brothers to proceed with the construction work.

The site of the factory was at Calgarth Park, one mile north-west of Windermere, on the edge of White Cross Bay. Construction of the factory on 28 acres of wood and farmland was swift. The main hangar had the distinction of being the biggest unsupported span in the country and was capable of housing nine Sunderlands. Along the main road to Troutbeck Bridge a prefabricated village was also constructed. The village contained 243 bungalows, plus several hostels, to accommodate the influx of skilled workers, who were transferred from all over the country. The plant, which, would eventually employ nearly 2,000 workers, included many local people trained by Shorts.

L J Braithwaite, who lived at Balla Wray, remembers the factory being built. 'Across the opposite side of the lake they were building a large factory and I was to learn later that they would be building Sunderland Flying Boats there. But of course we didn't talk about it. I could see all that went on at Calgarth, as that was the name of the estate on which it was built. Finally the first Sunderland was brought out onto the slipway. After some considerable number of days it suddenly appeared on the water. It wasn't long then before it was airborne, and more were to follow, but the first one is the one that sticks in your memory.

Once they had got the system organised the flying boats began to be moored over our side of the lake in Wray Bay. Boats were not allowed on the lake in those days but we used to swim out to the Sunderlands and on some occasions used the floats as diving platforms until the patrol came and chased us off with dire threats ringing in our ears.'

Production was principally the Sunderland III, which was the most prolific mark in RAF service. The plant would also cater for heavy battle damage repairs, overhauls and, later, modification work.

First flown in October 1937, the Sunderland was designed in response to the urgent need to replace the aging fleet of biplane flying boats in service with the RAF. This large four-engined flying boat was a military development of the 'C' Class Empire flying boat which served with Imperial Airways. The Sunderland was responsible for the destruction of at least 26 U-boats and many more claimed as shared kills with other aircraft or surface ships. Its defensive armament of three power-operated gun turrets and various other gun positions earned it the nickname 'flying porcupine' from the Germans. By the beginning of the Second World War three squadrons had been equipped with the Sunderland. 749 Sunderlands were eventually built, serving in various theatres throughout the war.

Post-war, the type took part in the Berlin Airlift and the Korean War, where Sunderlands based in Japan flew nearly 900 operational sorties. The Sunderland finally retired from RAF service in 1959 when the last aircraft were scrapped at RAF Seletar, Singapore.

All of the aircraft assembled at Windermere were the Sunderland III, represented here.

As soon as the factory was ready, the construction began of the first batch of 25 Sunderland IIIs. Delivered between September 1942 and January 1944, the first aircraft were given the RAF serials DP176 to DP200. Six of this batch were lost on operations, including DP176, which served only with 119 Squadron from Pembroke Dock, Pembrokeshire. Whilst on patrol over the Bay of Biscay, the Sunderland lost two propellers on 15th April 1943, ditched and foundered. DP177 of 10 Squadron RAAF was also lost over the Bay of Biscay, on 11th August 1943, after being attacked by several Junkers Ju88s. DP179 from the same squadron was lost in similar circumstances. DP181 of 423 Squadron crashed on landing at its home base of Castle Archdale in November 1943. This particular aircraft had a brush with the Luftwaffe on 14th September 1943, whilst on patrol over the Bay of Biscay. The pilot, Flg Off. H C Jackson, and crew of DP181 were on an 'Operation Percussion' sortie, which involved anti-submarine searches instead of convoy escort patrols. Halfway through the sortie, a Focke Wulf Fw200 Condor was spotted three miles ahead. The big German anti-shipping aircraft disappeared into the clouds only to reappear less than 3,000 yards behind the Sunderland. The Condor opened fire with its 20mm cannon at approximately 1,500

231

yards. At a range of 300 yards, the Sunderland's rear gunner fired over 800 rounds from his four 0.303 Browning machine guns, which carried only 1,000 rounds per gun. The German and the RCAF rear gunner both missed their targets and the Condor disappeared back into the clouds rather than continue the fight. DP182 of 343 Squadron ditched in the South Atlantic, capsized and blew up on 2nd February 1944. DP183 of 330 Squadron disappeared on a patrol on 20th March 1943. Two others were lost in training accidents, both from 4 (Coastal) Operational Training Unit at Invergordan in the Highlands. DP178 went missing on a night training exercise on 14th March 1945 and DP197 crashed into a hill at Groagh-a-Croinoch in Sutherland on 15th August 1944; remnants of this aircraft were recently displayed at an exhibition in the Lake District.

The remainder of this initial batch served with various units, including DP187, which went on to serve with the French Aéronavale for many years. DP191, after conversion to a Sunderland V, was transferred to the RNZAF and served into the mid 1960s.

First impressions of Windermere, surrounded by mountains, indicate that it would be quite a dangerous place to land a 20-ton Sunderland. However, a north-south wind generally blows up and down the lake, making take-offs and landings much easier. Often the water was so calm that a motor boat would travel up the lake to furrow a wake so that the pilot could judge his height better over the surface. The lake had plenty of room as well and rumour has it that one pilot actually took off across the lake, skimming the summit of the Coniston Old Man by a few feet!

Another clause, which was endorsed by Lord Beaverbrook, was that only the absolute minimum amount of flying be undertaken from the lake. All aircraft that were produced at the factory were flown directly out to 57 Maintenance Unit, based at Wig Bay in Dumfries and Galloway. It was here that all test flying of the new Sunderlands was carried out, far away from the tranquil Lake District. Crews who flew out of Windermere were under strict instructions that only in the event of a major emergency should they turn back to the lake. All 35 aircraft produced by the factory were tested at 57 MU, which, by the beginning of 1944, was changed to No 1 Flying Boat Servicing Unit (FBSU).

The second batch of ten Sunderland IIIs was delivered to the RAF between February and July 1944. Given the serials EJ149 to EJ158, several were delivered in time to see operational service. One particular aircraft from this batch scored one of the most significant U-boat victories of the Second World War. EJ150 'W', which served only with 201 Squadron, was flying an anti-submarine patrol over the Bay of Biscay on 18th August 1944. Piloted by Flt Lt L H Braystock DSO, DFC, the crew spotted U-107, commanded by Ltn Karl-Heinz Fritz, on the surface, west of La Rochelle. The Sunderland quickly attacked the submarine, sinking her immediately, with the loss of all 58 hands. U-107 had a remarkably successful career under three different commanders from when she began patrolling the Atlantic in 1940. The U-boat sank 43 ships during her career, totalling 243,000 tons; the Allies did not mourn her loss.

Two Sunderlands from the second batch were lost in flying accidents. EJ154, from 461 Squadron, crashed on landing at Pembroke Dock on 13th December 1944 and EJ157 caught fire on take-off from Castle Archdale in Northern Ireland on the 12th May 1945. The last sighting of a Windermere-produced aircraft was at the Hemswell Battle of Britain Air Display on the 15th September 1956. Sunderland V EJ153 'R' of 230 Squadron flew a dramatic display, pursued by three 'attackers'. Less than two months later, EJ153 was struck off RAF charge and scrapped.

The Windermere factory also carried out conversions of the Sunderland III to the Sunderland V standard. Additional equipment when fitted to the Sunderland IIIs, significantly increased the aircrafts' weight and air crews were having to run the Pegasus engines at combat power just to maintain normal flight. This resulted in high engine fatigue and it was RAAF Sunderland crews that suggested that the Pegasus be replaced by the more powerful 1,200 hp Pratt and Whitney Twin Wasp. These engines were readily available, as they were already in RAF use with the Consolidated Catalina and Douglas Dakota. Successful trials were conducted in February 1944 and, as expected, the new engines provided significantly greater performance without affecting the aircraft's range. The new Twin Wasp aircraft was designated the Sunderland V and 155 were built from new; a further 33 were converted from the Sunderland III, several of these at Windermere.

Many who worked at Windermere described it as a 'garden factory', surrounded by beautiful trees and rhododendron bushes. For those who enjoyed the countryside, the idea of working next to a vast lake, where you could cycle to work without any thought for the fact that the world was still at war, was a wonderful experience. Not everyone agreed: several workers returned to the Rochester factory, unimpressed by the lack of shops and the cool reception emitted by the local people. Once jobs became available, this attitude changed.

The only Short Shetland ever built descended onto Lake Windermere in early 1945. This giant flying boat was the largest aircraft in the country at the time.

The only reminders of the war were the occasional exercise by the Hawkshead Home Guard, who would take to their boats under the cover of darkness and test the security of the factory. A single bomb was dropped by the enemy near Troutbeck, killing a sheep; however the factory itself operated completely unseen by the eyes of the Luftwaffe. One worker recalled seeing a Sunderland which had been damaged after a sortie to Norway arriving at Windermere for repair. The rear gun turret was shot to pieces and the blood stains from the rear gunner were still to be seen. Over 30 Sunderlands were received in a similar condition through the war.

In early 1945, the lake witnessed the arrival of the largest British-built aircraft ever flown. Short Shetland DX266, weighing in at 125,000lbs, twice the weight of a Sunderland, landed with plenty of room to spare. All nine Sunderlands in the hangar at the time had to be removed to accommodate the enormous Shetland. The plan was to build the giant flying boat at Windermere during the post-war years, safeguarding the plant and the many jobs which went with it. Unfortunately, the flying boat, which had dominated world air transport before the Second World War, now received no further interest. Neither BOAC nor the RAF wanted the Shetland, the latter being content with a surplus of Sunderlands. DX266 was the only Shetland

An original path to a jetty, which was probably for the pilot boats, is still intact as well as remnants of the jetty itself. (Author)

ever built and Short's flying boat production came to a conclusion.

With the war at an end, the Friends of the Lake District reminded the Air Ministry of its promise to dismantle the factory. Despite this, the local council retained the prefabs at Troutbeck Bridge to house the many servicemen returning to the area. A serious proposal was made to turn the now vacated Short's factory into a textiles producer. This

The main slipway from the factory is now used for sailing boats rather than flying boats. (Author)

idea attracted a lot of support from the local community, who were suffering because of the factory's closure. Many opposed the demand made by the Friends of the Lake District for its dismantling. A letter published in the *Westmorland Gazette* stated that for the Friends to assert that a tree-shrouded works defiled the area was 'quite absurd'. 'I will go so far as to say that seven out of every ten visitors to Windermere would be totally unaware of its existence.'

The factory, still unused, was finally dismantled in the early 1950s. Built on 15 ft deep foundations, the Ministry of Agriculture refused to pay for the costly work involved to excavate them. This prevented the site from being returned to agriculture and many blamed the 'Friends' group for the 'eyesores' of concrete which were left behind.

Today, the concrete foundations can still be seen; apron areas and slipways were also left behind. The site is now the location of the White Cross Bay Caravan Park and, surrounded by trees, the park is as unobtrusive as the original factory. Remnants of the factory complex can still be seen today including the slipway, concrete roads and a couple of buildings in the surrounding woodlands.

A single airworthy example of a Sunderland returned to the lake during the 1990 Windermere Festival, bringing back pleasant memories for some who worked at this unique factory.

20
CIVILIANS
AT WAR

Neither Cumbria nor the Isle of Man would suffer at the hands of the Luftwaffe during the Second World War. Only a few civilians in Cumbria, relative to other counties, were killed as a direct result of bombing and none was recorded on the Isle of Man. However, as in the rest of the country, restrictions were put into place and, even in the most rural of areas, the effects of the conflict were felt.

Being an island, the Isle of Man lent itself perfectly for the siting of prisoner of war and internment camps. A pair of internment camps was first sited on the island during the First World War but many more were built during the second. People held in these camps included political detainees held under Section 18B of the Defence (General) Regulations, which gave the government the power to imprison without charge or trial. Many were held for a few months while others were held for the entire war, including members of the British Union of Fascists and the IRA. Over 4,000 women and children were held on the Isle of Man as well, many until the war ended. On 30th September 1941, a disturbance at a camp near Peel caused by 20 Fascists resulted in the guard being strengthened. The offending inmates were transferred to a more secure camp near Liverpool.

The Isle of Man was never specifically targeted by the Luftwaffe but, during the Belfast Blitz, in late 1940 into 1941, the island lay in the bombers' path. A significant number of high explosive and incendiary bombs were dropped on the island, but none gave the impression of being deliberate. Many of the bombs that fell were simply being discarded by the German bombers as they began the long flight home.

Equally, Cumbria was never strategically attacked, although it did claim to be the first county in the north of England to be bombed. In July 1940, bombs fell near the village of Kirkcambeck, eight miles north of Brampton. The only casualties were a Clydesdale mare, three sheep and ten chickens. A more serious attack the same month killed seven in Maryport school. At Carleton, south-east of Carlisle, a single device fell in November 1940. A high explosive bomb with a delayed timer fitted fell at Sewells Farm; the device took over 30 minutes to explode. More bombs fell at Harraby near Carlisle in May 1941 – none of them exploded – and other isolated incidents were reported throughout the county. Over 20 incendiary bombs fell onto Scotby, east of Carlisle, causing damage to several buildings as well as claiming the life of Ernest Rowe on 11th March 1943. Carlisle was the largest built-up area in the county during the Second World War and, like the Isle of Man, the city was seen as an opportune place to unload any remaining bombs. Accidents relating to the war effort also claimed lives in the county. An explosion ripped through the Broughton Moor bomb dump in 1944. Blamed on an unstable naval mortar, the blast killed eleven civilians.

As a direct result of the German bombing campaign, a feature that was to change thousands of people's lives and their gardens was the distribution of personal air raid shelters. The most prevalent type was the Anderson, named after the Home Secretary, Sir John Anderson. They were issued free to any household that earned less than £250 per

A common sight in many back gardens during the war years was the Anderson Personal Air Raid Shelter. Many people living in towns preferred to take cover in the communal shelters that could supply cover for an entire street.

238

year and could provide protection from blast and flying shrapnel from falling bombs, but not from a direct hit. Easy to construct, they were made of curved steel, which was bolted together, dug into the ground and then covered with at least three feet of soil. They were cold, small and prone to flooding but, from June 1940, they saved many lives.

Rationing was introduced from January 1940 and with it came the daily chore of dealing with ration cards, joining queues and chasing items that, only a few months earlier, were easy to purchase. Butter, sugar, bacon and ham were the first items to be rationed, but potatoes, bread, offal and fish were in plentiful supply.

On the 14th May 1940, Sir Anthony Eden, the Secretary of State for War, made a 'call to arms' broadcast which highlighted the threat of a potential German invasion. The vast majority of able-bodied men were already serving in the forces, so Eden announced the formation of a new home defence force called the Local Defence Volunteers (LDV). Less than 24 hours later, over a quarter of a million men had enrolled in the LDV and, by July, this had risen to over one million. Initially ribbed as *Look, Duck and Vanish* the LDV was renamed by Winston Churchill on 23rd July 1940 and became the Home Guard.

The Home Guard was initially poorly equipped, their only arms being a variety of garden and farm implements and the occasional shotgun. Uniforms and weapons had improved by 1941 and the introduction of standard army battledress, along with the issue of rifles shipped over from Canada, gave the Home Guard a more businesslike appearance. Although they were never taken seriously by other regular army units, had Hitler invaded there is no doubt the Home Guard would have put up a staunch defence.

The period leading up to the fall of France in mid 1940 was called the 'phoney war', after which civilians of Britain were, for the first time, about to experience war at first hand. The many training exercises that the Observer Corps, civil defence wardens, first aid parties and firemen had received would now be put to the test.

'Dig for Victory' was the government's campaign to encourage people to turn their gardens into vegetable patches and the addition of fresh vegetables to dinner plates made life more bearable. The Armed Forces also took part in the Dig for Victory campaign, even though they had no orders to do so. Often making use of good agricultural land, airfields lent themselves to the production of large areas of vegetables. Jurby, for example, turned over areas of land, effectively turning it into a farm. This greatly increased the variety of foodstuffs available to the local airmen. Heaton Park in Carlisle was a good

People were encouraged to turn their gardens into allotments and grow as many different vegetables as possible.

example of digging for victory at work; the park was set with potatoes, eventually yielding a 32-ton crop.

The Women's Land Army was also active in Cumbria; by the war's end, the unarmed force totalled 100,000 helping to turn over an extra six million acres in the country to agriculture. The Timber Corps was also formed in Grizedale Forest, staffed mainly by women, who were nicknamed 'Lumber Jills'. The Women's Institute was one of many groups which organized 'scrap drives', collecting pots, pans and anything that could be melted down. Although hardly any of the metal collected on these drives was actually used for the production of military equipment, they raised the morale of the general public, who felt that they were doing their bit for the war effort. Victory Weeks were another method of involving the public and an effective way of raising money for aircraft and ships. The population of Carlisle raised the £5,000 needed to pay for a Spitfire, which was appropriately named 'City of Carlisle'. Another group in the county, called the West Cumbria Spitfire Fund, raised enough to buy a Spitfire IIB named 'Scawfell'.

The authorities now prepared to receive their share of the planned 3.5 million evacuees who were to leave the country's major cities, in Cumbria's case the north-east and Barrow. Both areas were industrial targets and were suffering heavy bombing raids from late 1940

Thousands of evacuees descended upon Cumbria from towns and cities in the North-East, Barrow and much further afield.

through to early 1942. However, only 1.5 million families across the country actually joined the scheme. The first part of this vast operation was code-named 'Pied Piper' and involved many hundreds of thousands of pregnant women, children, teachers and helpers who were moved into the country. Mill Hill School in north London was taken over as a military hospital on the outbreak of the Second World War, and the school was evacuated to St Bees, where it remained until the end of the war in 1945. The evacuation had been pre-planned at the time of the Munich Crisis in 1938 and approximately 216 pupils continued their education in relative safety from enemy raids. Roedean public school from Brighton was moved to Keswick, as was St Katharine's teacher training college from Liverpool.

Economically, the war brought many advantages to local and national business alike. The construction of so many airfields in such a short space of time brought lucrative contracts to the big construction companies and also a large amount of work to smaller firms and individuals. The most famous local company that benefited the most from the massive expansion of airfields was John Laing, based in Carlisle. Wartime construction turned the firm into a multi-million-pound business almost overnight. Individual local people bought lorries and went to work transporting various items, including wood, sand and gravel, to help in the construction of the airfields. Although most airfields were constructed in an average of ten months, the Air Ministry paid well and many people reaped the rewards. Once a new airfield was opened, the influx of airmen would come as quite a shock to the local villagers, as the average population of an RAF station was approximately 2,000 people. The most obvious trader to benefit from this was the local publican, who during the war years could range from someone who had a beer barrel set up inside a house to a fully equipped pub.

Other 'war work' was introduced into the county, including munitions factories, aircraft component production and flying equipment. High Alloys in Distington provided a shadow factory for aircraft parts and K Shoes' Netherfield factory was involved in producing a variety of equipment. Their factory in Kendal was awarded several government contracts to produce aircraft covers, tents, service boots, kit bags, gaiters and RAF flying boots with hidden compartments for escape materials. K Shoes also produced ATS and WAAF shoes, both British and US Army officers' shoes and finally demobilisation shoes. By the war's end, the company had produced over 250,000 flying boots and nearly 30,000 kit bags.

Civilian staff manned the large Aircraft Storage Units (ASU) at Silloth and Kirkbride. Each employed over 700 people as well as many more on the airfields themselves. All four Satellite Landing Grounds in Cumbria employed on average 40 people each. The Shorts factory on Windermere may have had its opponents, but it offered new careers for many local people and, at its peak, the factory employed over 2,000 civilians.

When the Allies invaded mainland Europe on 6th June 1944, life on the home front began to improve. The nation could now taste victory, the national press claiming that the war would be over by Christmas. This was obviously a bold statement but the blackout restrictions were partially lifted in October 1944 and the Home Guard was disbanded on 1st November. The war raged on for nearly a year after D-Day, finally ending on 8th May 1945, the day was called 'Victory in Europe' (VE) Day and was treated as a holiday and celebrated by a multitude of street parties and parades. The People's War had come to an end, Churchill announcing, 'This is your victory'.

His Majesty King George VI, as he had done the day war broke out, addressed the nation on 8th May. 'Armed or unarmed, men and women, you have fought, striven and endured to your utmost.' Over 65,000 British civilians were killed and another 86,000 had been wounded fighting the 'People's War' on the home front.

APPENDIX

RAF and FAA units stationed at airfields in
Cumbria and the Isle of Man during the
Second World War

Andreas (IOM)

457 Sqn: From Jurby 3rd October 1941, to Redhill 23rd March 1942. Aircraft – Spitfire IIa, Spitfire Vb.

275 Sqn: Detachment from Valley, 30th November 1941 to 25th April 1944, departed for Warmwell, although detachments alternated with Eglinton. Aircraft – Lysander IIIa, Walrus I, Walrus II, Defiant I, Defiant Ia, Anson I and Spitfire Vb.

452 Sqn: From Kenley 23rd March 1942, to Australia 31st May 1942. Aircraft – Spitfire Vb.

825 Sqn: From Lee-on-Solent 1st April 1942, to Lee-on-Solent 8th April 1942. Aircraft – Swordfish I, Swordfish II.

93 Sqn: Re-formed 1st Jun 1942, to King's Cliffe 8th September 1942. Aircraft – Spitfire Vb.

808 Sqn [Transit]: From Stretton 16th October 1942, to Peterhead 20th October 1942. Aircraft – Fulmer II.

No11 Air Gunners School: Formed 2nd May 1943, to Jurby 19th September 1946. Aircraft – Martinet, Anson, Master, Wellington, Spitfire VII.

772 Sqn [B Flt]: From Ronaldsway 17th April 1945, to Ronaldsway 6th September 1945. Aircraft – Sea Otter.

772 Sqn [Det]: From Nutts Corner 7th March 1946, to Jurby 15th August 1946. Aircraft – Seafire L.III, Mosquito PR.XVI, Mosquito B.25, Mosquito PR.34, Anson I.

Anthorn

1 Aircraft Receipt & Dispatch Unit: 7th September 1944 to January 1958. Aircraft – Hellcat, Firefly, Avenger, Gannet, Sea Balliol, Firebrand, Seafire, Sturgeon, Harvard, Martinet, Sea Hawk, Sea Fury, Barracuda, Sea Hornet, Dominie, Tiger Moth, Anson, Oxford, SG.38 Glider.

Brayton

39 Satellite Landing Ground: Opened June 1941 for 12 MU. Closed 31st January 1946.

12 Maintenance Unit: Aircraft – Wellington, Fortress, Spitfire, Halifax, Mitchell, Vengeance.

Burnfoot (RLG)

15 Elementary Flying Training School: RLG from July 1940 to 9th July 1945. Aircraft – Magister, Tiger Moth.

Crosby-on-Eden

59 Operational Training Unit: Formed 20th February 1941, to Milfield 2nd August 1942. Aircraft – Hurricane, Master, Battle TT.

9 (Coastal) Operational Training Unit: From Aldergrove 6th September 1942. Disbanded 11th August 1944. Aircraft – Beaufighter VI, Beaufighter XIc, Beaufort, Oxford, Anson, Lysander, Martinet.

109 (Transport) Operational Training Unit: Formed 1st Aug 1944 from part of 9 OTU, redesignated 1383 (Transport) CU on the 10th August 1945. Aircraft – Dakota, Oxford, Horsa.

1383 (Transport) Conversion Unit: Formed 1st August 1945 ex 109 OTU. Disbanded 6th August 1946. Aircraft – Dakota III.

105 (Transport) Operational Training Unit: Single flight from Bramcote 8th August 1945 incorporated into 1383 CU. Aircraft – Dakota.

Great Orton

55 Operational Training Unit: Satellite airfield from 20th October 1943 to 26th January 1944 (main unit at Annan). Aircraft – Hurricane, Master.

1 (Coastal) Engine Control Demonstration Unit: From Longtown 17th November 1943, to Aldergrove on the 19th December 1943. Aircraft – Wellington.

4 Tactical Exercise Unit: 'B' Sqn 26th January to 28th March 1944. Aircraft – Hurricane.

281 Sqn: Detachments from Tiree February 1944 to February 1945. Aircraft – Warwick I.

3 Tactical Exercise Unit: 28th March 1944 to May 1944. Aircraft – Hurricane, Typhoon.

6 Operational Training Unit: Satellite airfield for Silloth June 1944 to April 1945. Aircraft – Wellington, Anson, Oxford, Martinet.

282 Sqn: Detachments from St Eval between September 1944 to March 1945. Aircraft – Warwick I.

Navigators' "W" Holding Course: From Haverfordwest 1st October 1944, to Killadeas 12th April 1945.

1333 Conversion Unit: Detachments and dropping zone from 1945 to 1947. Aircraft – Dakota.

219 Maintenance Unit: Satellite storage depot (sub-site) 4th May 1945 to 20th May 1947.

249 Maintenance Unit: Air ammunition park 27th May 1945 to 15th Aug 1952.

60 Maintenance Unit: RSU detachment 31st July 1946 to 1950.

Hall Caine

Drogue dropping area and later relief landing site

5 AOS: Aircraft – Battle, Henley.

5 B&GS: Aircraft – Battle, Henley.

Hornby Hall

9 Satellite Landing Ground: Opened 1st April 1941 for 22 MU.

22 Maintenance Unit: 1st April 1941 to 31st July 1945. Aircraft – Blenheim, Hurricane, Sea Hurricane, Wellington, Hudson, Anson, Mustang, Botha.

18 Maintenance Unit: February 1942 to 15th May 1942. Aircraft – Wellington, Battle, Hurricane, Whirlwind.

12 Maintenance Unit: January 1942 to May 1942. Aircraft – Wellington.

Hutton-in-the-Forest

8 Satellite Landing Ground: Opened 1st June 1941 for 22 MU.

22 Maintenance Unit: 1st June 1941 to 1st September 1945. Aircraft – Blenheim, Hudson, Botha, Hurricane, Ventura, Wellington, Mustang.

12 Maintenance Unit: 14th March 1942 to May 1945. Aircraft – Wellington.

50 Wing: From Silloth on the 1st June 1941. Established at Hutton Hall. Moved to Geltsdale, Wetheral on the 15th August 1941.

Jurby (IOM)

5 Armament Training Station: From Penrhos 16th September 1939, redesignated No5 AOS 18th September 1939.

5 Air Observers' School: Formed 18th September 1939 from 5 ATS, disbanded 1st February 1944. Aircraft – Blenheim, Battle, Henley, Anson.

166 Sqn: Detachment from Abingdon April 1940. Aircraft – Whitley III.

5 Flying Training School: Armament training detachment from Sealand 2nd January 1940 to 12th January 1940. Aircraft – Audax, Oxford.

5 Bombing & Gunnery School: Formed 1st December 1939 ex 5 AOS, reverted to 5 AOS 19th July 1941. Aircraft – Blenheim, Hampden (formerly Hereford), Anson.

12 Flying Training School: Armament training detachment from Grantham 18th January 1940 to 5th February 1940. Aircraft – Anson, Audax.

4 Group Pool Squadron: From Abingdon 16th February to April 1940. Aircraft – Whitley III.

11 OTU: Detachment from Bassingbourn 16th March 1940 to July 1940. Aircraft – Wellington .

10 OTU: 'C' Flight detachment 6th April 1940 to 10th September 1940. Aircraft – Whitley.

Central Flying School: Detachment, night flying 5th June 1940 to 13th June 1940. Aircraft – Battle Trainer.

215 Sqn: Detachment from Bassingbourn October to November 1940. Aircraft – Wellington I.

307 Sqn: From Kirton-in-Lindsey 7th November 1940 to Squires Gate 23rd January 1941. Aircraft – Defiant I.

258 Sqn: From Acklington 1st February 1941 to Valley 17th April 1941. Aircraft – Hurricane I.

312 Sqn: From Valley 25th April 1941 to Kenley 29th May 1941. Aircraft – Hurricane I.

302 Sqn: From Kenley 29th May 1941 to Church Stanton 7th August 1941. Aircraft – Hurricane I, Hurricane IIb.

457 Sqn: From Baginton 7th August 1941 to Andreas 3rd October 1941. Aircraft – Spitfire I, Spitfire IIa; converted to Spitfire IIA September 1941.

Armament Synthetic Development Unit: From Dumfries 1942 to Manby June 1943. Aircraft – Wellington, Warwick.

Air Navigation & Bombing School: Formed 1st February 1944 from 5 AOS, redesignated 5 ANS 31st May 1945. Aircraft – Anson, Magister, Martinet.

Wellington Conversion Flight (AN&BS): October 1944 to May 1945: Aircraft Wellington III, Wellington X.

5 Air Navigation School: Formed 31st May 1945 ex AN&BS to Topcliffe 17th September 1945.

772 Sqn [Det]: From Anthorn for detachment 15th August 1946 to 21st December 1946. Aircraft – Mosquito.

11 Air Gunners' School: From Andreas 19th September 1946, disbanded 15th October 1947.

(No.1) Initial Training School: Both Wings No1 at Wittering & No2 at Digby 17th April 1950, disbanded 10th September 1953.

RAF Officer Cadet Training Unit: Formed 10th September 1953, taking over commitment of OCTU Millom and becoming RAF OCTU 1st Apr 1954 to at least July 1959.

Kingstown (Carlisle)

38 Elementary & Reserve Flying Training School: Formed 1st July 1939, disbanded 3rd September 1939. Operated by Border Flying Club.

3 Air Observer & Navigator School: From Desford 24th November 1939 to Weston-super-Mare 3rd June 1940. Aircraft – Anson.

1 Anti-Aircraft Co-Operation Unit: Exercise in July and August 1940. Aircraft – Henley.

15 Elementary Flying Training School: From Redhill 2nd June 1940, disbanded 31st December 1947. Aircraft – Magister, Battle, Tiger Moth.

6 Anti-Aircraft Co-Operation Unit: March 1941 to February 1942. Aircraft – Leopard Moth, Magister, Lysander, Tiger Moth.

189 Gliding School: Formed by June 1945, disbanded by October 1947. Aircraft – Slingsby Cadet I and II.

Kirkbride

12 MU: Formed 5th June 1939 as a civil-manned ASU storage unit, disbanded 30th June 1960. Aircraft – Tutor, Hart, Magister, Seafox, Audax, Battle, Anson, Hector, Hampden, Spitfire, Botha, Hudson, Gauntlet, Queen Bee, Roc, Swordfish, Tiger Moth, Dominie, Wellington, Halifax, Airacobra, Ventura, Mitchell, Mustang, Havoc, Baltimore, Boston, Fortress, Kingfisher, Vigilant, Bermuda, Liberator, Vengeance, Oxford, Albemarle, Martinet.

Polish Grading & Testing Flight: From Redhill on the 3rd June 1940 whilst still affiliated to 15 EFTS at Carlisle/Kingstown, absorbed into 1 (Polish) Service FTS at Hucknall 30th November 1940. Aircraft – Battle, Magister.

1 (Coastal) Operational Training Unit: RLG for Silloth from November 1940 to July 1941. Aircraft – Hudson.

3 (Coastal) Operational Training Unit: Wellington & Whitley section from Chivenor/Silloth, May 1940. Cranwell 29th July 1941.

4 Ferry Pilots' Pool ATA: Sub-pool, became 16 FPP by July 1941.

16 Ferry Pilots' Pool/Ferry Pool ATA: Formed July 1941 ex sub-pool 4 FPP, disbanded late September 1945. Aircraft – Proctor, Anson.

Air Transport Auxiliary Air Movements Flight: Scheduled services for urgent spares between White Waltham and the aircraft storage units at Aston Down, Cosford, Hawarden and Kirkbride.

6 OTU: Satellite airfield for Silloth from October 1943 to May 1944. Aircraft – Wellington.

Longtown

59 Operational Training Unit: Satellite airfield for Crosby-on-Eden 14th July 1941 to 6th August 1942. Aircraft – Hurricane, Master.

41 Sqn: From Debden to Llanbedr 11th August 1942. Aircraft – Spitfire Vb.

55 Operational Training Unit: Satellite airfield (main unit at Annan) 28th April 1942 to 20th October 1943. Aircraft – Hurricane, Master.

1 (Coastal) Operational Training Unit: Night flying from Silloth 7th July 1942 to early 1943. Aircraft – Hudson

9 (Coastal) Operational Training Unit: Satellite for Crosby-on-Eden 6th September 1942 to 27th October 1943 and 5th January 1944 to 11th August 1944. Aircraft – Beaufighter, Beaufort.

6 OTU: Satellite for Silloth from 16th October 1943 to 5th January 1944. Aircraft – Wellington.

1 (Coastal) Engine Control Demonstration Unit: Formed 19th October 1943 within 1674 HCU, to Great Orton 17th November 1943. Aircraft – Wellington.

1674 Heavy Conversion Unit: Entire unit with the exception of the Liberator Flight from Aldergrove 19th October 1943, to Aldergrove 7th July 1944. Aircraft – Halifax, Liberator, Fortress.

1332 Conversion Unit: Formed 5th September 1944, to Nutts Corner 7th October 1944. Aircraft – Stirling, Liberator, York.

1521 Beam Approach Training Flight: From Wymeswold 20th October 1945, disbanded 1st April 1946. Aircraft – Oxford.

1383 (Transport) Conversion Unit: Satellite airfield, 15th November 1945 to 30th March 1946. Aircraft – Dakota.

Millom (Haverigg)

2 Bombing & Gunnery School: Formed 20th January 1941, redesignated 2 AOS 1st June 1941. Aircraft – Botha, Anson, Battle, Oxford.

CFS Flight: From Manby 11th February 1941, departure unknown. Aircraft – Battle.

2 Air Observers' School: Re-formed 1st June 1941 from 2 B&GS, redesignated 2 (O)AFU 18th February 1942. Aircraft – Botha, Anson, Oxford, Battle TT.

R Flight, No1 Anti-Aircraft Co-Operation Unit: From Squires Gate 13th September 1941 to Cark 7th January 1942. Aircraft – Henley, Defiant.

822 Sqn: In transit from Gosport to Hatston 25th to 27th January 1942. Aircraft – Swordfish II.

2 (Observers') Advanced Flying Unit: Formed 18th February 1942 ex 2 AOS, disbanded 9th January 1945. Aircraft – Anson I, Defiant I, Defiant II, Lysander, Martinet I, Tutor, Moth, Mosquito B.20.

776 Sqn: Detachment from Speke 30th December 1942 to 21st April 1944 and 27th October to 4th January 1945. Aircraft – Dominie I, Chesapeke I, Blackburn Skua II

Officer Cadet Training Unit: Formed 1st September 1952 as an additional (second) OCTU, disbanded and committed to OCTU Jurby.

Ronaldsway (IOM)

1 Ground Defence Gunners' School: From North Coates 1st July 1940, redesignated 3 RAF Regiment School June 1942, re-formed at Filey February 1943.

1 Ground Defence Gunners' School Target Towing Flight: From North Coates 1st July, to Hutton Cranswick February 1943. Aircraft – Wallace, Hart, Gauntlet.

3 RAF Regiment School: Formed June 1942 at Douglas from 1 GDGS with flying section at Ronaldsway, closed February 1943 as 1 GDGS.

747 Sqn: From Fearn 14th July 1944, to Crail 15th November 1945, 'B' Flt remaining until 20th December 1945. Aircraft – Barracuda II, Anson.

713 Sqn: Re-formed 12th August 1944, disbanded 20th December 1945. Aircraft – Barracuda II, Barracuda III.

710 Sqn: Re-formed 7th October 1944, disbanded 20th December 1945. Aircraft – Barracuda II, Barracuda III.

725 Sqn [Det 4]: Detached from Eglinton October/November 1944. Aircraft – Martinet TT.1, Reliant.

822 Sqn: From HMS Rajah 15th Nov 1944, to Lee-on-Solent 18th November 1944. No Aircraft.

836 'A' Flt: From MV Empire MacRae 23rd December 1944, to Maydown 26th December 1944. Aircraft – Swordfish I, Swordfish II.

772 Sqn [B Flt]: From Ayr 5th January 1945 to 17th April 1945, and 6th September 1945 to 10th January 1946. Aircraft – Hurricane, Corsair III, Reliant I, Swordfish II, Martinet TT1, Boston III, Fairey Firefly I

836 'U' Flt: From MV Empire MacRae 16th January 1945, to Maydown 17th January 1945. Aircraft – Swordfish I, Swordfish II.

705 Sqn: Re-formed 7th March 1945, disbanded 24th June 1945. Aircraft – Swordfish III.

Silloth

22 Maintenance Unit: Formed 5th June 1939 as a civil-manned ASU, disbanded 31st December 1960. Aircraft – Dragon, Hereford, Oxford, Skua, Spitfire, Gipsy Moth, Audax, Mentor, Anson, Wellington, Vega Gull, Hudson, Vildebeest, Harvard, Hurricane, Botha, Harrow, Stirling, Battle, Shark, Swordfish, Blenheim, Liberator, Ventura, Fortress, Mustang, Argus, Vigilant, Bermuda, Sea Hurricane, Oxford, Mosquito.

215 Sqn: Detachments from Bassingbourn September/October 1939. Aircraft – Wellington I.

Coastal Command Landplane Pilots' Pool: Formed 1st November 1939, redesignated 1 (Coastal) OTU 1st April 1940. Aircraft – Anson, Hudson, Botha, Beaufort.

Civilian Repair Organisation: Cunliffe-Owen Aircraft Ltd, from at least 23rd November 1939.

1 (Coastal) Operational Training Unit: Formed 1st April 1940, to Thornaby 24th March 1943. Aircraft – Hudson, Anson, Blenheim, Beaufort, Wellington, Whitley, Oxford, Fortress.

320 Sqn: Detachment from Leuchars October 1940. Aircraft – Anson I.

3 (Coastal) Operational Training Unit: From Chivenor, December 1940, Cranwell 29th July 1941. Aircraft – Wellington, Whitley.

No50 Wing: Re-formed 21st April 1941, to Hutton Hall 1st June 1941.

Civilian Repair Organisation: Scottish Aviation Ltd, from 19th July 1941.

6 Operational Training Unit: From Thornaby 10th March 1943, to Kinloss 18th July 1945. Aircraft – Wellington VII, Wellington XI, Wellington XIII, Wellington Ic, Wellington III, Wellington X, Wellington XII, Wellington XIV, Anson, Oxford, Lysander TT, Martinet TT.

6 Operational Training Unit Czech Flight: From Thornaby 10th March 1943, disbanded 31st August 1943. Aircraft – Wellington.

6 Operational Training Unit Polish Flight: From Thornaby 10th March 1943, transferred to 3 (Coastal) OTU Thornaby, returned 11th January 1944, absorbed into 6 (Coastal) OTU at Silloth. Aircraft – Wellington.

Preliminary Signals Flight: From Thornaby 10th March 1943, transferred to No12 RS 8th December 1943. Aircraft – Oxford, Anson, Tiger Moth.

1353 Flight: Detachment from 1st October 1945 to January 1946. Aircraft – Vengeance, Spitfire LFIX, Hurricane IIC.

5 Ferry Pool: Formed 15th October 1945, disbanded 25th May 1950. Aircraft – Various.

60 Maintenance Unit: RSU detachment 27th June 1946, to Great Orton 31st July 1946.

Wath Head (Jenkins Cross)

10 Satellite Landing Ground: Opened 1st May 1941.

12 Maintenance Unit: From Kirkbride 1st May 1941 to 12th January 1944. Aircraft – Hampden, Botha, Wellington, Halifax, Mitchell.

18 Maintenance Unit: 12th January 1944 to 1st December 1945. Aircraft – Wellington.

Windermere

Short Sunderland III assembly, repair and modification work.

BIBLIOGRAPHY

Andreas, *Air 28/658 (TFCC)*; *Air 29/1*

Bombing Ranges (IOM), *Air 2/12518*

Brayton, *Air 29/970*

Carlisle, *Air 29/973 14MU*

Crosby, *Air 29/612*; *Air 29/684 (59 OTU)*; *Air 29/705*

Great Orton, *Air 29/682 (55 OTU)*

Hornby Hall, *Air 28/982*

Hutton in the Forest, *Air 28/982*

Jurby, *Air 29/545 (5 AN&BS etc)*

Kingstown, *Air 2/6989 (15 EFTS Crest)*; *Air 29/47 (6 AACU)*; *Avia 2/678 (Aerodrome Licences, 1934–37)*; *Avia 2/1196 (Aerodrome Licences, 1937-41)*; *BT 31/35647/297991 (Border Flying Club)*

Kirkbride, *Air 29/970*

Longtown, *Air 29/611*; *Air 29/614*; *Air 29/875*; *Air 29/970*

Millom, *Air 28/557*; *Air 29/508*; *Air 29/544 (2 AOS)*

Ronaldsway, *ADM 1/12904*; *ADM 1 16441*; *ADM 1/13588*; *Air 29/26*; *Air 29/751*; *HO 45/24254*

Silloth, *Air 28/692*; *Air 29/982*

Wath Head, *Air 29/970*; *Air 29/978 (Dumfries)*

Windermere, *Air 28/866*

Avro Lancaster, Harry Holmes, Airlife

Avro One, J. A. Robinson, Old Forge Publishing

Bomber Squadrons of the RAF, P. J. R. Moyes, MacDonald

British Built Aircraft Vol.5, Ron Smith, Tempus Publishing Ltd

Britain's Military Airfields 1939–45, David J. Smith, PSL

Carlisle Airport, Paul R. Wiggins, Solway Aviation Society

Fields of Deception, Colin Dobinson, English Heritage

Fighter Command Losses 1939–41, Norman Franks, Midland

Fighter Squadrons of the RAF, John D. R. Rawlings, MacDonald

Lakeland Aviation and Airfields, Ken Davies, Regional Publications

Losses of the US 8th & 9th Air Forces, Bishop & Hey, Bishop Book Productions

Manx Aviation in War and Peace, Gordon N. Kniveton, Manx Experience

Military Airfields in the British Isles, Steve Willis & Barry R. Holliss, Willis-Holliss

RAF Aircraft Files, Various, Air Britain

RAF Flying Training & Support Units, Sturtivant, Hamlin & Halley, Air Britain

RAF Squadrons, Wg Cdr C. G. Jefford, Airlife

Royal Air Force, Thetford, Putnam

The Bomber Command War Diaries, Martin Middlebrook & Chris Everitt, Midland

The British Bomber since 1914, Francis K. Mason, Putnam

The Squadrons of the FAA, Sturtivant, Air Britain

The Squadrons of the RAF, Halley, Air Britain

World Aircraft WW2, Part 1, Sampson Low

World Aircraft WW2, Part 2, Sampson Low

INDEX

15 Elementary (and Reserve) Flying Training School (ERFTS /EFTS) 15, 48–51, 122–129, 131–133, 138, 191
38 ERFTS 12, 121–122
4 Ferry Pilots' Pool (ATA) sub pool 140, 142
16 Ferry Pilots' Pool/Ferry Pool (FP) 142–143, 146, 147, 152, 157
5 FP 219
1353 Flight 219
1458 Flight 26
1634 Flight 195
5 Flying Training School (FTS) 102
12 FTS 102
189 Gliding School 131
1 Ground Defence Gunners' School (GDGS) 15, 190–192, 195
1 Ground Gunners' School (GGS) 192
4 Group Pool Squadron 102
1674 Heavy Conversion Unit 17, 75, 164, 165, 166
1 Initial Training School 120
12 Maintenance Unit (MU) 13, 45, 47, 86, 88, 135–137, 141, 143, 146, 149, 153, 154, 156, 157–158, 218, 221–223, 225–226
14 MU 132, 133

18 MU 19, 45, 86, 87, 88, 139, 226
22 MU 13, 86, 88–96, 135 *passim*, 202–206 *passim*, 207, **209–220** *passim*
24 MU 136
32 MU 128
48 MU 214
57 MU 232
60 MU 80
219 MU 78, 80
247 MU 131
249 MU 78
2 (Observers') Advanced Flying Unit 178, 183, 184
Officer Cadet Training Unit 120, 185
1 Operational Training Unit (OTU) 147
6 OTU 78, 154, 165, 166, 215, 216–218
10 OTU 102
11 OTU 102, 103
27 OTU 111
55 OTU 16, 75, 142, 161–165 *passim*
59 OTU 15, 16, 52–58, 142, 160–162
1 (Polish) Service Flying Training School 138
3 RAF Regiment School 193
15 Reserve Flying School 133
3/4 Tactical Exercise Unit (TEU) 76
105 (Transport) OTU 68, 70

109 (Transport) Conversion Unit (CU) 16
1383 (Transport) CU 16, 70–71, 167
105 (Transport) OTU 67, 170
109 (Transport) OTU 67–70
1383 (CU) 16

Royal Navy/Fleet Air Arm Units

1 Aircraft Receipt and Dispatch Unit 19, 36, 38–39
1 Naval OTU 197–198
705 199
710 198, 200
713 197, 200
725 198
747 197, 198, 200
772 32, 33, 39, 120, 199
776 179, 183
801 39
802 39
807 39
808 28
812 39
813 39
822 198
824 39
825 24–25
836 199

Dutch Naval Squadrons

860 40
861 40